Tourism Marketing:
On Both Sides of the Counter

Tourism Marketing:
On Both Sides of the Counter

Edited by

Metin Kozak, Luisa Andreu, Juergen Gnoth, Sonja Sibila Lebe and Alan Fyall

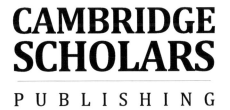

Tourism Marketing: On Both Sides of the Counter,
Edited by Metin Kozak, Luisa Andreu, Juergen Gnoth, Sonja Sibila Lebe and Alan Fyall

This book first published 2013

Cambridge Scholars Publishing

12 Back Chapman Street, Newcastle upon Tyne, NE6 2XX, UK

British Library Cataloguing in Publication Data
A catalogue record for this book is available from the British Library

ISBN (10): 1-4438-4259-1, ISBN (13): 978-1-4438-4259-4

CONTENTS

Introduction viii

Part 1: Destination Image and Branding

Chapter One 2
Images of Israel within a Cross-cultural Perspective
Maria D. Álvarez and Sara Campo

Chapter Two 20
Content Analysis of Slogans for Tourist Destinations
Gökçe Özdemir Bayrak and Metin Kozak

Part 2: Tourist Satisfaction and Experience

Chapter Three 42
Low-season Tourist Satisfaction at Traditional Mediterranean Resorts
Joan B. Garau and Sara Campo

Chapter Four 57
Determinants of the Co-created Destination Experience
Tatiana Chekalina, Matthias Fuchs and Maria Lexhagen

Part 3: Social and Environmental Consumption in Tourism

Chapter Five 80
Tourists' Perceptions of Tourism Development in Nature Areas
Carla Silva, Elisabeth Kastenholz and José Luís Abrantes

Chapter Six 98
Responsibility in Festivals and Events: A Competitive Advantage
Henri Kuokkanen

Chapter Seven... 115
Hey Look, I'm a Green Consumer: Online Social Visibility
and the Willingness to Pay for Carbon Offsetting Schemes
François J. Dessart, Luisa Andreu, Enrique Bigné and Alain Decrop

Part 4: Information and Communication Technologies in Tourism

Chapter Eight.. 138
Improving the Tourism Experience by Empowering Visitors
João V. Estêvão, Maria João Carneiro and Leonor Teixeira

Chapter Nine.. 156
Modeling Information Asymmetries in Tourism
Rodolfo Baggio and Jacopo A. Baggio

Chapter Ten 175
Maintaining the Reputation of Review Sites in Travel and Tourism
Brita Schemmann and Eric Horster

Part 5: Innovation and Competitiveness

Chapter Eleven 188
Innovation Orientation and Performance in Spanish Hotels
Sara Campo, Ana M. Díaz Martín and María J. Yagüe Guillen

Chapter Twelve 203
Innovation: A Primary Competitive Tool to Success at Tourism
Destinations
Marica Mazurek

Chapter Thirteen.. 222
New Product Development in Alpine Destinations
Ruggero Sainaghi

Chapter Fourteen 241
Creativity and Innovation in Tourism: The Role of Events
Tonino Pencarelli, Mirella Migliaccio, Simone Splendiani
and Francesca Rivetti

Chapter Fifteen 261
How Hotels can Learn from Failures: An Integrated Service Recovery
System
Ana M. Díaz Martín, María Leticia Santos Vijande,
Leticia Suárez Álvarez and Ana B. del Río Lanza

Subject Index 279

INTRODUCTION

The initial idea for this book originated from papers submitted for presentation at the 4th Advances in Tourism Marketing Conference (ATMC 2011) held in Maribor, Slovenia, 6-9 September 2011. Under the conference theme of "Transforming Experiences: Tourism Marketing from both Sides of the Counter", the conference set out to build on the success of the three previous Advances in Tourism Marketing conferences; the first hosted in 2005 by Mugla University in Akyaka (Turkey), the second hosted in 2007 by the Universitat de València (Spain), and the third hosted in 2009 by Bournemouth University (United Kindom).

As a direct result of the first conference held in Turkey, Kozak and Andreu (2006) published the book *Progress in Tourism Marketing*; in 2009, Kozak, Gnoth and Andreu published the book *Advances in Destination Marketing* which came about in direct response to papers presented at the Valencia Conference in 2007; and in 2009, Fyall, Kozak, Andreu, Gnoth and Lebe published the book *Marketing Innovations for Sustainable Destinations* with papers presented at the Bournemouth Conference in 2009.

As with the previous three books, the editors of this book, with the assistance of many colleagues who willingly gave their time to serve as reviewers for papers submitted to the ATMC 2011, selected those papers for the chapters in this book. The editors would like to acknowledge the contribution of the authors who submitted a chapter after discussing their papers in Maribor. The themes of the papers of this book fell within five topic areas: destination image and branding; tourist satisfaction and experiences; social and environmental consumption; information and communication technologies; and innovation and competitiveness in tourism.

Part 1: Destination Image and Branding

As is the case of Israel, presented in Chapter 1, and even when the initial image is negative, **Alvarez and Campo** argue that information used to promote the destination may improve the image of both the tourism destination and the country. The authors reveal that tourism marketing and communication efforts can be used as a vehicle for building international relations and can help overcome negative perceptions and stereotypes that affect a country's image.

Destination branding can enhance the strategic positioning of the destination. In Chapter 2, **Bayrak and Kozak** argue that branding a destination starts with understanding its uniqueness. This forms the basis of the brand, followed by emphasizing its values as expressed in a suitable logo and slogan so as to make it more recognizable and attractive to potential tourists. A content analysis of 812 destination marketing organizations, makes the authors emphasize that, as effective communication tools for branding destinations, slogans are likely to strengthen brand images and create distinctiveness among other destinations.

Part 2: Tourist Satisfaction and Experience

As **Garau and Campo** mention in Chapter 3, tourist destinations have a strong need to gather reliable indicators of competitiveness such as consumer satisfaction. Taking this into account, Chapter 3 provides a multi-dimensional scale for measuring tourist satisfaction during the low season. Research findings indicate that three main variables exert a strong influence on overall tourist satisfaction: accommodation; natural, cultural and urban setting; and restaurants at the destination.

Following the recent contributions of the Service Dominant Logic in service research, Chapter 4 emphasizes the role of customer experiences in tourism destinations. **Chekalina, Fuchs and Lexhagen** propose a destination experience model integrating destination resources, value-in-use and destination loyalty. In order to validate the model, they conduct empirical research with international guests at a Swedish ski destination. Research findings suggest that that value-in-use mediates the relationship between customers' perceptions of destination attributes and future behavioral intentions.

Part 3: Social and Environmental Consumption in Tourism

Environmental sustainability and social responsibility in tourism are research topics of high relevance in tourism marketing. This book contains three chapters related to this topic. Chapter 5 analyzes the social, economic and environmental impacts of tourism development in nature areas. After conducting a literature review on the impacts of tourism, **Silva, Kastenholz and Abrantes** develop a tourism impact measurement scale for assessing a wide set of tourism impact parameters. Using a quantitative study of 315 tourists in European nature destinations, the authors validate a scale with three dimensions: positive socio-cultural impacts, positive economic impacts and negative social impacts.

In Chapter 6, **Kuokkanen** deals with festival organizers when planning socially responsible and sustainable actions. Specifically, this chapter both explores the level of communication of responsible actions by festival organizers in Finland and, investigates whether any link between responsibility and visitor numbers can be established. The author concludes that use of responsibility in communication is not well adopted by most Finnish festivals and there is a call for further research on customer expectations of responsibility in this domain.

The growth of the environmentally oriented segments of tourism suggests the necessity to uncover their drivers. Chapter 7 explains the factors that influence the consumption of a pro-environmental tourist service, namely carbon offsetting schemes. Specifically, **Dessart, Andreu, Bigné and Decrop** analyze the role of visibility of consumption as well as other traditional determinants of pro-environmental consumption. Using a hypothetical scenario to build an experimental approach, results suggest that online social visibility raises the willingness to pay for green products. Moreover, general environmental concern is a good predictor of the willingness to pay for carbon offsetting schemes.

Part 4: Information and Communication Technologies in Tourism

The competitiveness of destinations is highly determined by their capacity to satisfy information needs of local actors and visitors through information communication technology applications. Focusing on destination management systems (DMSs), in Chapter 8, **Estêvão, Carneiro and Teixeira** analyze how advanced DMSs are enabling visitors to play a more active role in building their experiences through the implementation of Web 2.0 functionalities. By means of a content analysis, this chapter analyzes how selected DMSs use a variety of Web 2.0 tools, i.e., blogs, photo sharing, rating of tourism products, website rating, reviews and video sharing.

Traditionally, tourism has been characterized as an information asymmetric market in which tourists have lower level of information than their suppliers. However, as **Baggio and Baggio** recognize in Chapter 9, Web 2.0 environments have reversed the asymmetry and a traveler is now often able to fully evaluate the products on offer even more so than the supplier. The authors present an agent-based model for examining the two possible asymmetric conditions. Results are discussed with respect to possible strategies to be adopted by both buyers and sellers in order to re-balance satisfaction and earnings. When consumers have a strong source of information about all aspects and services offered, there is a risk for suppliers to lose a percentage of revenues due to their inability to fully understand the market value of what they offer.

The impact of consumer-generated reviews in tourism marketing has been widely assessed in the last few years, but reputation management and different forms of control used by these review platforms have not received much attention. As discussed in Chapter 10, tourism-related review sites should implement a sustainable and effective control system to generate trustworthy reviews and therefore maintain the reputation of the site. **Schemmann and Horster** describe three different control mechanisms focusing on registered users, actual customers, or verifying the credibility before the reviews are published.

Part 5: Innovation and Competitiveness

In the tourism industry, empirical knowledge about the effects of innovation in tourism enterprises and tourism destinations is needed. Innovation has become a critical factor for firms to keep growing and fight against increasing competition and environmental uncertainty. In Chapter 11, **Campo, Díaz Martín and Yagüe Guillen** analyze the impact of innovation orientation in the Spanish hotel sector on different types of business performance. Among their findings, the importance of investing in innovation to improve the hotel services in the medium and long term is demonstrated.

Chapter 12 focuses on tourism destinations. With two specific case studies from Slovakia and Austria, **Mazurek** analyzes how innovation is a competitive tool for enhancing the competitive advantage of tourism destinations.

Collaboration between tourism destinations and local firms is also a key factor to enhance the competitive positioning of destinations. Chapter 13 explores some critical conditions that destination management organizations must manage in order to become a focal organization for local firms. Using a case study in an Alpine destination, **Sainaghi** shows that, in the presence of rigid cost structures and high demand elasticity, it is possible to modify competitive results, by working on collaborative strategies.

Positioning events as creative and innovative tourism products, in Chapter 14, **Pencarelli, Migliaccio, Splendiani and Rivetti** analyze the conceptual links between creativity, innovation, and tourist areas. Focusing on the two perspectives of destination and organization level, this chapter also uses cases of Italian events as examples, highlighting underlying creative and innovative processes.

Information systems designing and monitoring procedures of recovering from service failures are considered as an invaluable way of learning. In Chapter 15, **Díaz Martín, Santos, Suárez** and **del Río** identify the dimensions of an Integrated Service Recovery System. One of the dimensions, response to failures, is comprised of a learning-innovation initiative. The authors highlight that failure management is a continuing process, and based on the systematic detection and analysis of all failure-related information which provides a valuable source of learning for improving future provision of services.

Co-editors:
Metin Kozak, Luisa Andreu, Juergen Gnoth,
Sonja Sibila Lebe and Alan Fyall

PART 1:

DESTINATION IMAGE AND BRANDING

CHAPTER ONE

IMAGES OF ISRAEL
WITHIN A CROSS-CULTURAL PERSPECTIVE

MARIA D. ALVAREZ AND SARA CAMPO

Abstract

A cultural approach to image studies suggests that for places, multi-layered images may exist and countries may be viewed differently from a political and economic point of view or from a tourist destination perspective. This study seeks to determine the effect of tourism promotional brochures on the country and destination image of Israel, as two different constructs. The research follows a quasi-experimental research design and analyzes the effect of printed brochures on the opinions regarding Israel. Additionally, the study compares this influence for samples from two different countries whose people are expected to have varied views regarding Israel. The focus of the paper is on the extent to which efforts geared at creating a positive destination image may also be effective in changing other aspects of the image of a country.
Keywords: country image, destination image, image construction, marketing communication, information sources.

1. Introduction

Recent theoretical developments in the field of marketing that stress the blurring of the roles of marketers and consumers have determined that destinations are not fixed, but created through a process in which tourists also participate (Saraniemi & Kylänen, 2011). Thus, socio-cultural processes are at the heart of tourism, as culture and history influence the construction of imagery about people and places (Pritchard & Morgan, 2001). Image is formed through the "construction of a mental representation of a destination on the basis of information cues delivered by the image formation agents and selected by a person" (Tasci & Gartner,

2007, p. 414). A cultural approach suggests that places receive their meaning and identity through socio-cultural dynamics and there may be co-existing multilayered images (Saraniemi & Kylänen, 2011). At the same time, individuals may rely on varied sources and perspectives when evaluating a place from a cultural, political and economic perspective, or from a tourism point of view.

In accordance with this line of thought, the tourism-related literature has recently begun to differentiate the image of a country from a social, economic and political perspective, and that of the place as a tourist destination. In general, a positive relationship between country and destination image could be expected, since the country image influences the image of products that are made in there, including tourism products (Martin & Eroglu, 1993; Nadeu *et al.*, 2008). However, studies carried on Nepal (Nadeau *et al.*, 2008), Rusia (Stepchenkova & Morrison, 2008) and Turkey (Campo & Alvarez, 2010) have determined that certain countries may be perceived as attractive destinations, while they may also be viewed as economically underdeveloped or politically undesirable. Therefore, a comprehensive management of the country brand requires an understanding of whether "these two images [country and destination] can be separated in the minds of potential travelers" (Stepchenkova & Morrisson, 2008, p. 559) and of how they are managed so that they remain distinct from each other.

While for some countries such as Turkey, individuals seem to be able to differentiate between a negative country image and a positive destination image (Campo & Alvarez, 2010), this may not always be the case. Avraham (2009) points out that the problematic public image of Israel creates a difficult challenge for both the Government and the Ministry of Tourism. From a political point of view, Israel's image is based on its position of power and control with regards to the Palestinians (Avraham, 2009). Furthermore, the international media often portrays Israel as a war zone and a place of conflict (Beirman, 2003), which influences the perceptions regarding the security for tourists. Therefore, for a country such as Israel, faced with continuous image crises, marketing and media strategies become even more important.

The objective of this chapter is to understand the difference between country and destination image in Israel, as a country subject to continuous crises, and to determine how tourism-related promotional strategies may have an effect on modifying both the country and the destination image. In particular, the impact of printed tourist brochures on the creation of Israel's distinct images is determined through the use of experimental methodology. The focus of this paper is on the extent to which efforts geared at creating a positive destination image may also be effective in changing other aspects of the country's image, with potential benefits in terms of international relations, attracting investment and trade. Thus, tourism may act as a valuable context to comprehend broader societal and political issues (Saraniem & Kylänen, 2010).

Additionally, the chapter aims at providing a cross-cultural comparison of the images of Israel among individuals of two different countries, namely Turkey and Spain, to determine to what extent cultural differences may influence the degree to which people are receptive to additional information regarding a given place, and change their perceptions accordingly. Therefore, the research follows an interpretative perspective that analyzes how individuals respond to promotional messages and information transmitted by marketers (Arnould & Thompson, 2005). In this sense, the study compares the perceptions that the Turkish and Spanish nationals have regarding Israel, and who differ from each other in terms of culture, religion and political interaction with Israelites.

2. Literature Review

Kotler and Gertner (2002, p. 251) define the image of an area as "the sum of beliefs and impressions people hold about places. Images represent a simplification of a large number of associations and pieces of information connected with a place. They are a product of the mind trying to process and pick out essential information from huge amounts of data about a place." This conceptualization has been followed by researchers both in connection to country as well as destination image. In this sense, the literature agrees that image is formed by a cognitive component, including the opinions and beliefs that the individual holds regarding a country or a destination, and an affective dimension, based on the emotions and feelings they arouse in the individual (Baloglu & Mangaloglu, 2001; Baloglu & McCleary, 1999; Hosany et al., 2007;. Laroche et al., 2005; Mackay & Fesenmaier, 2000; Stern & Krakover, 1993; Uysal et al., 2000; Verlegh & Steenkamp, 1999). Both components form the overall image (Lin et al., 2007; San Martín & Rodríguez del Bosque, 2008). However, image is not universal and may not be perceived in the same manner as individuals with varied motives and cultural values may view the same place differently (San Martín & Rodríguez del Bosque, 2008). Furthermore, a socio-cultural perspective states that the meaning of the destination is determined by tourists as producers, who create the sense of the place through their practices and discourses (Saraniemi & Kylänen, 2011). Thus, destinations are constructed through a combination of cultural, political, social and economic relationships (Saraniemi & Kylänen, 2011).

Research on destination image has significantly increased in recent years (Ballantyne *et al.*, 2009) although these studies have mainly examined the concept of image, its dimensionality and its relationship to other behavioral variables such as satisfaction and loyalty. However, research that centers on determining how to change the negative image of a country or a destination are far less common. For example, Qu *et al.* (2011) stress the importance of measuring the image of places such as Oklahoma that are viewed as "flat, dusty and windblown" (p. 466). These authors apply a conceptual model of image to measure the perceptions regarding the place, and provide recommendations for the positioning and differentiation of the destination, but they do not mention how the initial image could be changed.

On the other hand, Stepchenkova and Morrison (2008) determine that although American tourists know very little about Russia as a tourist destination, their perceptions are mainly negative. These authors conclude that image is a dynamic concept that changes when the tourists visit the destination. In their study, they find a significant difference regarding Russia's image between those who have previously visited the country, and those who have not, and who usually have a stereotyped perception. Similarly, other research also concludes that visiting the destination may change the initial perceptions regarding the place (Alvarez *et al.*, 2009). However, the question of how to encourage individuals to visit the destination when the initial perception is negative is still in need of investigation. Thus, the influence of information sources and tourism promotional tools on the image of the country and destination, and their ability to change a negative opinion about the place is an interesting area of research.

Gunn's (1972) pioneer research determines that the image of a place is created internally through experience and visitation, or externally, through exposure to various information sources. Following Gunn, more recent research (for example Baloglu, 2001) determines that familiarity and knowledge play an important role in the formation of destination image. Familiarity is not only based on previous experience at the destination, but it may also be obtained through the knowledge that these individuals may have about the place, even though they may not have visited it (Stepchenkova & Morrison, 2008). Some studies (Chon, 1991; Dann, 1996; Pearce, 1982; Phelps, 1986) suggest that tourists' perceptions of the destination positively change when the individual receives additional information or visits the place. However, different conclusions are obtained in research on destinations that have an unclear image, such as the former Soviet Union (Pizam *et al.*, 1991). Stepchenkova and Morrison (2008) explain this divergence by differentiating between the first journey to the place, which brings about the major image modification, and the subsequent visits, during which the perceptual change may be lower. Furthermore, the initial perceptions and stereotyped prejudices may also be reinforced after the visit, due to the individual's selective attention and retrieval of information that is consistent to prior beliefs (Fisher & Price, 1991).

In addition to previous experience, external information sources may influence or change the image of the destination, and that of the country. Gartner (1993) determines that tourist information sources may be classified into eight categories, depending on their degree of autonomy and control by the marketer. Thus, least autonomous sources are paid sources, such as TV and printed advertisements, whereas news and information received through word of mouth are at the other end in the spectrum, being less dependent on the marketer. Some studies have stated that the more neutral sources of information may have a greater effect on the formation of destination image, due to their increased credibility (Butler, 1990; Kim & Richardson, 2003). These include movies and news, which are also important because of their accessibility to a wider audience (Kim & Richardson, 2003) and their ability to not only transmit but also interpret the information (Hall, 2002). In contrast, in Alvarez and Campo's (2011) study, the marketer-controlled promotional source was found to have a greater influence than the more autonomous news item on the image of Turkey. As tourism organizations strive to affect the perceptions regarding the destination and increase visitation, a communication mix that includes advertisements in broadcast and printed media, the Internet, books, movies and travel programs may all be used to manage the image of a place (McCartney *et al.*, 2008).

In particular, visual information concerning the destination is considered to be especially effective, as it provides the opportunity for a vicarious experience of tourist services. Therefore, promotional material that includes visual cues may communicate the various aspects of the destination to people who have not visited it before (Tasci & Gartner, 2007). According to a recent study (Alvarez & Campo, 2011), the audio-visual promotional information positively influences both the image of the country and that of the tourist destination for developing nations that have a negative country image. Past research also determines the importance of photographs in tourism promotional material and travel literature, as it allows for comparison between different destinations (MacKay &

Fesenmaier, 1997). Furthermore, visual content may also influence perceptions regarding the experiences to be obtained at the destination, as associations between pictures and certain experiences may be created (MacKay & Fesenmaier, 1997). Molina *et al.* (2010) also stress the significance of tourist brochures as effective in conveying the image of a given destination.

In line with this literature, the current study analyzes the effect that the promotional tourist information in the form of brochures may have on Israel's country and destination image. Moreover, the influence of cultural factors that may cause individuals from dissimilar countries to respond differently to new and additional information is taken into consideration. Therefore, the next section examines existing studies regarding Israel, and the implications that successive crises have had on its image and competitiveness in tourism.

Since the formation of Israel as a nation state, it has been subject to both conflicts and terrorist attacks that have undermined its tourism industry, since the media often depicts the country as a "'war zone' or a 'hot spot'" (Beirman, 2003, p. 95). Israel has been a site for pilgrimage and tourism for 3,000 years, and it offers a rich variety of historical and archeological resources, as well as a wealth of natural beauties and attractive shores (Beirman, 2003). Despite the potential for varied and alternative tourism, including religious, cultural and diving tourism, the industry in Israel has been characterized by cycles of crisis and recovery (Mansfeld, 1999). Political conflicts and violent incidents that have occurred periodically in Israel have been the cause of a decrease in tourist arrivals and revenues, even though very few fatalities have occurred, so that the actual risk for individuals traveling to Israel is small (Fielding & Shortland, 2005). In this regard, a study of news reporting Israeli conflicts via television determined that individuals are more likely to react to reports about violent events in the media, than to actual increases in conflict intensity in the country (Fielding & Shortland, 2009).

The political conflicts and the perceptions of power in Israeli policies have also resulted in a negative public image of the country. This has led Israel to be ranked last among 35 countries, according to the Anholt Nations Brand Index in 2006 (Anholt, 2006, cited in Appel *et al.*, 2008). In this study, Israel's evaluation was especially low in relation to its people, who were defined as unwelcoming, and in terms of its activities regarding international peace and security (Anholt, 2006, cited in Appel *et al.*, 2008). In addition, the individuals surveyed expressed a much lower willingness to visit Israel than some of the other countries included in the research (Anholt, 2006, cited in Appel *et al.*, 2008). Although Israel has worked to overcome its perceptions of being an unsafe and dangerous destination through specific campaigns and focus on religious tourism (Beirman, 2000), it continues to be influenced by incessant crises and negative media coverage.

A developing country with attractive tourist resources such as Turkey in Europe, Jordan and Syria in Africa or Cuba in America, may not be able to modify its macro-economic situation in the sort term, but may manage to separate its country and destination image. Thus, these nations may focus on their image as tourist destinations to increase their demand for tourist services, which may in turn bring not only economic benefits but also help to improve their country image through improved knowledge and information. Similarly, Israel has many attractions and resources that include a wealth of natural resources, its history and diverse culture, and its ties to Jewish, Christian and Muslim traditions (Avraham, 2009). Providing individuals in target countries with better and more detailed information regarding these aspects may not only increase interest in the place and the probability of a visit in relation to other competing alternatives (Bigné et al., 2001), but it may also benefit the more general country image. In this line, Avraham (2009) determines that one of Israel's media strategies has been to expand the country's image through the promotion of Israel's achievements in different fields that include science, technology and culture. The current research may add to the knowledge on this topic by determining the extent to which efforts to promote the destination at the international level may also influence other aspects of the country's image.

3. Methodology

In accordance to the above literature, the objective of this research is to assess the effect of printed tourist promotional brochures on the country and destination image of Israel, as a nation faced with continuous image crises. With this objective in mind, a 2 x 2 quasi-experimental design was used. The data were collected through a survey administered to university students in two different countries, Turkey and Spain, where it is foreseen that the perceptions about Israel would be dissimilar. In this sense, Pizam et al. (2002) stress historical and current international relations between pairs of nations as influencing the attitude and perceptions of their citizens towards the other country.

Even though both countries where the research was conducted are secular, the Turks, as a predominantly Muslim nation, are expected to have more negative views regarding Israel than the mainly Catholic Spanish.

Furthermore, although in the past Turkey has been most supportive of Israel within the Eastern Mediterranean and Middle Eastern region, in the recent years, this relationship has become conflictive. The Turkish Prime Minister Erdogan has been much more critical and less sympathetic to Israel, and the media in the country has also gradually increased its criticism of Israel policies. In contrast, Spain has shown a more neutral approach to Israel, which may also be explained by the greater geographical distance between the two countries and the lower stake that Spain holds in the region.

The two universities in Turkey and Spain, where the research was carried out, are both public and located in the largest city of their respective country (Istanbul and Madrid). The researchers collected the data at several public access points of the two universities, sequentially assigning the students passing by to the experimental or the control group. Using a questionnaire, respondents were required to evaluate Israel, both as a country and as a tourist destination. The subjects in the experimental group were asked to examine printed brochures on Israel's tourist attractions before filling in the survey. In contrast, the individuals in the control group received no information prior to completing the questionnaire.

The brochures employed as stimulus in the research were obtained from the Israeli consulate in Istanbul. These materials were in English, although they included little written text and were dominated by pictures and photographs. Containing several pages, the brochures portrayed the various destinations and attractions throughout Israel. After pre-testing the leaflets obtained, one was selected as the research stimulus. The same brochure was used both in Turkey and Spain.

The perceptions regarding Israel as a country and as a destination were based on an overall evaluation of the respondents using a 7-point semantic differential scale (varying between totally negative and totally positive) by means of the following question: "What is your overall evaluation of Israel as a country (or as a tourist destination)? The intention of the respondents to visit Israel was assessed through the following three questions measured on a 7-point Likert-type scale: "I intend to visit Israel in the near future," "I would choose Israel as the destination for my next vacation," and "I would prefer to visit Israel as opposed to other similar destinations." Additionally, the level of knowledge regarding Israel in general and in its relation to historical, cultural, political, and economic aspects was determined through a 7-point Likert-type scale.

A total of 542 valid surveys were obtained (300 in Turkey and 242 in Spain). In the Turkish sample, 50% of the respondents were exposed to the stimulus (printed brochure) before completing the questionnaire, whereas 50% only filled in the survey. Among the Spanish respondents, 49.6% of the sample was included in the experimental group, versus 50.4% who were in the control group. The age and gender distribution is similar for both samples, with a mean age of 22 and a slightly higher percentage of females (52.7% of the sample in Turkey and 59.3% of the sample in Spain were women).

4. Results

This study seeks to measure the effect of additional information, in the form of printed promotional brochures, on the country and destination image of Israel. Therefore, the respondents' level of information regarding various aspects of Israel prior to the provision of the stimulus was evaluated. For this purpose, those who had been exposed to added information through the promotional leaflet were excluded from this analysis. Table 1 provides a comparison between the Spanish and Turkish respondents. The findings indicate that the level of information regarding Israel prior to the administration of the stimulus is low for both samples; however, Spanish students report a significantly higher knowledge on all aspects of Israel except political and economic issues, than their Turkish counterparts.

Table 1 - Perceived Knowledge of Israel for Two Samples

	Mean[a] Turkey	Mean[a] Spain	Mean difference	Sig.
Historical aspects	3.15	3.61	0.46	0.01
Cultural aspects	3.12	3.70	0.57	0.00
Political aspects	4.29	3.60	0.69	0.00
Economic aspects	3.71	2.99	0.72	0.00
Tourism attractions	2.36	3.18	0.82	0.00
General knowledge	3.38	3.66	0.28	0.05

[a] 1= Totally uninformed; 7 = Totally informed.

The results of the quasi-experimental research determine the influence of the promotional stimulus on the image change of Israel, both as a country and as a destination, and on the preference for and intention to visit the place. Table 2 summarizes the differences obtained between the experimental and control groups. It is interesting to note that the evaluations regarding Israel are low although the assessments regarding the country as a destination are relatively higher. However, for those individuals exposed to the printed brochure, the evaluations of Israel as a country and as a destination are more positive, while they also show a higher intention to visit the place. On the other hand, the exposure to the additional promotional information does not significantly change the preference for Israel versus other similar destinations.

Table 2 - Mean Differences between Groups

	Control group	Experimental group	T
My opinion about Israel as a country is	2.90 (std. dev. = 1.21)	3.19 (std. dev. = 1.13)	-2.86 (sig. 0.00)
My opinion about Israel as a tourist destination is	3.36 (std. dev. = 1.30)	4.06 (std. dev. = 1.24)	-6.34 (sig. 0.00)
I intend to visit Israel in the near future	2.70 (std. dev. = 1.79)	3.03 (std. dev. = 1.77)	-2.14 (sig. 0.03)
I would choose Israel as the destination for my next vacation	2.40 (std. dev. = 1.60)	2.89 (std. dev. = 1.68)	-3.45 (sig. 0.00)
I would prefer to visit Israel as opposed to other similar tourist destinations	2.63 (std. dev. = 1.70)	2.88 (std. dev. = 1.64)	-1.74 (sig. 0.08)

To evaluate the image changes and preferences in two countries, the means comparison is carried out by segments (Table 3). The findings indicate that the Turkish respondents have a more negative opinion regarding Israel, both as a country and destination, and a lower preference for and intention to visit the country than those individuals in the Spanish sample. However, although the administration of the promotional stimulus significantly increases the evaluations of Israel as a country and destination in both samples, it does not significantly change the intention to visit and the preference for the place among the Spanish respondents. In contrast, Turkish individuals' intention to visit the place and preference for Israel is enhanced after exposure to the printed brochure.

Table 3 - Mean Differences between Groups for Each Country

	TURKISH SAMPLE			SPANISH SAMPLE		
	Control Group	Experimental group	t	Control Group	Experimental group	t
My opinion about Israel as a country is (1= negative; 7 = positive)	2.51 (std. dev. = 1.24)	2.81 (std. dev. = 1.08)	-2.16 (sig. 0.03)	3.39 (std. dev. = 0.98)	3.67 (std. dev. = 1.00)	-2.14 (sig. 0.03)
My opinion about Israel as a tourist destination is (1= negative; 7 = positive)	3.07 (std. dev. = 1.31)	3.90 (std. dev. = 1.36)	-5.37 (sig. 0.00)	3.73 (std. dev. = 1.20)	4.26 (std. dev. = 1.03)	-3.63 (sig. 0.00)
"I intend to visit Israel in the near future" (1 = totally disagree; 7 = totally agree)	2.35 (std. dev. = 1.76)	2.77 (std. dev. = 1.85)	-1.97 (sig. 0.04)	3.13 (std. dev. = 1.74)	3.36 (std. dev. = 1.61)	-1.03 (sig. 0.30)
"I would choose Israel as the destination for my next vacation" (1 = totally disagree; 7 = totally agree)	2.33 (std. dev. = 1.78)	3.03 (std. dev. = 1.88)	-3.27 (sig. 0.00)	2.48 (std. dev. = 1.35)	2.71 (std. dev. = 1.38)	-1.32 (sig. 0.18)
"I would prefer to visit Israel as opposed to other similar tourist destinations" (1 = totally disagree; 7 = totally agree)	2.35 (std. dev. = 1.77)	2.77 (std. dev. = 1.75)	-2.06 (sig. 0.04)	2.97 (std. dev. = 1.54)	3.01 (std. dev. = 1.24)	-0.21 (sig. 0.83)

Table 4 - Mean Differences between Countries

	CONTROL GROUP			EXPERIMENTAL GROUP		
	Turkey	Spain	T	Turkey	Spain	t
My opinion about Israel as a country is (1= negative; 7 = positive)	2.51 (std. dev. = 1.24)	3.39 (std. dev. = 0.98)	-6.26 (sig. 0.00)	2.81 (std. dev. = 1.08)	3.67 (std. dev. = 1.00)	-6.66 (sig. 0.00)
My opinion about Israel as a tourist destination is (1= negative; 7 = positive)	3.07 (std. dev. = 1.31)	3.73 (std. dev. = 1.20)	-4.26 (sig. 0.00)	3.90 (std. dev. = 1.36)	4.26 (std. dev. = 1.03)	-2.38 (sig. 0.01)
"I intend to visit Israel in the near future" (1 = totally disagree; 7 = totally agree)	2.35 (std. dev. = 1.76)	3.13 (std. dev. = 1.74)	-3.63 (sig. 0.00)	2.77 (std. dev. = 1.85)	3.36 (std. dev. = 1.61)	-2.75 (sig. 0.00)
"I would choose Israel as the destination for my next vacation" (1 = totally disagree; 7 = totally agree)	2.33 (std. dev. = 1.78)	2.48 (std. dev. = 1.35)	-0.72 (sig. 0.47)	3.03 (std. dev. = 1.88)	2.71 (std. dev. = 1.38)	1.54 (sig. 0.12)
"I would prefer to visit Israel as opposed to other similar tourist destinations" (1 = totally disagree; 7 = totally agree)	2.35 (std. dev. = 1.77)	2.97 (std. dev. = 1.54)	-2.98 (sig. 0.00)	2.77 (std. dev. = 1.75)	3.01 (std. dev. = 1.24)	-1.16 (sig. 0.24)

Table 4 analyses the differences between the Turkish and Spanish students taking into consideration their membership in the control or experimental group. The findings determine that the change in the Turkish students' evaluation of the destination and their intention to visit the place is greater than that of the Spanish respondents. Nevertheless, the original assessment (prior to the provision of the stimulus) of the Turkish sample is significantly lower than that of the Spanish students. Therefore, the results determine that the initial negative opinion regarding Israel and the lower preference and intention to visit the destination on behalf of Turkish students is somehow offset by the access to additional printed information. However, this change is not enough to reach the results displayed by the Spanish sample.

5. Conclusion

Information used to promote the destination may improve the image of both the destination and the country, even when the initial image is negative, as is the case of Israel. The comparison of perceptions regarding Israel in two different countries with varied religious values and different international relations with Israel, such as Turkey and Spain, shows that these cultural and political differences influence the image of the country and the destination. Specifically, Israel's image is more positive in Spain than in Turkey. However, the relative influence of the destination's promotional tools is greater among the Turks, who hold a more negative initial image. Additionally, tourist promotional tools are unable to increase the choice of the place as the next vacation destination or its preference among other competing destinations among the Spanish sample. In contrast, the positive preference change is stronger among the Turks.

These findings indicate that the tourist promotional tools may positively affect a destination's image, but it may not be enough to attract tourists to that place. To appeal to potential tourists, the destination needs to be preferred to other competing places. As Qu et al. (2011) explain, "consumers are generally offered various destination choices that provide similar features such as quality accommodations, beautiful scenic view, and/or friendly people. Therefore, it is not enough for a destination to be included in the evoked set; instead, the destination needs to be unique and differential to be selected as a final decision" (p. 465). Thus, the reason as to why the promotional material increases the preference for the destination in the Turkish sample may be related to the selection of the specific promotional materials that may be more suited to the Turkish taste.

The tourist promotion chosen as stimulus in the research may not be so attractive for the Spanish people. Additionally, Spaniards may not consider Israel as a better alternative to other more popular destinations in Spain, such as countries that share the same language and culture (Latin America) or a recent history and proximity (Portugal, France and Italy). As Qu *et al.* (2011) state, the key lies in developing the country brand with a strong positioning in which consumers perceive a clear difference between competing products in the same category. A tourist destination included in the country's umbrella brand needs to be unique, distinctive and difficult to replace (Qu *et al.*, 2011).

In the case of Israel, it is necessary for this country to find its own positioning that reflects the key components of a destination brand, its rational (head) and emotional (heart) benefits and associations, together with its brand personality (Morgan & Pritchard, 2004). This positioning strategy should start with the identification of the important elements that differentiate Israel from its competitors in each of its potential markets (Crompton *et al.*, 1992).

The study also adds knowledge to the ways in which tourism may be used as a vehicle to enhance a country's image, not just from the perspective of tourism, but in relation to a number of other aspects. This research supports the conclusion that tourism-related marketing and communication activities aimed at increasing the number of foreign visitors to the destination may have effect in other areas as well. Thus, in the case of Israel, tourist brochures are found to influence not only how the country is seen from a tourism-related perspective, but also from the economic, political and social point of view. Therefore, tourism may be used as a vehicle of international relations and could help overcome negative perceptions and stereotypes affecting a country's image (Alvarez *et al.*, 2009; Light, 2007). Further research needs to be carried out to understand the influence that the various tourist information sources have on a country's image, as well as on its destination image.

References

Alvarez, M.D., & Campo, S. (2011). Controllable versus uncontrollable information sources: Effects on the image of Turkey. *International Journal of Tourism Research*, 13, 310-323.

Alvarez, M.D., Inelmen, K., & Yarcan, Ş. (2009). Do perceptions change? A comparative study. *Anatolia*, 20(2), 401-418.

Anholt, S. (2006). *Global survey confirms Israel is the worst brand in the World*. Retrieved May 2008 from www.nationbrandindex.com/ nbi_q306-usa-press-release.phtml.

Appel, R., Irony, A., Schmerz, S., & Ziv, A. (2008). Cultural diplomacy: An important but neglected tool in promoting Israel's public image. Working Paper. The Interdisciplinary Center Herzliya Lauder School of Government, Diplomacy and Strategy. Retrived April 2011from http://portal.idc.ac.il/en/Argov/Documents/Cultural_Diplomacy.pdf

Arnould, E.J, & Thompson, C.J. (2005). Consumer culture theory (CCT): Twenty years of research. *Journal of Consumer Research*, 31(4), 868–882.

Avraham, E. (2009). Marketing and managing nation branding during prolonged crisis: The case of Israel. In A. Fyall, M. Kozak, L. Andreu, J. Gnoth, & S.S. Lebe (Eds.), *Marketing Innovations for Sustainable Destinations* (pp. 230-242). Oxford: Goodfellows.

Ballantyne, R., Packer, J., & Megan, A. (2009). Trends in tourism research. *Annals of Tourism Research*, 36(1), 149-152.

Baloglu, S. (2001). Image variations of Turkey by familiarity index: informational and experiential dimensions. *Tourism Management*, 22(2), 127-133.

Baloglu, S., & Mangaloglu, M. (2001). Tourism destination images of Turkey, Egypt, Greece, and Italy as perceived by U.S.-based tour operators and travel agents. *Tourism Management*, 22(1), 1-9.

Baloglu, S., & McCleary, K.W. (1999). A model of destination image formation. *Annals of Tourism Research*, 26(4), 868-897.

Beirman, D. (2000). Destination marketing: The marketing of Israel in Australia and the south-west Pacific. *Journal of Vacation Marketing*, 6(2), 145-153.

—. (2003). *Restoring Tourism Destinations in Crisis: A Strategic Marketing Approach*. Oxford: CABI Publishing.

Bigné, J.E., Sánchez, M.I., & Sánchez, J. (2001). Tourist image, evaluation variables and after purchase behaviour: Inter-relationship. *Tourism Management*, 22(6), 607-616.

Butler, R. (1990). The influence of the media in shaping international tourist patterns. *Tourism Recreation Research*, 15, 46–53.

Campo, S., & Alvarez, M.D. (2010). Country versus destination image in a developing country. *Journal of Travel and Tourism Marketing*, 27(7), 749-765.

Chon, K.S. (1991). Tourism destination image modification process: Marketing implications. *Tourism Management*, 12(1), 68-72.

Crompton, J.L., Fakeye, P.C., & Lue, C.C. (1992). Positioning: The example of the Lower Rio Grande Valley in the winter long stay destination market. *Journal of Travel Research*, 31(2), 20–26.

Dann, G.M.S. (1996). Tourists' images of a destination – An alternative analysis. *Journal of Travel and Tourism Marketing*, 5(1/2), 41-55.

Fielding, D., & Shortland, A. (2005). Are Americans more gung-ho than Europeans? Evidence from tourism in Israel during the Intifada. *University of Otago Economics Discussion Papers*, No. 0506.

—. (2009). Does television terrify tourists? Effects of US television news on demand for tourism in Israel. *Journal of Risk and Uncertainty*, 38, 245-263.

Fisher, R.J., & Price, L. (1991). International pleasure travel motivations and post-vacation cultural attitude change. *Journal of Leisure Research*, 23(3), 193-208.

Gartner, W.C. (1993). Image formation process. *Journal of Travel and Tourism Marketing*, 2(2/3), 191-215.

Gunn, C. (1972). *Vacationscapes*. Bureau of Business Research, Austin, TX: University of Texas.

Hall, C.M. (2002). Travel safety, terrorism and the media: The significance of the issue-attention cycle. *Current Issues in Tourism*, 5(5), 458-466.

Hosany, S., Ekinci, Y., & Uysal, M. (2007). Destination image and destination Personality. *International Journal of Culture, Tourism and Hospitality Research*, 1(1), 62-81.

Kim, H., & Richardson, S.L. (2003). Motion picture impacts on destination images. *Annals of Tourism Research*, 30(1), 216-237.

Kotler, P., & Gertner, D. (2002). Country as brand, product and beyond: A place marketing and brand marketing perspective. *Journal of Brand Management*, 9(4/5), 249-261.

Laroche, M., Papadopoulos, N., Heslop, L.A., & Mourali, M. (2005). The influence of country image structure on consumer evaluations of foreign products. *International Marketing Review*, 22(1), 96-115.

Light, D. (2007). Dracula tourism in Romania: Cultural identity and the State. *Annals of Tourism Research*, 34, 746-765.

Lin, D.H., Morais, D.B, Kerstetter, D.L., & Hou, J.S. (2007). Examining the role of cognitive and affective image in predicting choice across natural, developed, and theme-park destinations. *Journal of Travel Research*, 46, 183-194.

MacKay, K.J., & Fesenmaier, D.R. (1997). Pictorial element of destination in image formation. *Annals of Tourism Research*, 24(3), 537-565.

Mansfeld, Y. (1999). Cycles of war, terror, and peace: Determinants and management of crisis and recovery of the Israeli tourism industry. *Journal of Travel Research*, 38, 30-36.

Martin, I.M., & Eroglu, S. (1993). Measuring a multi-dimensional construct: Country image. *Journal of Business Research*, 28, 191-210.

McCartney, G., Butler, R., & Bennett, M. (2008). A strategic use of the Communications mix in the destination image-formation process. *Journal of Travel Research*, 47(2), 183-196.

Molina, A., Gómez, M., & Martín-Consuegra, D. (2010). Tourism marketing information and destination image management. *African Journal of Business Management*, 4(5), 722-728.

Morgan, N., & Pritchard, A. (2004). Meeting the destination branding challenge. In N. Morgan, A. Pritchard, & R. Pride (Eds.) *Destination Branding: Creating the Unique Destination Proposition* (2nd ed.) (pp. 59-78). Burlington, MA: Elsevier Butterworth-Heinemann.

Nadeau, J., Heslop, L., O'Reilly, N., & Luk, P. (2008). Destination in a Country Image Context. *Annals of Tourism Research*, 35(1), 84-106.

Pearce, P.L. (1982). Perceived changes in holiday destinations. *Annals of Tourism Research*, 9, 145-164.

Pizam, A., Fleisher, A., & Mansfeld, Y. (2002). Tourism and social change: The case of Israeli ecotourists visiting Jordan. *Journal of Travel Research*, 41, 177-184.

Pizam, A., Jafari, J., & Milman, A. (1991). Influence of tourism on attitudes: US students visiting the USSR. *Tourism Management*, 12, 47-54.

Phelps, A. (1986). Holiday destination image-the problem of assessment: An example developed in Menorca. *Tourism Management*, 7(3), 168-180.

Pritchard, A., & Morgan, N. (2001). Culture, identity and tourism representations: Marketing Cymru or Wales? *Tourism Management*, 22(2), 167-179.

Qu, H., Kim, L.H., & Im, H.H. (2011). A model of destination branding: Integrating the concepts of the branding and destination image. *Tourism Management*, 32(3), 465-476.

San Martín, H., & Rodríguez del Bosque, I.A. (2008). Exploring the cognitive–affective nature of destination image and the role of psychological factors in its formation. *Tourism Management*, 29(2), 263-277.

Saraniemi, S., & Kylänen, M. (2011). Problematizing the concept of tourism destination: An analysis of different theoretical approaches. *Journal of Travel Research*, 20(2), 133-143.

Stepchenkova, S., & Morrison, A. M. (2008). Russia's destination image among American pleasure travelers: Revisiting Echtner and Ritchie. *Tourism Management*, 29, 548-560.

Stern, E., & Krakover, S. (1993). The formation of composite urban image. *Geographical Analysis*, 25, 130-246.

Tasci, A.D.A., & Gartner, W.C. (2007). Destination image and its functional relationships. *Journal of Travel Research*, 45, 413-425.

Uysal, M., Chen, J., & Williams, D. (2000). Increasing state market share through a regional positioning. *Tourism Management*, 21(1), 89-96.

Verlegh, P.W.J., & Steenkamp, J.B.E.M. (1999). A review and meta-analysis of country-of-origin research. *Journal of Economic Psychology*, 20(5), 521-546.

CHAPTER TWO

CONTENT ANALYSIS OF SLOGANS FOR TOURIST DESTINATIONS

GOKCE OZDEMIR BAYRAK AND METIN KOZAK

Abstract

Tourism authorities or professionals practice a unique approach of marketing destinations and enhancing their value with the use of branding strategies. The initial scope of this study is to identify how destinations differentiate themselves through slogans while seeking to create a distinctive and unique position in relation to other competing destinations. This chapter examines the list of available slogans on websites as branding attributes of 812 destinations that are listed as the members of Destination Marketing Association International. The data collection procedure through content analysis includes checking the links of destination websites in terms of slogans and ranking the terms used in slogans based on the frequency of each word. The assessment of results indicates that differentiating destinations and creating a valuable brand image through slogans is not an easy process. While being effective communication tools for branding destinations, slogans are likely to strengthen brand images and to communicate through websites that attract millions of visitors throughout the world. **Keywords:** destination marketing, destination branding, destination websites, slogans.

1. Introduction

Branding provides a consistent image that makes a product stand on and easy to be identified. Thus, branding is expected to add value to a product (Kozak & Baloglu, 2011; Vellas & Becherel, 1999). Virtually, according to Nilson (2000, p. 62), all products/services can be differentiated and, thus, have the potential to be branded. Over the past few decades, marketing destinations have been very competitive and more significant than earlier where places used to be branded in a similar manner as products and services. In this sense, destination authorities have begun paying more attention to branding in order to differentiate themselves from their competitors. It is clear that destinations have many benefits and advantages when they implement a brand strategy through differentiation, which is an important key to gaining success.

The branding of destinations is affected by culture, history, economics, and politics, all of which make it a complex activity. Thus, destination branding is not a task of the public sector, but fairly a collaborative responsibility of the destinations' key stakeholders. Countries, regions, cities, resorts, and towns that seek to build reputation and prestige are keenly devoted to spending time and money toward re-branding themselves with an aim of capturing a very profitable share in the tourism industry. Destinations that rely heavily on tourism, by all means, pay more attention to branding than others do. Branding a destination starts with understanding its uniqueness, which the brand will be based on, and then emphasizing its value by developing a logo and a slogan in order to make it more recognizable and attractive to prospective tourists.

In a particular reference to the context of business tourism, major cities are usually the places that attract the highest proportion of domestic or international tourists visiting a country; for example, Wales, London, Istanbul, Paris, and New York. It is well known that Paris is a major factor in drawing millions of tourists to France. Generally speaking, major cities in Europe and Asia are usually the capital cities as well. Therefore, they attain a higher rate of recognition due to their association with politics, resulting in a high rate of visibility in the local or international media. Istanbul as a major urban destination, despite not being a capital, is revealed as being a highly recognized metropolitan city of Turkey. Jensen and Korneliussen (2002) contend that particular places or cities in a country, such as London, Paris, Rome, and Istanbul, can act as "halos" or "summary constructs" for the entire country and would be enough to draw the attention of potential visitors.

Every city has its own name, which can be used as an analog to a brand for products and services. Next, branding strategies take into account direct and indirect competitors, incorporating positioning strategies. In addition, the assessment of city branding includes evaluations of marketing activities such as advertising effectiveness, positioning analysis, competitive performance analysis, and market segmentation. In the evaluation of alternatives in the tourism and travel industry, decision makers are bombarded with choices that are easily substitutable, because more and more cities try to attract visitors to gain economic benefits. Most places emphasize the attributes of attractiveness such as friendly people, beautiful scenery, or nice facilities, which no longer assist potential visitors to distinguish between and choose from among competing cities. Therefore, it is crucial for countries to differentiate themselves from others by fostering their unique identity or personality, which is based on their core values.

This chapter attempts uncovering what differentiates each destination in terms of slogans compared with their counterparts. Thus, the proposed study assesses the competitive positions of 812 cities and their brand equity. The study includes a series of destination assessment criteria with regard to major destinations' slogans; for example, Vienna, Bratislava, Prague, Budapest, Paris, Rome, Madrid, Berlin, Athens, London, Brussels, and Amsterdam. It also includes the level of their top-of-mind awareness and attractiveness in an effort to develop a potential unique brand for each of these destinations in the future. This effort of defining the current and potential constituents of brands comprises a comprehensive study of searching for the relevant information that is available on the Internet about various destinations' slogans. At this stage, content analysis includes the assessment of slogans as well as logos for each destination. This process helps us not only evaluate the general structure of destinations but also see which part/s of their characteristics and identities are promoted to constitute overall branding in the international market.

2. Literature Review

Brands are more than just names and symbols. They represent consumer perceptions and feelings about a product and its performance (Kotler & Armstrong, 2006). According to Randall (2000, p. 4), a brand has an existence that is more than an actual product or service. In a similar vein, Kotler and Keller (2006, p. 275) define branding as endowing products and services with the power of a brand. Branding is also considered a method that is used to identify quality products. Whether new or old, a brand should be relevant to people's needs, and its emotional appeal, saliency, and perceived performance need to be stronger than those of its rivals (Morgan & Pritchard, 2000). In order to attain a successful brand, destinations should be different in terms of many aspects (Ritchie & Crouch, 2003). Therefore, branding is all about creating differences.

Keegan and Green (2005) suggest that information about products and brands is derived from a variety of sources and cues, including advertising, publicity, and sales personnel. In contrast with the homogeneity and standardized nature of corporate brands, branded spaces and cities valorize cultural diversity and project images which attempt to convince people that they are relatively unique, distinctive, and original (Gotham, 2007). According to Keller (1998), from an economic perspective, brands also allow consumers to lower search costs for products both internally and externally. Keller (1998) also states that if consumers recognize a brand and have some knowledge about it, then they do not have to engage in a lot of additional thought or processing of information to make a product-related decision. On the other hand, as Morgan and Pritchard (2000) imply, consumers need to be bonded to the brand attitudinally, and a brand's rational and emotional benefits need to be communicated through strong and consistent brand communications. Therefore, authorities should develop images on the objective information to assist consumers while making their final decisions (Kendall & Gursoy, 2007).

Previous research in the field of tourism branding has gained attention mostly with regard to destinations (Blain *et al.,* 2005; Cai, 2002; Cai *et al.,* 2007; Ekinci & Hosany, 2006; Gnoth, 2007; Hankinson, 2004a, 2005; Kozak & Baloglu, 2011; Lee *et al.,* 2006; Pike, 2005, 2009; Williams & Palmer, 1999). On the other hand, branding studies also include tourism (Clarke 2000), hospitality (Mangan & Collins, 2002), package holidays (Westwood *et al.,* 1999), and distribution channels (Woodward, 2000). A number of researchers have studied destination brands in a general sense (e.g., Cai *et al.,* 2007; Gnoth, 2007; Pike, 2005), whereas others have concentrated on different aspects such as brand images (Hankinson, 2004a; Hankinson, 2005), brand personality (Ekinci & Hosany, 2006; Hosany, *et al.,* 2006; Murphy, *et al.,* 2007), brand equity (Boo *et al.,* 2009), brand logo (Hem & Iversen, 2004), positioning, and branding (Kendall & Gursoy, 2007; Pike, 2009). In addition, some studies also contribute to the destination branding through the Internet (Lee *et al.,* 2006; Williams & Palmer, 1999).

The literature illustrates that branding operations also focus on countries apart from cities in general (Kozak & Baloglu, 2011) or on particular countries such as Britain (Hall, 2004), New Zealand (Morgan *et al.,* 2003), or Denmark (Ooi, 2004); whereas some others focus on branding nations (Fan, 2006), for instance, branding states such as Oregon (Curtis, 2001), branding regions, for instance, Central and Eastern Europe (Hall, 1999), Western Australia (Crockett & Wood, 1999), the Alps (Pechlaner *et al.,* 2007), Pays Cathare (Woods and Deegan, 2003), or Alto Minho (Edwards, Fernandes, Fox & Vaughan, 2003). Additional empirical evidence suggests branding the countryside such as Surrey Hills (Niininen *et al.*, 2007) and branding rural destinations (Cai, 2002). There are also several examples of research conducted on city branding issues (Phillips & Schofield, 2007; Trueman, 2004; Merrilees *et al.*, 2007).

Olins (2003) points out the importance for a country's position in the world in many aspects, living in a global world in which all countries communicate all the time, sending several messages throughout different communication channels. Faulkner, Moscardo and Laws (2000) state that branding, as for the country, provides a way of building an emotional link between products and consumers, appealing to holidaymakers' self-image and lifestyle concepts. In addition, according to Gnoth, (2007), branding a destination means offering place values for tourism consumption.

Goeldner *et al.* (2000, p. 653) define a destination brand to be "a name, symbol, logo, word mark or other graphic that identifies and differentiates the destination; conveys the promise of a memorable travel experience that is uniquely associated with the destination; and serves to consolidate and reinforce the recollection of pleasurable memories of the destination experience." In fact, the marketing of many destinations does not begin from a zero base (Hankinson, 2004a). Pechlaner, Raich and Zehrer (2007) explain reasonable brand management as contributing extensively to a destination's success or failure and ensuring an effective use of resources to actively maintain and reinforce unique values of the products as signified by the brand. Morgan *et al.* (2005) propose that a successful destination branding initiative should comprise trust, quality, and lifestyle connotations that consumers can associate with. Place branding, therefore, inevitably becomes a coordinated process rather than a managed activity (Hankinson, 2004b). Branding a destination is also difficult, because brand managers are not in control of the image that can also be affected by the experience of tourists within a destination.

In his study, Baker (2006) points out that a destination or place brand requires constant care, consistency, and commitment to produce the strong and meaningful brand identity that over time will become an asset and be very difficult for competitors to copy. Nevertheless, brand names, logos, and slogans are the key elements of the brand and strongly facilitate brand recognition and awareness. Kohli *et al.* (2007) suggest that logos, whether stylized depictions of brand names or more abstract designs, serve as visual cues for faster processing and universal recognition of brands across different languages and cultures. On the other hand, as Murphy, Benckendorff and Moscardo (2007) indicate, destinations need to embark on the branding process to fully understand the concept in the sense that it requires more than developing logos and slogans if tourists' visiting behavior is to be influenced. It is important that the brand reveals the actual value of the destination and what it really is in consistency with the slogan. Since the brand plays a role in giving the impression what the destination stands for, it is vital to reflect the true view of the destination.

As for tourist destinations, brand names are the actual names of destinations, and a destination name is almost never changed from slogans and logos. In addition, Kohli *et al.* (2007) explain slogans as being the most dynamic element of a brand's identity, the one most easily and most often altered, when needed. According to Lee *et al.* (2006), the slogan, which is a summary of the brand personality of a destination, needs to reflect the brand image. As Keller (1998) stresses, slogans are about phrases that communicate descriptive or persuasive information about the brand. Pike (2005) also considers a slogan as the necessary public articulation of the brand positioning strategy of a destination.

Thus, slogans are effective tools that are used in the enhancement of brand images apart from names and logos. The perception of a destination can, therefore, be changed by an attractive slogan that represents the experience as a whole. According to Avraham (2004), a good slogan may be used for many years and through several different campaigns. Avraham (2004) emphasizes the importance of slogans in delivering messages and defines good slogans as laying out a destination's vision, reflecting its spirit, and creating enthusiasm and momentum. In this manner, logos with slogans contribute to the brand image of a destination and encourage the volume of visits while positioning it in the minds of tourists. Therefore, slogans that consist of word phrases should be creative as well as appealing to draw attention and ease the decision-making process of tourists in favor of a destination. However, creating memorable slogans that complement the destination brand with a name and a logo can contribute toward changing the perceptions of tourists.

3. Methodology

The purpose of this chapter is to analyze the slogans of the destination brands extracted from the websites of the destination marketing organizations **(DMOs)** that are the members of the Destination Marketing Association International (DMAI). The list of the DMOs and their websites has been taken from this organization, because it is considered the world's largest association of destination marketing organizations. DMAI, founded more than 90 years ago, is dedicated to improving the effectiveness of more than 2,800 professionals from more than 650 destination marketing organizations in more than 30 countries (http://www.destinationmarketing.org/page.asp?pid=20). The study, which was completed in March 2009, contains surfing on 812 DMO websites and analyzing the slogans of destinations mentioned on the main page to persuade tourists in terms of vocational visits. Therefore, the links listed on the website of DMAI were used to reach the destination websites to collect the slogans. The authors failed to reach 75 links, as they were not functioning due to unknown reasons.

While communicating with the positioning strategy, a destination can choose whether to develop a unique selling proposition or create a message based on a couple of differentiators. This study has not taken into consideration the different strategies of branding while developing slogans. The study has also excluded from the analysis terms such as "destination," "place," "county," "country," "city," "village," the prepositions, and the articles in order to concentrate on words defining the meaning of destinations. In addition, the names of destinations repeated in the slogans have been excluded from the analysis.

The websites were checked by the two coders for the availability of slogans. Subsequently, a list of collected slogans was compared with each other. As implied by Hall and Valentin (2005), at least two coders are necessary during the process of content analysis in order to avoid the possible appearance of any confusion and misunderstanding. In fact, when a difference about slogans was detected, the websites of the related destinations were checked once more by the two coders. In a subsequent stage, the phrases were content analyzed. Accordingly, frequently used terms were identified, as content analysis is considered an effective and quantitative textual method that is used for analyzing slogans.

The use of content analysis in studying image and representation is much greater, as it has been increasingly used as a tool in examining the effectiveness of tourism websites and analyzing the Web traffic (Hall & Valentin, 2005). In the same study conducted by Hall and Valentin (2005), content analysis and its application by the researchers in many subfields of tourism research ranging from advertisement identification with regard to gender and place issues to the Web has been discussed. In addition, content analysis as a method of qualitative research has been widely used in tourism studies, particularly over the recent years (Cai *et al.*, 2004; Lee *et al.*, 2006; Roney & Özturan 2006; Choi *et al.*, 2007; Govers & Go 2005; Özdemir & Gök 2010; Benckendorff, 2006). While conducting research in tourism, content analysis is mainly focused on collecting information from websites and analyzing it accordingly.

According to Purdue (2001), the designing of websites and the features of Internet marketing contribute to the recognition of a brand image, the effective delivery of messages, and the perceived quality of products and services. In addition, as Liao *et al.* (2006) imply, websites and their quality play a vital role in creating a brand reputation, with their concurrent advantages of convenient global access, interactivity, and easily updated information. Consequently, websites are visited independently by researchers to search for the slogans of destinations, if available, in order to analyze their context in terms of the words used. Therefore, this study includes the collection of data by visiting the target addresses listed on the DMAI in March 2009 and by clicking on each of the listed links to gain an access into the list of destination slogans. Finally, the scope of this study is to emphasize the core words used in slogans and their meanings to convey a message to domestic or international tourists.

4. Results

The study covers 812 DMOs from all over the world that are the members of DMAI. The DMOs in continents range from America with 719 members to Europe with 73, Asia with 8, Australia with 6, and Africa with 6 members. Destination marketing organizations affiliated to DMAI range from regions, cities, towns, states to counties. This study does not take into account the types of destinations but rather destinations regardless of their types. As Pike (2008) points out, travelers are now spoilt for their choice of destinations, which should compete for attention in markets cluttered with the messages of substitute products as well as rival places. Therefore, destination marketers should pay attention toward creating effective slogans due to the target market they identify.

Since it is almost impossible to represent every attribute, destination marketers should develop a clear understanding of the message communicated through slogans. Thus, an analysis is aimed at identifying slogans that differentiate destinations from competing ones and enhance the brand image. When the terms of slogans are analyzed, it is apparent that the words amount to 598 and all are chosen especially to create a slogan which should represent the destination. Some slogans are short and simple [I Amsterdam, Visit Brighton, Historically dynamic (Istanbul), heart of the new west (Calgary)]; whereas others use long and complicated sentences to express a welcoming attitude [There is no place in the world like Sydney, U just have to be here! (Surrey)]. These words specifically try to highlight the attractiveness of destinations, convey the benefits of the destination experience, and create a sympathetic impression.

On the other hand, some slogans and logos simply facilitate destinations to be distinguished from their counterparts while emphasizing the uniqueness that tourists could value. It is certain from a variety of words communicated that destinations have efforts to stand out from others by their unique slogans. An attempt of creating slogans refers to the efforts of destination marketers to be differentiated from competitors in the international tourism arena. Emphasizing the uniqueness of destinations or the most important attribute is considered as a key for destination marketers. As a result, tourists will likely choose the one that most meets their needs, wants, and expectations.

Some destinations' slogans appear to be very simple and easy to remember, including the names of destinations such as *I Amsterdam*, *Visit Brighton*, *Visit Malta*, *Korea Sparkling*, *Only Lyon*, *Only Vegas*, *Cardiff Caerdydd*. Others consist of several words, including the names of destinations such as *I feel sLOVEnia*, *There is no place in the world like Sydney*, *MADrid about you*, *That's so LA*. Some other slogans are designed in the form of not emphasizing the names in slogans to represent destinations such as *make no little plans* (Chicago), *The Mediterranean as it once was* (Croatia), *U just have to be here!* (Surrey), *Historically dynamic* (Istanbul), *Touch your heart* (Taiwan), and *Heart of the new west* (Calgary).

Some slogans include verbs that seek convincing tourists to make decisions in favor of traveling to the destination, for example, "visit," "play," "follow," "welcome," "reserve," "touch," "go," "change," "travel," "stay," "escape," "plan," and "experience." Therefore, pulling tourists to have a memorable experience is done though slogans that reflect the image of destinations and represent brand values. Words expressed by destination marketers are used to create an effective slogan that is an important attribute of branding practices. Reflecting the image with an appropriate slogan facilitates the success of destination marketing. The destination product is intangible, and a slogan is a branding message that makes it tangible. Destination authorities, therefore, should try to encourage their potential visitor segments by establishing an attractive slogan that is promoted through Websites by underlining the appeal of destination products.

Table 1 - Ranks for the words of slogans

Terms	Frequency	Terms	Frequency	Terms	Frequency
Visit	42	Stay	4	Smart	2
Excellent	17	Unspoiled	4	Perfect	2
Welcome	16	Inspiring	3	Refreshing	2
Heart	13	Different	3	Possible	2
Adventure	12	High	3	Good	2
Real	11	New	3	Easy	2
Experience	10	Road	3	Cool	2
Fun	10	Business	3	Closer	2
Play	10	Choice	3	Better	2
World	9	Turn	3	Unique	2
History	8	Discovery	3	Small	2
Capital	8	Future	3	Charm	2
Natural	7	Pure	3	Choose	2
Life	7	Meet	3	Pace	2
Home	7	Coastal	3	Opportunity	2
Lake	7	Plan	3	Meeting	2
Coast	7	Center	3	Park	2
Conferences	6	Tour	3	Kingdom	2
Escape	6	Mystic	3	Passion	2
Big	5	Step	3	Historic	2
Beach	5	Trip	2	Birthplace	2
Culture	5	People	2	Travel	2
Nature	5	Ground	2	Convention	2
Time	5	Valley	2	Living	2
Seasons	5	Like	2	Room	2
Gateway	5	Hospitality	2	Heartland	2
Spirit	5	Rhythm	2	Blues	2
Right	4	Art	2	Wine	2
Side	4	University	2	Rising	2
Treasure	4	Heritage	2	Wild	2
River	4	Rock	2		

Table 1 displays the words used for each destination slogan. The list contains 277 different words used in destinations' slogans among 598 words. Ranks for the words are listed in Table 1 with "visit," "excellent" and "welcome" having the top frequencies. For instance, "visit" is the most mentioned frequent word for being repeated 42 times to define a destination internationally; whereas "excellent" is the second most frequent word for the slogans of destinations with a frequency of 17. In addition, "welcome" is the third most frequent word defining the hospitality of destinations. The frequency of the 51 words used in slogans ranges from 3 to a maximum of 42, such as "time," "season," "life," "natural," "fun," "heart," "adventure," "world," "history," and "capital.. On the other hand, there are 41 words used twice, such as "wine," "easy," "wild," "better," "unique," and "choose." Finally, as a result of individual efforts for differentiation in the message conveyed by slogans, 186 words are used only once among 599 words in total. For instance, words such as "simple," "go," "ski," "colorful," "affordable," "never," "convenient," and "sparkling" are among the less frequently used applications that are chosen to generate an image about a destination.

In order to strengthen the study of slogans, Table 2 shows a list of selected logos to emphasize the usage of slogans with logos and points out how they mutually strengthen the induced image to create a strong and consistent brand. Logos are considered to be limited in creating an image, because they lack the inherent ability to say much about the product (Kohli *et al.*, 2007). Furthermore, this study emphasizes that slogans can bridge this gap, and can and should say something about the image of the product, thereby making it possible to communicate what the brand is about. As can be observed from the list of logos in Table 2, they are mostly colorful drawings, including a special handwriting of the destination name and sometimes the slogan as well. In order to create a distinctive image, the destination authorities are more concerned about putting the logos and slogans in harmony with the message they communicate.

Therefore, the creation of destination brands should address slogans as well as logos, as the expression of brands through coherent drawing and words is likely to influence the perception of tourists. With the examination of 812 destinations, it can be identified that destination marketers may not benefit from slogans to differentiate their attributes as much as they can. In fact, some destinations do not use a slogan and ignore the advantages of having a slogan. In addition, it is surprising that the number of destinations which do not mention any slogan on their websites accounts to 261.

5. Conclusion

Branding is about creating a value for the destinations in accordance with a powerful and distinctive strategic vision. Since there are many competing destinations, branding the destination derived from differentiation should be the key act for strengthening their viability in the international marketplace. In fact, a successful branding campaign or an initiative can enhance the competitiveness of the destination and distinguish the destination from its rivals in the global tourism market. Due to the complexity of the destinations as a product in nature, it might be a risky strategy to rely on a unique selling proposition. However, the development of the communication message based on a number of similar characteristics, such as the majority of the competition, can also create confusion and make the decision-making process of prospective tourists problematic.

It is fairly difficult to differentiate destinations in the global tourism industry. Generally speaking, destinations offer similar tourism products to some extent; so, it is crucial for a destination to make up a story with an emotional appeal, reflecting the unique experience they are going to have by visiting the destination. Therefore, marketers pursue a unique approach of marketing destinations and enhancing their market value with the use of branding. According to Cai (2002), the name of a destination brand is relatively fixed by the actual geographical name of the place. As Morgan *et al.*, (2005) imply, destination names amount to brands and help consumers in evaluating products and making purchasing decisions. On the other hand, slogans and logos are important elements of a brand that are used to tangibilize the destination product. Not only slogans but also logos should be determined by the destination marketers after conducting a detailed search about the right ones to communicate the offered benefits of destinations and their image. Both slogans and logos should be recognizable and memorable with their main features.

In a general sense, this chapter examines the terms of slogans used to express the brand image of destinations as a continuation of Richardson and Cohen's (1994) study which states that tourism destination advertising slogans fail to communicate unique selling propositions, because destinations themselves are geologically and culturally diverse entities whose many and diverse appeals cannot be captured in a single slogan. Pike (2005) explains as to why brand positioning through slogans is complex and challenging while focusing on six reasons; specifically, destinations are multidimensional, stakeholders of markets are heterogeneous, who decides on the slogan is critical, the balance between community consensus and brand theory is important, measuring brand loyalty, and funding problems.

According to Pike (2009), slogans and logos are likely to be short lived, and do not effectively differentiate the destination from competing places that offer similar benefits. Lee *et al.* (2006) analyzed slogans of 50 U.S. states in addition to visuals, graphics, verbal expressions, and the sites' Web-based brand-building elements. They found that the more clearly the tourism slogan of each state reflects the USP of the brand, the more efficient a message it tends to deliver. Pike (2004b) also held an exploratory analysis of the proposition content of the NTO, STO, and RTO slogans of 244 destinations by categorizing the key terms used in each slogan. Likewise, Pike (2004a) conducted a research about the content of slogans used by New Zealand RTOs to determine the extent to which they have been ephemerally indifferent and, therefore, categorized the slogans by their unique selling propositions, such as superiority, discovery, nature, water, and climate. In a similar vein, Lee *et al.* (2006) categorize and analyze the state tourism slogans in terms of unique selling propositions building and market targeting. Study findings show that almost all states emphasize nature and culture/heritage. The study by Worden (2001) examines the meaning of Malaysia's slogan in the context of cultural policies of the Malaysian state in the 1970s and 1980s; whereas Marcella (2010) seeks to examine the extent to which the holiday experiences of the six Dutch Caribbean islands are differentiated in their presentation of individual country narratives, images, logos, and slogans on their official destination homepages.

Derived from the study, destinations try to stand out from their competitors by the words they use in slogans to express an attractive place to visit. They also emphasize the unique features through slogans to create distinctiveness among other destinations. Probably, destinations that offer very similar products differentiate themselves by offering similar but better products with an enhanced experience resulting from a high performance. Considering the group of destinations under investigation, it has been observed that many destination marketers seek to attract tourists through slogans whereby 261 destinations (almost one-third) attempt to create one slogan. On the other hand, it is argumentative that all destinations could create a special slogan or a logo that do not look like each other and remind other destinations with similar slogans. Since the creativity has its own limits, slogans and logos that represent the basic and narrow view of destinations should be supported by many other brand elements.

On the other hand, there are some limitations that should be considered. First, the data were collected in the year 2009 from destination homepages. Slogans available for destinations but not accessible through Websites could not be evaluated. Second, inactive Websites at the time of examination were not added to the research. In spite of these limitations, results are expected to be helpful for developing a unique brand for each city included in this study. Depending on these results, the authorities are able to define a distinctive position to market their cities in the international arena or conduct cooperative marketing with other cities with similar offerings. Destination marketers should pay strict attention for differentiators and positioning variables not to be alike in terms of the communication message sent. Inevitably, as the number of claims for brands increases, it will be more complex for consumers to remember the key point of messages, particularly in today's communication environment. For example, it might be viable for Paris to keep its distinctive and unique position while joint branding is to be conducted for other cities with similar attributes and identities such as Prague, Budapest, Bratislava, and Bucharest. Since branding a city involves keeping the core values, identities, and sense of place of a city per se, this study of developing EU city brands will also serve a social benefit for the whole European community in preserving their authentic identities.

Table 2 - Examples of Logos for Destinations

References

Avraham, E. (2004). Media strategies for improving an unfavorable city image. *Cities,* 21(6), 471-479.

Baker, B. (2006). http://www.destinationbranding.com/articles/Places_New_Brand_Fron tier.pdf, September 10.

Benckendorff, P. (2006). An exploratory analysis of traveler preferences for airline website content. *Information on Technology and Tourism*, 8, 149-159.

Blain, C., Levy, S.E., & Ritchie, J.R.B. (2005). Destination branding: Insights and practices from destination management organizations, *Journal of Travel Research*, 43, 328-338.

Boo S., Busser, J., & Baloglu, S. (2009). A model of customer-based brand equity and its application to multiple destinations. *Tourism Management*, 30, 219-231.

Cai, L., Card, J.A., & Cole, S.T. (2004). Content delivery performance of World Wide Web sites of US tour operators focusing on destinations in China. *Tourism Management,* 25, 219-227.

Cai, L.A. (2002). Cooperative branding for rural destinations. *Annals of Tourism Research*, 29(3), 720–742.

Cai, L.A., Qiu, H.L., & Guoxin, L. (2007). Towards a competitive destination brand in a mass market. *Tourism Analysis,* 12, 463 – 471.

Choi, S., Lehto, X.Y., & Morrison, A.M. (2007). Destination image representation on the Web: Content analysis of Macau travel related websites. Tourism Management, 28, 118-129.

Clarke, J. (2000). Tourism brands: an exploratory study of the brands box model. *Journal of Vacation Marketing,* 6(4), 329-345.

Crockett, S.R., & Wood, L.J. (1999). Brand Western Australia: A totally integrated approach to destination branding. *Journal of Vacation Marketing*. 5(3), 276-289.

Curtis, J. (2001). Branding a state: The evolution of brand Oregon. *Journal of Vacation Marketing*, 7(1), 75-81.

Daye, M. (2010). Challenges and prospects of differentiating destination brands: The case of the Dutch Caribbean islands'. *Journal of Travel & Tourism Marketing*, 27(1), 1-13.

d'Hauteserre, A. (2001). Destination branding in a hostile environment. *Journal of Travel Research*, 39, 300-307.

Edwards, J., Fernandes, C., Fox, J., & Vaughan, R. (2003). Tourism brand attributes of the Alto Minho, Portugal. In D. Hall & G. Richards (eds.), *Tourism and sustainable community development.* Routledge.

Ekinci, Y., & Hosany, S. (2006). Destination personality: An application of brand personality to tourism destinations. *Journal of Travel Research,* 45(2), 127-139.

Fan, Y. (2006). Branding the nation: What is being branded? *Journal of Vacation Marketing,* 12(1), 5-14.

Faulkner, B., Moscardo, G., & Laws, E. (2000). *Tourism in the 21st century: Lessons from experience*, Continuum, London.

Gnoth, J. (2007). The structure of destination brands: Leveraging values. *Tourism Analysis,* 12, 345–358.

Govers, R., & Go, F.M. (2005). Projected destination image online. Website content analysis of pictures and text. *Information Technology & Tourism*, 7, 73-89.

Goeldner, C.R., Ritchie, J.R.B, & McIntosh, R.W. (2000). Tourism: *Principles, practices, philosophies*, John Wiley, USA.

Gotham, K.F. (2007). (Re)Branding the Big Easy: Tourism rebuilding in Post-Katrina New Orleans, Urban Affairs Review, 42(6), 823-850.

Hall, C.M., & Valentin, A. (2005). Content Analysis. In Ritchie B.W., Burns P. & Palmer C., *Tourism research methods: Integrating theory with practice* (pp.191-210), Oxon: CABI.

Hall, D. (1999). Destination branding, niche marketing and national image projection in Central and Eastern Europe. *Journal of Vacation Marketing,* 5(3), 227-237.

Hall, J. (2004). *Branding Britain. Journal of Vacation Marketing,* 10(2), 171-185.

Hankinson, G. (2004a). The brand images of tourism destinations: A study of the saliency of organic images. *Journal of Product & Brand Management*, 13(1), 6-14.

—. (2004b). *Re*lational network brands: towards a conceptual model of place brands. *Journal of Vacation Marketing*, 10(2), 109-121.

—. (2005). Destination brand images: A business tourism perspective. *Journal of Services Marketing,* 19(1), 24-32.

Hem, L.E., & Iversen, N.M. (2004). How to develop a destination brand logo: A qualitative and quantitative approach. S*candinavian Journal of hospitality and tourism,* 4(2), 83-106.

Hosany, S., Ekinci, Y., & Uysal, M. (2006). Destination image and destination personality: An application of branding theories to tourism places. *Journal of Business Research*, 59, 638–642.

Jensen, Ø., & Korneliussen, T. (2002), Discriminating perceptions of a peripheral 'Nordic Destination' among European tourists, *Tourism and Hospitality Research*, 3(4), 319-330.

Keegan, W.J., & Green, M.C. (2005). *Global marketing,* 4th ed., NJ: Prentice Hall.

Keller, K.L. (1998). *Strategic brand management: Building, measuring, and managing brand equity*, NJ: Prentice-Hall.

Kendall, K.W., & Gursoy, D. (2007). A managerial approach to positioning and branding: Eponymous or efficient. *Tourism Analysis*, 12, 473–483.

Kohli, C., Leuthesser, L., & Suri, R. (2007). Got slogan? Guidelines for creating effective slogans. *Business Horizons,* 50, 415-422.

Kotler, P., & Keller, K.L. (2006). *Marketing management*, NJ: Pearson Prentice Hall.

Kotler, P.,& Armstrong, G. (2006). *Principles of marketing,* NJ: Prentice Hall.

Lee, G, Cai, L., & O'Leary, A.J.T. (2006). WWW. branding states. US: An analysis of brand-building elements in the US state tourism websites. *Tourism Management,* 27(5), 815-828.

Liao, C., To, P., & Shih, M. (2006). Website practices: A comparison between the top 1000 companies in the US and Taiwan, *International Journal of Information Management*, 26, 196–211.

Mangan, E., & Collins, A. (2002). Threats to brand integrity in the hospitality sector: Evidence from a tourist brand international. *International Journal of Contemporary Hospitality Management*, 14(6), 286-293.

Maynard, M., & Tian, Y. (2004). Between global and glocal: Content analysis of the Chinese web sites of the 100 top global brands. *Public Relations Review*, 30, 285-291.

Merrilees, B., Miller, D., Herington, C., & Smith, C. (2007). Brand Cairns: An insider (resident) stakeholder perspective. *Tourism Analysis,* 12(5/6), 409–418.

Morgan, N., & Pritchard, A. (2000). *Advertising in tourism and leisure*, Oxford: Butterworth-Heinemann.

Morgan, N., Pritchard, A., & Piggott, R. (2003). Destination branding and the role of the stakeholders: The case of New Zealand. *Journal of Vacation Marketing,* 9(3), 285-299.

Morgan, N., Pritchard, A., & Pride, R. (2005). *Destination branding: Creating the unique destination proposition*, Oxford: Elsevier Butterworth-Heinemann.

Murphy, L., Benckendorff, P., & Moscardo, G. (2007). Destination brand personality: Visitor perceptions of a regional tourism destination. *Tourism Analysis*, 12, 419–432.

Nilson H.T. (2000). *Competitive branding*, NY: John Wiley.

Nininen, O., Hosany, S., Ekinci, Y., & Airey, D. (2007). Building a place brand: A case study of Surrey Hills. *Tourism Analysis,* 12, 371–386.

Olins, W. (2003). *On brand*, Slovenia: Thames & Hudson.

Ooi, C. (2004). Poetics and politics of destination branding: Denmark. *Scandinavian Journal of Hospitality and Tourism,* 4(2), 107-128.

Özdemir, G., & Gök, O. (2010). Evaluating popular city destinations' websites: A framework for website assessment. *Tourism Analysis*, 14(6), 809-819.

Pechlaner, H., Frieda, R., & Zehrer, A. (2007). The Alps: challenges and potentials of a brand management. T*ourism Analysis,* 12, 359–369.

Phillips, L., & Schofield, P. (2007). Pottery, pride, and prejudice: Assessing resident images for city branding *Tourism Analysis,* 12(1), 397-407.

Pike, S. (2004a). Destination positioning slogans: analysis of themes used by New Zealand regional tourism organizations. In J. Wiley (ed.) *Proceedings of the Australian and New Zealand Marketing Academy Conference*, 29 November - 1 December 2004, Victoria University, New Zealand.

—. (2004b). Destination brand positioning slogans towards the development of a set of accountability criteria. *Acta Turistica*, 16(2), 102-124.

—. (2005). Tourism destination branding complexity, beyond products brand management. *Journal of Product & Brand Management,* 14(4), 258-259.

—. (2008). Destination marketing: An integrated marketing communication approach, Oxford: Butterworth-Heinemann.

—. (2009). Destination brand positions of a competitive set of near-home destinations. *Tourism Management*, 30(6), 857-866.

Purdue, R.R. (2001). Internet site evaluations: The influence of behavioral experience, existing images, and selected website characteristics. *Journal of Travel and Tourism Marketing,* 11(2/3), 21-38.

Randall, G. (2000). *Branding: A practical guide to planning your strategy*, London: Logan Page.

Richardson, J., & Cohen, J. (1994). State slogans: The case of the missing USP. *Journal of Travel & Tourism Marketing.* 2(2&3), 91-110.

Ritchie, J.R.B., & Crouch, G.I. (2003). *The competitive destination: A sustainable tourism perspective*, Oxon: CABI.

Roney, S.A., & Özturan, M. (2006). A content analysis of the web sites of Turkish travel agencies. *Anatolia,* 17(1), 43-54.

Trueman, M., Klemm, M., & Giroud, A. (2004). Can a city communicate?. Bradford as a corporate brand. *Corporate Communications: An International* Journal, 9(4), 317-330.

Vellas, F., & Becherel, L. (1999). *The international marketing of travel and tourism: A strategic approach,* London: Macmillan.

Westwood, S., Morgan, N., Pritchard, A., & Ineson, E.(1999). Branding the package holiday – the role and significance of brands for UK air tour operators. *Journal of Vacation Marketing*, 5(3), 238-252.

Williams, A.P., & Palmer, A.J. (1999). Tourism destination brands and electronic commerce: Towards synergy?. *Journal of Vacation Marketing*, 5(3), 263-275.

Woods, M., & Deegan, J. (2003). A warm welcome for destination quality brands: The example of the Pays Cathare region. *International Journal of Tourism Research*, 5, 269–282.

Woodward, T. (2000). Using brand awareness and brand image in tourism channels of distribution. *Journal of Vacation Marketing*, 6(2), 119-130.

Worden, N. (2001). Where it all began: The representation of Malaysian heritage in Melaka. *International Journal of Heritage Studies*, 7(3), 199-218.

http://www.destinationmarketing.org/page.asp?pid=20

PART 2:

TOURIST SATISFACTION AND EXPERIENCE

CHAPTER THREE

LOW-SEASON TOURIST SATISFACTION AT TRADITIONAL MEDITERRANEAN RESORTS

JOAN B. GARAU AND SARA CAMPO

Abstract

This chapter presents the design and validation of an instrument for measuring low-season tourist satisfaction at a traditional Mediterranean holiday destination, the island of Mallorca. The said survey-based satisfaction scale was developed after conducting a review of literature and following in-depth interviews with tourism experts. Subsequently, it was tested out on a representative sample of tourists for validation purposes and also to determine whether modifications had to be made to the scale. The results indicate that three variables exert a strong, significant influence on overall tourist satisfaction: accommodation at the destination; the natural, cultural and urban setting; and restaurants at the destination. **Keywords:** tourist satisfaction, measurement scale, low season, traditional Mediterranean destinations.

1. Introduction

Tourist destinations have a strong need to gather reliable competitiveness indicators. Customer satisfaction is considered to be one of the most powerful indicators, since high customer satisfaction levels will probably indicate high future profits (Anderson & Sullivan, 1990), and tourist satisfaction has been proved to exert a positive influence on destination loyalty (Anderson & Sullivan, 1990, Cronin *et al.*, 2000, Stauss & Neuhaus, 1997) through a positive image of the destination, its recommendation to other customers, repeat visits, increased expenditure and a reduction in price sensitivity. Due to their seasonality, traditional Mediterranean resorts also experience big changes in the composition of the tourism demand throughout the year (Garau, 2002), generating different tourist satisfaction scenarios, depending on the season.

Taking into account the importance of the satisfaction variable, if customer-oriented policies are to be applied at tourist destinations, it is crucial for them to have reliable measurement tools at their disposal, capable of assessing customer satisfaction. Generally these instruments are designed for use during high-season frameworks. However, circumstances, interests, and tourists' travel motivations tend to vary from season to season and certain measurements may therefore be inappropriate.

This chapter presents a measurement model specifically designed to measure low-season tourist satisfaction, based on tourists' evaluations of their experiences, with reliability tests and a discussion of the implications.

More specifically, our chapter presents the results of a pilot test conducted at a leading traditional holiday destination – Mallorca – during the low season. The objectives were as follows: from a review of literature and interviews with tourism experts, to determine what aspects of the tourism experience should be measured and how; to design an initial data-gathering instrument, incorporating aspects identified in literature and other input from discussions with tourism experts; to conduct a pilot test of the measurement instrument; to determine the validity of different measurement scales in order to validate the instrument; to identify factors with a distorting effect on the expected results, perhaps because satisfaction is being analysed during the low season; and, finally, to make any necessary adjustments so as to ensure a reliable tourist satisfaction measurement tool.

2. The Concept of Tourist Satisfaction

For some decades now, satisfaction has been one of the most commonly analysed constructs in the marketing literature (Fournier & Mick, 1999; Szymnasky & Henard, 2001). During the last decades, over 15,000 articles were published on customer satisfaction/dissatisfaction (Peterson & Wilson, 1992). However, given the variety of different ways in which satisfaction is conceptualized, this poses a problem for researchers when choosing the most fitting definition, developing valid measurement tools, and comparing empirical results (Giese & Cote, 2000).

When an analysis is made of different definitions of satisfaction, some slight nuances can be observed in the methods used to measure it (Campo & Yagüe, 2009a). These discrepancies mainly concern: (1) the nature of the reply or state of satisfaction, (2) aspects or mechanisms involved in generating satisfaction, and (3) the purchase or consumption stage when satisfaction occurs.

One of the most widely used definitions is Oliver's (1981). He defines satisfaction as "an evaluation of the surprise inherent in a product acquisition and/or consumption experience. In essence, the summary psychological state resulting when the emotion surrounding disconfirmed expectations is coupled with the customer's prior feelings about the consumption experience" (Oliver, 1981, p. 27). This definition refers to the fact that a customer's evaluation of a specific purchase is an emotional one. He also cites how this evaluation is made: by comparing what is received after making the purchase with what was expected when the service is used.

This definition is based on a pioneering theory, according to which satisfaction is derived from a comparison of pre-purchase expectations and post-purchase or post-consumption perceptions. This comparison is known as disconfirmation (Oliver, 1980; 1981), and it can be positive, null or negative. Models based on this theory (see the literature review in Campo & Yagüe, 2009a) claim that the variables that exert a direct influence on satisfaction are disconfirmation (Cadotte *et al.*, 1987) and customer expectations, with this last variable exerting a lesser influence (Oliver, 1981).

Previous studies (Yi, 1990; Yi & La, 2003) demonstrate that, in addition to these two variables (disconfirmation and expectations), customer perceptions are also directly influential in generating satisfaction. Likewise, they show that customer expectations and customer perceptions have an indirect impact on satisfaction through disconfirmation. Lastly, some authors, like Anderson and Sullivan (1990), separate the effect of positive and negative disconfirmation on satisfaction, finding that the second has a greater impact on customer satisfaction.

Churchill and Surprenant (1982) define satisfaction as "an outcome of purchase and use resulting from the buyer's comparison of the rewards and costs of the purchase in relation to the anticipated consequences" (Churchill & Surprenant, 1982, p. 493). According to this definition, the evaluation process is mainly a cognitive-evaluative one, carried out after the product's purchase, and the product is assessed by comparing the benefits of its purchase with associated costs.

This idea of satisfaction is based on the concept of perceived utility, as seen by the customer, and the determinants of satisfaction are identified as being the benefits perceived by the customer and incurred costs when the product is purchased. This is the approach followed by Campo and Yagüe (2007, 2009) and Campo and Garau (2008).

Although the expectation-disconfirmation paradigm is normally used as a theoretical basis in understanding satisfaction, there are serious drawbacks to measuring it, because a mechanism is needed to record customer expectations prior to the purchase stage, in addition to their post-purchase perceptions. Consequently, attempts to measure expectations and contrast them with perceptions have gradually been replaced by efforts to measure customers' perceived level of satisfaction. Indeed, from comparative studies of results based on the disconfirmation theory and others based on perceived utility, better results are seen to be achieved in the second case (Anderson & Sullivan, 1990; Churchill & Suprenant, 1982).

Among more up-to-date definitions of satisfaction, reference must be made to the interpretation put forward by Anderson et al. (1994): "An overall evaluation based on the total purchase and consumption experience with a good or service over time" (Anderson et al., 1994, p. 54). This definition and other latter ones do not explicitly describe how this evaluation is made by customers. Instead, they focus on what the customer actually evaluates. In this case, satisfaction with a specific transaction is equated by Anderson et al. (1994) with overall satisfaction with a service (Bolton & Drew, 1991; Garbarino & Johnson, 1999), and customer satisfaction is defined as a cumulative assessment, dependent on all past purchases made by the customer. According to some authors (e.g. Jones & Suh, 2000), this approach is more accurate, since it is more efficient at explaining a customer's long-term behavioural intentions and the positive consequences of customer satisfaction.

The definitions outlined above focus on how customers evaluate satisfaction and what they evaluate; i.e. whether it is their last purchase or whether it is a cumulative assessment. What they fail to refer to, however, is the nature of this evaluation: whether it is cognitive, affective or a combination of both. Later definitions try to explore the exact nature of the evaluation process and they allude to the emotional component as being a determining factor in customer satisfaction, defining it as "an emotional state of mind after exposure to the opportunity" (Baker & Crompton, 2000, p. 787).

Finally, one group of authors believes that satisfaction is neither cognitive nor affective, but both things at the same time, and they purport that satisfaction should be defined as "the evaluation of an emotion" (Hunt, 1977, p. 459-60). This last definition encompasses concepts encapsulated in prior definitions, since it incorporates cognitive components (the evaluation) and emotional ones (emotions); it can refer to a specific purchase and/or to cumulative ones, because the emotional component can be a consequence of a specific purchase or a succession of purchases; and it implicitly incorporates the need for a purchase in evaluations of product satisfaction, because a product must necessarily be consumed for an evaluation to be made or an emotion felt.

3. Measuring Tourist Satisfaction

Given the differing definitions of satisfaction and the debate that has been aroused in literature, authors like Steenkamp *et al.* (1999), Garau (2009) or Campo and Garau (2010) suggest that satisfaction should be measured as a global assessment of the total purchase and customer experience. When this is put into practice, businesses tend to opt for one of two typical methods: either to record sales and complaints, or to measure customer satisfaction through a satisfaction survey. The former has serious drawbacks, because not all dissatisfied customers actually make a complaint and this method does not offer an insight into what aspects of the service need improving. The latter, on the other hand, is the method most commonly used by service sector companies.

Two main approaches are taken to surveys. In the first case, customers are considered to make a global one-dimensional evaluation of the experience (an approach taken by Hallowell, 1996; Soderlund, 1998; Yi, 1990; Zinz, 2001). Although this global one-dimensional measurement system is widely used, it has also been criticized in literature (Stauss & Neuhaus, 1997), mainly because if customers obtain the same level of satisfaction, it is assumed that they coincide in their opinions of differing aspects of the purchased product. This assumption is false. Even if individuals achieve the same level of satisfaction, they might differ in their opinions of these different aspects or even have opposite views.

The second option consists of regarding satisfaction as a multi-dimensional construct. This makes it possible to identify which attributes are more important for customers in generating satisfaction. Following this approach, customer satisfaction indexes have been developed at both a national and international level in Sweden (Fornell, 1992), the United States (Fornell, *et al.,* 1996), Norway (Andreassen & Lindestad, 1998) and Denmark (Martensen, *et al.*, 2000). In the tourist industry, studies can be found aimed at developing satisfaction scales, such as Millan and Esteban (2004) applied to travel agencies, and Kozak (2003, 2004) or Kozak and Rimmington (1999), who use a satisfaction index to analyse rival destinations. Similarly, a satisfaction scale was developed by Campo and Garau (2008[a]) and Garau (2009) for sun and sand destinations.

In this chapter, a mixed approach is taken. First, following the work of Campo and Garau (2008[a]), Garau (2009) and Campo and Garau (2010), a multi-dimensional satisfaction survey was developed that includes every aspect of a destination that is appraised when tourists decide how satisfied they are with it. At the same time, the survey also includes questions about the tourists' overall level of satisfaction, so as to identify the partial influence of each satisfaction component on overall satisfaction.

4. Methodology

To design the measurement instrument, an extensive review of literature was first conducted. Additionally, 20 in-depth interviews were held with a group of leading experts from the Balearic tourist industry, including members of the local hoteliers' association, the public authorities, SMEs, and academics, all representative of tourism in the Balearics today. These in-depth interviews were carried out during the months of August, September and October 2009.

The structure of the measurement instrument was designed using input from the literature review and from the above in-depth interviews. It initially included a set of descriptive tourist-typology variables, followed by the 38 variables shown in Table 1, directed at measuring tourist satisfaction with different aspects of the trip, such as the airport, accommodation, catering outside the accommodation centre, destination, beaches and leisure services. Lastly, the questionnaire included variables aimed at measuring overall tourist satisfaction with the trip.

The measurement system was based on 7-point Likert scales, with semantic equivalences ranging from 1=Totally dissatisfied to 7=Totally satisfied, 1=Not at all important to 7=Very important, and 1=Absolutely not to 7=Definitely. All the above input was used to draft a survey for subsequent use.

The survey was conducted in person at the departure gate of domestic and international flights leaving from Son Sant Joan Airport in Palma. The tourists were interviewed at the end of their holiday in the Balearics during the month of February 2010, more specifically between February 3rd and 20th 2010. To ensure a more representative sample, no more than 10 interviews were conducted per flight. During the fieldwork stage, 440 surveys were conducted. Once they had been checked, 40 were rejected because they were incomplete or because there was a problem of some kind with the answers. In the end, a final sample of 400 valid surveys was left.

Specifically, 38% of the final sample was made up of Germans (152), 29% were British (116), 22.5% were Spaniards (90), and 11% corresponded to other nationalities (44), reflecting the distribution of tourism to the Balearics by nationality. 220 of the individuals were male (55%) and 180 were female (45%). The age distribution, which highlighted the representativeness of different age groups, was fairly homogeneous, with 21.2% of the sample being under 30, 26.6% being aged between 31 and 45, 28.9% between 46 and 60, and 23.3% being over 60. 40.9% of the interviewees had secondary school studies and 35.9% held a university degree, while those with a low level of education (primary school studies) or postgraduate education (a master's degree or PhD) accounted for more minor percentages (14.2% and 9% respectively). Given the intrinsic nature of traditional holiday destinations, most of the tourists had visited the resort for leisure purposes (62.2%), followed by those on a visit to friends or relatives (14.5%), and people travelling for work purposes (12.7%) or to attend a congress (2.8%).

5. Results

In order to analyse the multi-dimensional aspect of satisfaction, a principal components analysis was conducted with the SPSS statistical package. Using the varimax rotation method, the original information, made up of 38 items or variables, was summarized into 7 factors, conserving 82% of the total explained variance. The results of the tests – a KMO equal to 0.67 (higher than the recommended value of 0.50) and Bartlett's test of sphericity with significance at p =0.000 - confirm the excellent fit of the exploratory factor analysis.

Factor 1 (F1), satisfaction with the airport, is made up of appraisals of different aspects of the destination airport (SA_1 to SA_5). This component obtained a Cronbach alpha of 0.895, much higher than the minimum recommended value of 0.70. To find out which variables are more influential in generating satisfaction with the airport, a regression analysis was conducted $_{(Eq1)}$, where overall satisfaction with the airport (SA) is the dependent variable and each of the other variables – the facilities (SA_1), treatment by staff (SA_2), signage (SA_3), the price/quality ratio (SA_4) and transfers (SA_5) – is an independent variable. The result of the regression model shows that 72.1% of satisfaction with the airport is explained by 5 of the independent variables included in the model (corrected R^2 =0.721).

$$SA = B + a_1 * SA_1 + a_2 * SA_2 + a_3 * SA_3 + a_4 * SA_4 + a_5 * SA_5 + error \quad \text{(Eq1)}$$

From the regression analysis and standardized beta coefficient $_{(Eq2)}$ that was obtained, the items that are most influential in generating tourist satisfaction with the airport were found to be the signage (a_3=0.287), price/quality ratio of products that can be purchased there (a_4=0.253), and treatment by the airport staff (a_2=0.216). The facilities exert a lesser influence. Transfers from the airport to the destination do not exert a significant influence on tourist evaluations, perhaps because not all tourists use these services.

$$SA = B + \underline{0.185} * SA_1 + \underline{0.216} * SA_2 + \underline{0.287} * SA_3 + \underline{0.253} * SA_4 + 0.045 * SA_5 + error$$

(Eq2)
(Significant values underlined p<0.05)

Factor 2 (F2), satisfaction with the accommodation (SAC), is made up of satisfaction with the facilities, with services at the accommodation centre, meals, treatment by staff, and the price/quality ratio (SAC_1 to SAC_5). It is particularly reliable, since it obtained a Cronbach alpha of 0.995. A regression analysis was also conducted to test the importance of each of the variables in factor 2 $_{(Eq3)}$. From the results of the regression model, 4 of the 5 significant variables explain 85.1% of the dependent variable, satisfaction with the accommodation (corrected R^2 =0.851). When satisfaction with the accommodation is rated, the significant variables are the price/quality ratio (SAC_5), meals (SAC_3), treatment by staff at the hotel (SAC_4) and, finally, the facilities (SAC_1). The "other accommodation services" variable was not very influential, perhaps because different guests tend to assess different aspects, possibly leading to contradictions in the replies.

$$SAC = B + \underline{0.181} * SAC_1 + 0.031 * SAC_2 + \underline{0.273} * SAC_3 + \underline{0.221} * SAC_4 + \underline{0.300} * SAC_5 + error$$

(Eq3)
(Significant values underlined p<0.05)

Factor 3 (F3), satisfaction with restaurants at the destination (SR), includes satisfaction with the amount/variety of restaurants, the treatment by staff at restaurants, the quality of the meals, the price/quality ratio at restaurants, and a fifth variable comprising satisfaction with the hospitality shown by the resident population (SR_1 to SR_5) $_{(Eq4)}$. An alpha reliability coefficient of 0.932 was obtained for this factor. From the results of the regression model, the 5 significant variables that make up the dependent variable (satisfaction with restaurants) explain 82.5% of the latter. The variables that contribute the most to tourist satisfaction with restaurants are the price/quality ratio (SR_4) and quality of the meals (SR_3), followed by the amount and variety of available restaurants (SR_1), treatment by staff at restaurants (SR_2), and the hospitality shown by the resident population (SR_5).

$$SR = B + \underline{0.172} * SR_1 + \underline{0.120} * SR_2 + \underline{0.300} * SR_3 + \underline{0.323} * SR_4 + \underline{0.090} * SR_5 + error \text{ (Eq4)}$$
(Significant values underlined p<0.05)

Factors 4 (F4) and 5 (F5). The fourth and fifth factors are very closely interrelated. F4 can be termed satisfaction with the natural/cultural setting and it includes satisfaction with the climate, scenery, towns and cities, and architectural heritage (Alpha = 0.91) (SN_1 to SN_4). F5 encompasses appraisals of the urban setting: its cleanliness, safety, peace and quiet, roads into urban areas, the price/quality ratio of services at the destination, child-friendly facilities at the destination, and public transport (Alpha = 0.929) (SE_1 to SE_7). The regression model indicates that satisfaction with the natural setting $_{(Eq5)}$ and satisfaction with the urban setting $_{(Eq6)}$ explain 57.4% and 72.4% of the variance in satisfaction with the destination respectively.

From the results of the regression model, the destination's architectural heritage (SN_4) and climate (SN_1) are seen to be the most influential factors in generating tourist satisfaction with the natural and cultural setting (SN). Child-friendly facilities (SE_6), peace and quiet (SE_3), roads into urban areas (SE_4), and public transport (SE_7) have a significant influence on tourist satisfaction with the urban setting. Cleanliness (SE_1) and safety (SE_2) do not have a significant influence on tourist satisfaction, perhaps because they are necessary prerequisites and so they are not judged by tourists unless they are negative.

$$SN = B + \underline{0.226} * SN_1 + \underline{0.166} * SN_2 + \underline{0.164} * SN_3 + \underline{0.299} * SN_4 + error \text{ (Eq5)}$$
$$SE = B + 0.037 * SE_1 + 0.014 * SE_2 + \underline{0.219} * SE_3 + \underline{0.205} * SE_4 + \underline{0.154} * SE_5 + \underline{0.265} * SE_6 \text{ }_{(Eq6)}$$
$$+ \underline{0.124} * SE_7 + error$$
(Significant values underlined p<0.05)

Factor 6 (F6), satisfaction with the beaches (SB), is made up of satisfaction with the water and sand, and it achieved an alpha of 0.897 (SB_1 to SB_2) $_{(Eq7)}$. The results of the regression model show that the quality of the water and sand play an important role in generating customer satisfaction with the beaches. Other variables that were included with a view to evaluating tourist satisfaction with the beaches do not form part of this factor (SB_3 to SB_8). This could be accounted for by the fact that the surveys were conducted during the low season and, although tourists can stroll along a beach and admire its transparent waters or clean sands, they cannot make use of other available services. Consequently, results relating to variables concerning beachside services must be interpreted with caution.

$$SB = B + \underline{0.489} * SB_1 + \underline{0.317} * SB_2 + error \quad \text{(Eq7)}$$
(Significant values underlined p<0.05)

Finally, factor 7 (F7) can be termed satisfaction with leisure activities (SL). This is made up of tourist assessments of the variety of leisure facilities, any sporting activities that were done, cultural attractions that were visited, the nightlife, and shopping activities. This factor also displays a high consistency, with an alpha of 0.091 (SL_1 to SL_5). From the results of the regression model $_{(Eq8)}$, the variables that exert the highest influence on satisfaction with leisure activities are seen to be satisfaction with the variety of services and facilities (SL_1), with the nightlife (SL_4), with shopping (SL_5) and with cultural (SL_3) and sporting activities (SL_2).

$$SL = B + \underline{0.270} * SL_1 + \underline{0.158} * SL_2 + \underline{0.159} * SL_3 + \underline{0.232} * SL_4 + \underline{0.194} * SL_5 + error \quad \text{(Eq8)}$$
(Significant values underlined p<0.05)

To analyse the influence of each of the factors on overall satisfaction, a step-by-step regression analysis was conducted, where the dependent variable is overall tourist satisfaction and the independent variables are each of the satisfaction factors. With this method, variables that turn out to be significant can be incorporated, while ones that are not significant can be rejected. This model explains 65.2% of the variance in overall satisfaction, and the coefficients of the regression model and variables excluded from it are shown in Table 2. The results indicate that three satisfaction variables exert a strong, significant influence on overall tourist satisfaction: firstly, accommodation at the destination (SAC); secondly the natural, cultural and urban setting (SN and SE); and thirdly restaurants at the destination (SR).

At the same time, tourist satisfaction with the airport (SA), beaches (SB) and leisure (SL) does not have a significant effect on overall satisfaction during the low season. This phenomenon could be attributable to the fact that low-season tourists are not affected by certain drawbacks thanks to the lower tourism demand, such as congested services or queues at the airport, and they probably benefit from more customized treatment at leisure facilities, without the problem of overcrowding. Consequently, tourists' perceptions of these services during the low season might differ from those of high-season visitors. The above point is particularly important in the evaluation of beaches and all the services available at them, since tourists cannot take advantage of these services during the low season due to the weather.

Table 1 - Regression model

Regression Model: Dependent variable: Overall satisfaction with the holiday	Non-standardized coefficients		Standardized coefficients	t	Sig.
	B	Standard error	Beta		
(Constant)	.886	.312		2.835	.005
Satisfaction with the destination (SN and SE)	.332	.079	.342	4.192	.000
Satisfaction with the accommodation (SAC)	.314	.062	.360	5.030	.000
Satisfaction with the restaurants (SR)	.221	.080	.236	2.759	.007

6. Conclusion

Based on a multi-dimensional approach, a model was developed to measure tourist satisfaction during the low season. Scales with a very high degree of validity and reliability were obtained.

By filtering the measurement scales, a valid and tested survey was obtained for measuring satisfaction during the low season. As might seem obvious for those familiar with traditional sun and sand tourist destinations, the results confirm that items with a strong potential influence on satisfaction ratings during the high season (e.g. beach-related factors) are not significant during the low season. Thus, if the measurement instrument is applied to other seasons, it should first be retested in each case so as to eliminate aspects that might be important in one season but are not relevant in another. As mentioned previously, ratings of services at beaches and excursions should logically be included in surveys conducted during the mid or high seasons.

It was also demonstrated that an instrument for measuring tourist satisfaction is a fundamental tool for policy-makers at destinations, since key aspects in generating satisfaction can be identified from surveys and these aspects can be prioritized with a view to improving satisfaction.

More specifically, in our case, the results indicate that three variables exert a strong, significant influence on overall tourist satisfaction:

accommodation at the destination; the natural, cultural and urban setting; and restaurants at the destination. If these services are outstanding, tourist satisfaction with Mallorca will be high. Likewise, by improving these variables, tourist satisfaction can be raised. Other information can also be ascertained from the results, such as the fact that tourist satisfaction with the airport, beaches and leisure does not have a significant effect on overall satisfaction, suggesting that, in principle, any improvement to them would not have a significant effect on satisfaction.

By regarding satisfaction as a multi-dimensional construct, each of the different aspects that comprise it can be individually worked on. For instance, if policy-makers wish to improve tourist satisfaction with the airport, attention must mainly be paid to the signing and products sold there, and staff at the airport must be trained to excel in the service offered to tourists.

Lastly, it should be remembered that it is more important to collect data from regular surveys over a period of time than simply to analyse a satisfaction survey's absolute ratings. In this way, it is possible to ascertain whether satisfaction levels have remained stable or whether they can be boosted, if necessary, and any shortcomings rectified if there is a drop in satisfaction.

References

Anderson, E.W., & Sullivan, M.W. (1990). The antecedents and consequences of customer satisfaction for firms. *Marketing Science*, 12(2), 125-142.

Anderson, E.W., Fornell, C., & Lehmann, D.R. (1994). Customer satisfaction, market share, and profitability: Findings from Sweden. *Journal of Marketing*, 58(July), 53-66.

Andreassen, W., & Lindestand, B. (1998). Customer loyalty and complex service. The impact of corporative image on quality, customer satisfaction and loyalty for customers with varying degrees of service expertise. *International Journal of Service Industry*, 9(1), 7-23.

Baker, D.A., & Crompton, J.L. (2000). Quality, satisfaction and behavioral intentions. *Annals of Tourism Research*, 27(3), 785-804.

Bolton, R.N., & Drew, J.H. (1991). A multistage model of customers' assessments of service quality and value. *Journal of Consumer Research*, 45 (April), 69-82.

Cadotte, G.R., Woodruff, R.B., & Jenkins, R.L. (1987). Expectations and norms in models of consumer satisfaction. *Journal of Marketing Research*, 24, 305-314.

Campo, S. & Yagüe, M.J. (2007). The formation of the tourist's loyalty to the tourism distribution channel: How does it affect price discounts. *International Journal of Tourism Research*, 9, 453-464.

—. (2009a). Exploring non-linear effects of determinants on tourist satisfaction. *International Journal of Culture, Tourism and Hospitality Research*, 3(2), 127-138.

Campo, S. & Garau, J. (2008): The influence of nationality on the generation of tourist satisfaction with a destination. *Tourism Analysis*, 13(1), 81-92.

—. (2010). The generation of tourism destination satisfaction. *Tourism Economics*, 16(3), 1-16.

Churchill, G.A., & Surprenant, C. (1982). An investigation into the determinants of customer satisfaction. *Journal of Marketing Research*, 19(November), 491-504.

Cronin, J. Jr., Brandy, M.K., & Hult, G.T.M. (2000). Assessing the effects of quality, value and customer satisfaction on consumer behavioral intentions in service environments. *Journal of Retailing*, 76(2), 193-218.

Fornell, C. (1992). A national customer satisfaction barometer: The Swedish experience. *Journal of Marketing*, 56(January), 6-21.

Fornell, C., Johnson, M.D., Anderson, E.W., Cha, J., & Bryant B.E. (1996). The American customer satisfaction index: Nature, purpose, and findings. *Journal of Marketing,* 60(October), 7-18.

Fournier, S., & Mick, D.G. (1999). Rediscovering satisfaction. *Journal of Marketing*, October, 5-28.

Garau J. (2002). Diversification through segmentation in Mediterranean tourism destinations. *Innovation in Tourism Planning.* Dublin: Tourism Research Centre, Dublin Institute of Technology.

—. (2009). *Tourist Satisfaction, Dissatisfaction and Place Attachment at Sun and Sand Tourism Destinations.* Doctoral Thesis. Departament d' Economia Aplicada. Universitat de les Illes Balears.

Garbarino, E., & Johnson, M.S. (1999). The different roles of satisfaction, trust, and commitment in customer relationships. *Journal of Marketing*, 63(April), 70-87.

Giese, J.L., & Cote, J.A. (2000). Refining consumer satisfaction. *Academy of Marketing Science*, 1, 1-24.

Hallowell, R. (1996). The relationship of customer satisfaction and relationship quality of customer retention. A critical reassessment and model development. *International Journal of Services Industry Management*, 7(4), 27-42.

Hunt, H.K. (1977). *Conceptualization and Measurement of Consumer Satisfaction and Dissatisfaction.* Cambridge, Mass: Marketing Science Institute.

Jones, M.A., & Suh, J.J. (2000). Transaction-specific satisfaction and overall satisfaction: An empirical analysis. *Journal of Service Marketing*, 14(2), 147-159.

Kozak, M. (2003). Measuring tourist satisfaction with multiple destination attributes. *Tourism Analysis*, 7(3-4), 229-240.

—. (2004). Measuring comparative performance of vacation destinations: Using tourists' self-reported judgements as an alternative approach. In G.I. Crouch, R.R. Perdue, H.P. Timmermans, & M. Uysal (Eds.), *Consumer Psychology of Tourism Hospitality and Leisure*, (pp. 285-302). Wallingford: CABI.

Kozak, M., & Rimmington, M. (1999). Measuring destination competitiveness: Conceptual considerations and empirical findings. *International Journal of Hospitality Management*, 18(3), 273-283.

Martensen, A, Gronholdt, L., & Kristensen, K. (2000). The drivers of customer satisfaction and loyalty: Cross-industry findings from Denmark. *Total Quality Management*, 11, 544-553.

Millán, A., & Esteban, A. (2004). Development of a multiple-item scale for measuring customer satisfaction in travel agency services. *Tourism Management*, 25(5), 533-546.

Oliver, R.L. (1980). A cognitive model of the antecedents and consequences of satisfaction decisions. *Journal of Marketing Research*, 17 (November), 460-469.

—. (1981). Measurement and evaluation of satisfaction processes in retail settings. *Journal of Retailing*, 57(3), 25-48.

Peterson, R.A., & Wilson, W.R. (1992). Measuring customer satisfaction: Fact or artefact. *Journal of the Academy of Marketing Science*, 20(1), 61-71.

Soderlund, M. (1998). Customer satisfaction and its consequences on customer behaviour revisited. The impact of different levels of satisfaction on word-of-mouth, feedback to the supplier and loyalty. *International Journal of Services Industrial Management*, 9(2), 169-188.

Stauss, B., & Neuhaus, P. (1997). The qualitative satisfaction mode. *International Journal of Services Industry Management*, 8(3), 236-247.

Steenkamp, J-B.E.M., Hofstede, F., & Wedel, M. (1999). A cross-national investigation into the individual and national cultural antecedents of consumer innovativeness. *Journal of Marketing*, 63, 55-69.

Szymnasky, D.M., & Henard, D.M. (2001). Customer satisfaction: A meta-analysis of the empirical evidence. *Journal of Academy of Marketing Science*, 29(1), 16-35.

Yi, Y. (1990). A critical review of consumer satisfaction. In V. Zeithaml (Ed.). *Review of Marketing*. Chicago, IL: American Marketing Association.

Yi, Y., & La, S. (2003). The moderating role of confidence in expectations and the asymmetric influence of disconfirmation on customer satisfaction. *The Service Industries Journal*, 23(5), 20-47.

Zins, A.H. (2001). Relative attitudes and commitment in customer loyalty models. *International Journal of Services Industrial Management*, 12(3), 269-294.

CHAPTER FOUR

DETERMINANTS OF THE CO-CREATED DESTINATION EXPERIENCE

TATIANA CHEKALINA, MATTHIAS FUCHS AND MARIA LEXHAGEN

Abstract

The aim of this chapter is to address the complex and dynamic concept of destination experience by viewing it through the lens of the value co-creation perspective. Destination experience is, therefore, conceptualized as the process and the outcome of transformation of destination attributes - including tangible and intangible resources and human assets - into the value-in-use for a customer. Exemplarily for a Swedish ski destination, the chapter shows that by monitoring unique destination and tourist-specific experience dimensions, the destination management organisation can control both the value-in-use for a customer and customer loyalty, upgrade and evaluate its marketing strategy, and, finally, discover innovation potentials for highly experiential tourism products. **Keywords:** destination experience, experience economy, value creation.

1. Introduction

The advancement of service marketing and management over the past decade has created a wide range of implications for tourism destination research and business practice and, particularly, offered a new framework for studying the tourism destination experience. Contemporary marketing and management research (Grönroos, 2000, 2008; Vargo & Lusch, 2004, 2008) focuses on customers and firm-customer relationships and, thereby, enables the re-evaluation of firm-centric models and concepts.

The present chapter applies the notion of value-in-use (Vargo & Lusch, 2004), which has become one of the central concepts for contemporary marketing and management, in order to develop and empirically validate a structural model of co-created destination experience. Since relationships between tourists and destinations develop in time and space, the understanding of inputs and outcomes of these relationships enriches the core concepts of tourism research and enables their transfer into both destination marketing and management practices.

The study goal is to contribute to the further development of the model proposing the co-created destination experience (Gnoth, 2007; Palmer, 2010). More precisely, the research question concerns how functional and intangible destination experience dimensions (i.e., destination resources) transform into emotional value experience.

2. Experience and Value for Customers within Firm-Customer Interactions

More than one decade ago, Pine and Gilmore (1999) declared the shift to the "Experience Economy" and, therefore, switched the focus from extracted commodities, manufactured goods and delivered services to staged experiences defined as memorable events, in which consumers are personally engaged. The notion of customer experience received much attention both among researchers and business practitioners. However, until now, customer experience remains one of the most vague and weakly defined concepts (Helkkula & Kelleher, 2010; Palmer, 2010).

Moreover, marketing and management scholars had already addressed the issue of customer experience as far back as the 1950s (e.g. Abbott, 1955; Alderson, 1957), while the roots of the experiential approach can even be traced back to the works of Alfred Marshall and Adam Smith (Holbrook, 2006). Particularly, Abbott (1955) proposed a utilitarian process-based view upon customer experience and identified 'satisfying experiences' as the desired outcome of the consumption of goods and services.

The discussion concerning customer experience gained new momentum in 1980s, when Holbrook and Hirschman (1982) introduced a phenomenological perspective towards the customer experience, which the authors expressed through the "Three Fs" of fantasies, feelings and fun. The experiential approach in marketing and management was boosted during the last two decades, when researchers drifted away from utilitarian towards more hedonic aspects of consumption (Gupta & Vajic, 2000; Palmer, 2010; Schmitt, 1999). Other researchers argued that a broadened view of the experience phenomenon is required and, therefore, proposed the notion of total customer experience, thus, covering all types of contacts between consumer and organisation, as well as the consumer's holistic experience (e.g., Harris, Harris, & Baron, 2003). However, Palmer (2010) suggests that such broad definitions of experience remain circular and, at the same time, they do not contradict Abbot's definition of experience viewed as an outcome of product consumption processes and customer's perception of the transformation of products into value.

More precisely, Palmer (2010) argues that both hedonistic motivators and "hygiene" factors comprise customer experience. Particularly, the conceptual framework for the construct of customer experience proposed by Palmer (2010) represents a sequential process of customer's attitude formation based on perception and affective interpretation of a diverse range of raw stimuli at the service encounter. These raw stimuli, therefore, are conceptualized as overlapping high order constructs, including tangible and process quality, brand relationships, as well as interpersonal relationships between a customer and the service provider's employees. Palmer (2010), particularly, emphasizes the importance of non-functional expectations communicated through brands. Furthermore, the author considers emotions as a source of information to evaluate stimuli and their contribution to the experience formation process.

However, Palmer (2010) also addresses a number of obstacles, which hamper the operationalization of the proposed model constructs and the use of quantitative measurement approaches. These problems, particularly, concern the complexity of context-specific variables, as well as the non-linearity and complexity of customer experiences, including the uncertainty regarding optimal experience levels (Fuchs & Weiermair, 2004). Additionally, the sequential nature of the proposed model and the assumed change of customer's attitudes over time impose practical obstacles for model validation using quantitative methods. At the same time Palmer (2010) acknowledges the possibility to operationalize the customer experience concept in consistency with the notion of value-in-use (Vargo & Lusch, 2004).

3. Value Co-creation and Customer Experience

Value-in-use has become one of the central concepts in contemporary marketing. It is contrasted to the value-in-exchange, which is captured by price and serves as an intermediary concept in the value creation process (Vargo & Lusch, 2004). While value-in-exchange is embedded in the product, which is exchanged, value-in-use is created when a product, a good or a service, is actually used. Therefore, value for a customer is created as a result of interaction between a firm and a customer by the total experience of all elements, including firm's resources, such as physical objects (e.g. goods), information, interactions with employees, systems, infrastructures, as well as other customers. In many cases these elements cannot be directly controlled by a firm (Grönroos, 2006, 2008).

Value-in-use discloses the purpose and the benefit of resource integration for the customer. The combination of resources used as an input for value creation is always unique. Therefore, value is unique, experiential, contextually interpreted and determined only by the beneficiary (Vargo & Lusch, 2008). According to Vargo and Lusch (2008), in the end, all economic and social actors, including individuals, families, firms, as well as societies and nations, interact in order to improve their own state of being. Hence, value is defined as an improvement of the beneficiary's well-being and its ability to fit in its environment (Vargo & Lusch, 2006, 2004; Vargo, Maglio, & Akaka, 2008). However, so far the relationship between customer experience and value for customer received only little attention in the marketing literature (Helkkula & Kelleher, 2010).

The relationship between value and experience is particularly addressed by Holbrook (2006), who defines the customer value as "an interactive relativistic preference experience" (ibid., 715), and, therefore, emphasises an interaction between an object (e.g., a product) and a customer, which entails "subjective hierarchical preferences based on an individual's situation-specific comparison of one object with another" (ibid., 715). Thus, the value for a customer is created, when products perform services, which in turn provide relevant value-creating experiences (Holbrook, 2006).

Helkkula and Kelleher (2010) revealed that the relationship between experience and value does not represent a linear value chain. Rather, it represents a complex circular and dynamic process of experiencing and perceiving value, which is influenced by both previous and current, as well as future imaginary consumption experiences. More precisely, the ongoing customer experience of a service influences customer perceived value, which, in turn, influences cumulative customer service experience (ibid., 48). Additionally, the customer value creation process on an individual level can intertwine with the value creation process of other customers. Therefore, the role of wider customer-to-customer relationships is stressed (Helkkula & Kelleher, 2010).

A broader approach to consider customer experience is developed by Baron and Harris (2010). The authors employ the idea that interaction between a customer and a given firm is only one of many interactions, which constitute customer's consumption experience. The authors introduce the notion of 'experience domain', which they define as "a field of knowledge, activity and discourse that stimulates consumers to engage in purposeful interactions with a network of organizations and consumer communities in the course of experiences that are collectively understood" (ibid., 520). A firm, therefore, should understand the value creation process from a customers' perspective and should identify, which interactions impact customers' well-being within an experience domain. A firm, which is able to explain the network of customer interactions and its place in this network, can act respectively to support customer's practices enhancing customer's perceived value and to deal with those interactions inhibiting value creation for the customer.

Therefore, the focus on value-in-use enables the application of a value co-creation perspective for developing a destination experience model. Particularly, it is proposed that customer experience firstly comprises interactions with various value-contributing resources which belong to a particular firm, to a customer or to other actors. Secondly, a customer experience includes the process of transformation of available resources into value. Finally, value-in-use is the result of resource transformation and the outcome component of customer experience. Value for customer (i.e., value-in-use), on the one hand, is individual and subjective (Vargo & Lusch, 2008). On the other hand, however, value is defined and communicated by a firm (e.g., a destination) through the brand (e.g. Gnoth, 2007) and collectively perceived by the consumer community (Helkkula & Kelleher, 2010).

4. Theoretical Framework and Conceptual Model

The value co-creation perspective towards understanding the experience as the process and the outcome of interactions between a tourist and a destination constitutes the very core of the concepts of tourism product and tourism destination. Smith (1994) proposed a five-level model of the generic tourism product. Accordingly, the 'physical plant', like resort hotels, the physical environment, tourism infrastructure and so on, forms the core of any tourism product. By contrast, services, hospitality, traveller's freedom of choice as well as physical, intellectual and emotional involvement of travellers in service consumption build the outer circles of the model. Murphy, Pritchard, and Smith (2000) refer to Smith (1994) when defining tourism destinations 'as an amalgam of individual products and experience opportunities that combine to form a total experience of the area visited' (ibid., 2000, p. 44).

Tourism literature increasingly addresses the co-creative nature of a destination experience. Accordingly, Larsen (2007) conceptualizes the tourist experience as a highly complex and purely individual psychological process and defines it as "a past personal travel-related event strong enough to have entered long-term memory" (ibid., 2007, p. 15). Other researchers, however, argue that destinations can actively design and to a great extent control tourist experiences (Ek, Larsen, Hornskov, & Mansfeldt, 2008; Mossberg, 2007).

While experiences exist only in consumers' minds, destinations and tourists co-create places where the tourist experience occurs. By doing so, destinations create 'experiencescapes' through substantive and communicative staging of those available elements of the physical environment devoted to tourism consumption. Thereby, tourists are particularly guided on how to assemble, use and interpret these elements and their total experience. Similarly, tourists co-create 'experiencescapes' by direct participation and allocation of own resources, including time, money, efforts and skills (Arnould, Price, & Tierney, 1998; Fuchs, 2004; Gnoth, 2007; Mossberg, 2007; Pettersson & Getz, 2009).

Fuchs (2004) proposes an efficiency model for tourism service processes, which is based on Parasuraman's (2002) model of synergistic service productivity. Accordingly, destination efficiency depends on the combination of the tourist's and destination's resources and determines benefits for both tourists and the destination. Moreover, an increase of resources from one actor reduces the required input from another actor. Particularly, if the destination's input of resources increases, a smaller input of tourist's resources is needed. Additionally, this relationship is moderated by the destination's ability to properly allocate the available destination's resources. Finally, the benefits received by tourists (i.e., service performance, satisfaction, etc.) as a result of a destination visitation directly convert into benefits for the destination in terms of increased sales, higher occupancy rates, market share, profits, and so on. (Fuchs, 2004).

Similarly, Cracolici and Nijkamp (2009) employ a resource-based view towards the destination considering tourist areas "as the 'supplier' of spatial tourist services with distinct attractiveness features (or attributes), which have to be managed effectively and efficiently, while the demander is the tourist-consumer who wishes to enjoy a holiday experience at least equal to – or even better than – his/her past holidays" (ibid., 337). The authors define tourist satisfaction as the tourist's feeling of well-being in relation to the holiday destination, including the total leisure experience, escape and relaxation for the mind, pleasurable unique experiences, physical well-being, etc. The ability of a tourist area to satisfy tourists' needs relatively better than other destinations is a measure to assess the relative attractiveness of competing destinations (Crouch, 2011).

Yet, in the literature there are only a few examples of empirical validation of tourist experience models on a destination level (Gountas, Mavondo, Ewing, & Gountas, 2011). For instance, Yuksel, Yuksel and Bilim (2010) examined how emotional associations and symbolic meanings of a destination visitation can explain the formation process of tourist satisfaction and loyalty. Moreover, a qualitative analysis by Kneesel, Baloglu, and Millar (2010) revealed the destination-specific combination of cognitive (i.e., functional) and affective (i.e., emotional) evaluations of the perceived images of four gaming destinations.

Therefore, the proposed destination experience model, on the one hand, focuses on destination-specific dimensions of complex tourism experiences, including tourism destination products and services, as well as various intangible characteristics of a destination and social interactions. On the other hand, the model considers the contribution of destination resources to the modification of tourist's state of being (i.e., the value-in-use of visitation). Finally, both resources provided by a destination and utilised by a tourist, as well as value-in-use for a tourist are related to the managerially relevant construct of destination loyalty (Figure 1).

The destination resources available for tourism consumption are widely addressed in the tourism marketing literature in terms of destination attributes (i.e., Echtner & Ritchie, 1993; Gallarza, Saura, & Garcia, 2002). Therefore, the construct remains fully consistent with Palmer's (2010) conceptualization of the 'raw stimuli' factors of customer experience. Thus, visitors' perception of a destination on the attribute level of destination resources consists of both tangible and intangible attributes of the destinations as well as human assets. The availability of resources is unique for every destination, while the combination of required and experienced resources is unique for every tourist and for a particular visitation context (Moeller, 2010; Palmer, 2010; Zabkar, Brencic, & Dmitrovic, 2010).

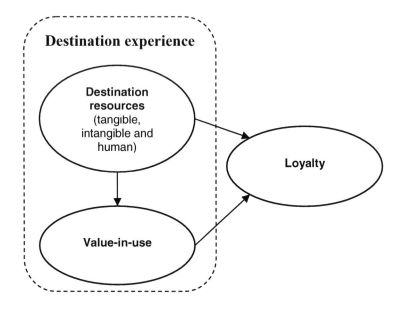

Figure 1. Conceptual model

The value-in-use for a tourist, on the contrary, represents the tourist's state of being as the result of visiting the destination. Sweeney and Soutar (2001) distinguish between four different dimensions of perceived value, including functional value in terms of price and value for money, functional value of product quality and performance, emotional value as the utility derived from the feelings or affection generated by a product, as well as social value in terms of the enhancement of a social self-concept. While the two dimensions of functional value represent a firm's resources within an interaction process between a firm and a customer (Grönroos, 2006, 2008; Moeller, 2010), both emotional and social value constitute the modification of a customer's state of being, and, therefore, represent value-in-use for a customer.

In a tourism context the value-in-use of a destination can be exemplified on the basis of Crompton's (1979) classification of benefits from destination visitation by tourists in terms of satisfying internal socio-psychological needs. These benefits include push motivation factors of destination visitation, such as escape from routine environment, exploration and evaluation of self, relaxation, social recognition, social interaction, novelty seeking, and knowledge among others (Crompton, 1979). From a more general perspective of positive psychology (i.e., Seligman & Csikszentmihalyi, 2000), the valued subjective experience of the event, which occurred in the past, is about well-being, contentment and satisfaction. In the present it is about flow and happiness, and towards the future it is about hope and optimism (Nawijn, 2011).

In order to operationalize and validate the proposed model, the conceptualization of the value-in-use of a destination visitation for a tourist is limited to the emotional (i.e., hedonic) value of destination visitation, assuming that hedonic value is of primary importance for mass tourism. However, it is acknowledged, that the scope of value-in-use of destination visitation is broader and, thus, includes social value, as well as other types of value dimensions, like, increased working capacity of a tourist after visitation as the result of relaxation, recreation or gained knowledge (Nawijn, Marchand, Veenhoven & Vingerhoets, 2010; Neal & Sirgy, 2004).

Tourism literature provides substantial evidence of positive relationships between visitor's perception of tangible and intangible destination attributes, the evaluation of visitation outcomes and tourist's behavioural intentions. For instance, Klenosky (2002) applies a means-end approach to empirically examine relationships between pull and push motivation factors of destination choice. Pull factors (i.e., historical and cultural attractions, natural resources, location, activities etc.) are considered as means, which can be employed to achieve rather abstract benefits (i.e,. ends), which correspond to travel pull motivation factors (i.e., fun and enjoyment, self esteem, excitement etc.). Similarly, Yoon and Uysal (2005) examine and empirically confirm structural relationships between push and pull motivation factors, destination satisfaction and loyalty.

Moreover, Chi and Qu (2008) provide empirical support for a strong and positive influence of attribute satisfaction on overall satisfaction. Chen and Tsai (2007) found that the relationship between trip quality (i.e. primarily constituted by the tourist's perception of functional destination attributes) and overall visitor's satisfaction is mediated by the construct of perceived value. The latter construct includes time value, money value and effort value. Del Bosque and Martin (2008) confirmed, that positive and negative emotions evoked by destination influence overall satisfaction. Finally, Zabkar et al. (2010) empirically verify the relationship between perceived quality of the destination' offerings, which is unique and a contextually dependent (i.e., formative) construct, as well as visitor satisfaction construct, which incorporates both cognitive and affective evaluation dimensions of tourist's state of being (i.e. including sense of joy, being pleased and delighted).

There has been a body of research confirming a positive relationship between tourist's perception of attribute-based destination performance and behavioural intentions towards the destination (Chi & Qu, 2008; Pike, Bianchi, Kerr, & Patti, 2010; Zabkar *et al.,* 2010). Finally, some other researchers also confirm that overall satisfaction (i.e., the tourist's state of being) directly influences the tourist's loyalty behaviour (Chen & Tsai, 2007; Chi & Qu, 2008; del Bosque & Martin, 2008; Faullant, Matzler, & Füller, 2008; Yoon & Uysal, 2005; Zabkar *et al.,* 2010). Most importantly, del Bosque and Martin (2008) found a direct positive relationship between positive emotions evoked by the destination experience and loyalty.

Thus, based on the briefly discussed literature, the following set of hypotheses can be formulated (Figure 1):

H1 The more positive the perception of destination resources, the more positive is the perception of emotional value from the destination visitation.

H2 The more positive the perception of destination resources, the stronger the loyalty to a destination.

H3 The more positive the perception of emotional value from a destination visitation, the stronger the loyalty to a destination.

5. Methodology

The list of measurement items describing destination resources and emotional value is deduced from the literature focusing on ski destinations (Faullant et al., 2008; Flagestad & Hope, 2001; Hudson & Shephard, 1998; Klenoski, Gengler, & Mulvey, 1993; Komppula & Laukkanen, 2009; Richards, 1996; Weiermair & Fuchs, 1999).

The list of items was farther updated based on a content analysis of destination brochures, web-sites, publications about the destination Åre in media, as well as tourists' comments in blogs. The intention was to deduce a list of tangible and intangible resources offered by Åre for international tourists as the input for co-creation of the destination experience, and to capture the type of emotional value of visitation communicated by the destination and narrated by previous visitors.

The evaluation of destination resources is operationalized as a higher-order construct consisting of four sub-dimensions, including the core destination product (i.e., skiing), complementary services (i.e., quality and service level of staff in accommodation facilities, restaurants and bars), level of prices and value-for-money, as well as intangible destination resources, such as family-friendliness, cleanliness and safety.

Operationalization of the emotional value construct reflects the findings of the qualitative study by Klenoski et al. (1993) regarding the value of ski destinations. Items were finally formulated based on the analysis of destination-specific qualitative data (i.e., brochures, blogs, articles in journals and newspapers). Four measurement items are employed to operationalize the construct, including "Åre is a thrilling winter destination", "Åre offers various winter experiences", "Åre offers fun and excitement" and "Åre brings you the joy of achievement".

Finally, destination loyalty (Oliver, 1997; 1999) is operationalized by four items. Willingness to recommend and willingness to come back are commonly used in the tourism literature (e.g., Chen & Tsai, 2007; Chi & Qu, 2008). At the same time, two additional items measuring the degree of destination attachment were introduced in order to strengthen the construct measurement (Back & Parks, 2003).

5.1 Data collection

The data collection process was organized in collaboration with business partners in Åre, a leading Swedish ski resort. The survey targeted only international guests. It was decided to approach international tourists after their visitation was over, when they had already returned home. The idea that a complex event, such as the experience of a destination stay and the related trip, should be evaluated when the experience is completed was expressed by Arnould and Price (1993). Furthermore, Palmer (2010) criticizes the widely adopted approach to evaluate service quality during or immediately following the consumption of (e.g., tourism) services and argues that customers' attitudes adjust over time. Thus, a web-survey was conducted to reach tourists after they returned home and had already had some time to reflect and evaluate their holiday stay.

In order to obtain an accuracy level of 95% at a significance level of 5% the sample size should be N=384 completed surveys (Finn, Elliott-White, & Walton, 2000). Thus, E-mails were randomly selected from the databases of two major destination stakeholders generating about 95% of Åre's international guest base.

The data was collected during April-May 2010. The number of fully completed questionnaires was 387. However, as the respondents were provided with a "don't know" option, the number of usable responses was lower. Finally, 329 cases with completed responses on items measuring destination loyalty were preserved for further analyses, which allow obtaining an accuracy level of 94.6% at a significance level of 5.4%. The share of missing values was particularly high for indicators measuring tourists' perception of various tangible and intangible attributes of the destination. Therefore, items with more than 10% of missing values were removed from the analysis. More concretely, this resulted in the exclusion of items measuring tourists' perception of various non-ski activities, such as after-ski, shopping, nightlife, indoor activities, like spa and bowling, as well as outdoor non-ski winter activities. The share of missing values among items preserved for analysis varies from 1% to 9%. Missing values were assigned with the score 3 (i.e., neutral).

Finally, the examination of z-scores revealed some outliers. Thus, according to Field (2005), 17 scores were substituted with "the next highest score plus one" (ibid, 2005). This type of score substitution affected four items while the share of adjusted scores does not exceed 2% per item.

5.2 Validating the theoretical model

Confirmatory factor analysis (CFA) was performed using AMOS 17.0 in order to validate the constitutive measurement constructs of the proposed theoretical model (Hair, Black, Barbin, Anderson, & Tatham, 2006). Table 1 shows the results of the CFA for the previously identified dimensions of the theoretical model. The results of the measurement model validation prove convergent and discriminant validity of the proposed model constructs.

Firstly, the theoretically proposed model constructs fit the data very well as both, Goodness of Fit Index (GFI) and Root Mean Squared Error of Approximation (RMSEA) score at 0.896 and 0.058, respectively. Secondly, all other fit measures (e.g. CFI, NFI) as well as composite reliability approve the model and satisfy recommended thresholds (Hair et al., 2006). Thirdly, all estimated regression weights (i.e., factor loadings) are relatively high (i.e., ranging from 0.600 to 0.902) and are significant (i.e., t-Values). Finally, Squared Multiple Correlations (SMC) demonstrate respectable portions and Average Variance Extracted (AVE) for five out of six model constructs ranks above the recommended threshold of 0.5 (Hair *et al.,* 2006).

In order to empirically test the significance of the hypothesised relationships among the validated model constructs reflecting the causal structure of the proposed model, a linear structural equation modelling

Table 1 - Validation of the Measurement Model

Constructs		Scale items	Composite reliability	Standardized Loadings	t Value (CR)	SMC	AVE
Destination resources	Skiing	Number and variety of ski slopes	0.799	0.746	-	0.556	0.503
		Safety in the ski area		0.618	10.428	0.382	
		Overall quality of skiing experience		0.845	14.087	0.714	
		Transportation at the mountain area (e.g., ski lifts, chair lifts, cable cars)		0.600	10.212	0.360	
	Service	Service level of the staff in accommodation facilities	0.749	0.650	-	0.423	0.427
		Service level of the staff in restaurants and bars		0.651	8.437	0.424	
		Overall quality of accommodation (e.g., hotel, cabin, apartment)		0.670	9.928	0.449	
		Quality of food and beverages		0.643	8.136	0.413	
	Value for money	Compared to other skiing destinations, visiting Åre is good value for money	0.873	0.902	-	0.814	0.774
		Overall, Åre as a skiing destination has reasonable prices		0.857	15.431	0.734	
	Intangible resources	Åre is family-friendly	0.852	0.747	-	0.558	0.658
		Åre is clean and tidy		0.887	14.747	0.786	
		Åre is safe and secure		0.794	13.751	0.630	

Emotional value	0.872	Åre is a thrilling winter destination	0.777	-	0.603	0.630
		Åre offers various winter experiences	0.802	14.304	0.643	
		Åre offers fun and excitement	0.836	15.083	0.698	
		Åre brings you the joy of achievement	0.759	14.380	0.576	
Loyalty	0.823	I would still come to Åre, even if it is more expensive than other ski resorts	0.616	-	0.379	0.541
		I will come back to Åre in winter within 2 years	0.761	10.448	0.579	
		I consider Åre to be my first choice of a ski resort	0.826	11.291	0.683	
		I will encourage friends and relatives to visit Åre in winter	0.723	10.101	0.523	

approach (SEM) using maximum likelihood (ML) estimation was applied (Steenkamp & Baumgartner, 2000; Hair *et al.*, 2006).

Figure 2 displays the obtained SEM results. First of all, normed-$\chi2$ statistics (i.e., χ^2/df) and incremental (i.e., CFI, NFI) as well as absolute fit indices (i.e., GFI, RMSEA, SRMR) rank well above recommended thresholds (Hair et al., 2006; Klein, 2005). Secondly, the model behaves according to theory as all hypothesized relationships are supported by the results gained by SEM. Thirdly, the model accounts for a substantial proportion of the variance (i.e., explanation power: SMC) in the endogenous constructs (Figure 2).

Thus, although relatively few variables were considered in the empirical analysis, based on the revealed results the proposed approach to measure co-created destination experience can be considered as valid and reliable. More precisely, SEM revealed that tourists' perception of the higher order construct "destination resources" positively affects the co-created construct of emotional value (i.e. $\beta= 0.785$, SMC= 0.617). While the latter construct serves as an intermediary variable, in turn, both variables explain destination loyalty very well (i.e. $\beta= 0.400$ and $\beta= 0.491$; SMC= 0.710).

6. Conclusion

The proposed destination experience model rests upon a value co-creation perspective on marketing strategy, and assumes that destination management organization can better understand the nature of the unique destination experience, including the contribution of the tangible, intangible and human resources of a destination to the value creation for attracted tourists.

The results of the study are in line with findings of previous tourism research, which confirmed that the tourists' evaluation of the outcomes of destination visitation (e.g., satisfaction) partially mediates the relationship between tourists' evaluations of destination attributes and tourists' behavioural intentions towards the destination (Chen & Tsai, 2007; Chi & Qu, 2008; del Bosque & Martin, 2008; Faullant et al., 2008; Zabkar et al., 2010; Fuchs, Chekalina & Lexhagen, 2011). Moreover, the present study proposed and empirically validated that the destination-specific emotional value of visitation (i.e., value-in-use) mediates the relationship between customers' perception of destination attributes and future behavioural intentions. The operationalization of the emotional value construct is guided by Klenoski et al.'s (1993) qualitative study, which empirically identified the emotional outcome dimensions of a ski winter holiday.

As argued, destinations co-create experiences of individual tourists through communicative staging of destinations, which is underlined by a unique configuration of destination resources and guidance on how to access and utilise available resources in order to obtain and create value. Accordingly, tourists may choose between available products and services. Hence, tourists experience destinations by utilizing destination products, services and additional tangible and intangible attributes and, consequently, evaluate whether their experience was valuable (i.e., value-in-use).

Therefore, destination managers have to combine and inter-relate knowledge bases about destination resources devoted to tourism consumption and the value-in-use of the destination for tourists. Moreover, the link between resources and value-in-use has to be clearly communicated through the brand (Gnoth, 2007; Vargo & Lusch, 2004). For instance, based on the present study, the destination management organization of the Swedish ski resort of Åre, can identify the attributive dimensions behind (i.e., emotional) value creation and destination loyalty, namely, value for money, service quality, skiing and intangible destination resources, such as family-friendliness, cleanliness and safety. Moreover, the study results clearly show the destination management, which specific (attributive) experience aspects are most responsible in the value co-creation and destination loyalty formation process, respectively. Finally, and probably most importantly, the crucial dimensions for co-creating (emotional) value can also be identified by the destination management. These include thrill, variety, and so on.

The main limitation of the presented study is the basic assumption that the emotional value construct is the core component of the value-in-use of a destination visitation. Since, both travel motivations and the scope of the value-in-use of the destination go far beyond hedonic benefits, other dimensions of value-in-use should, thus, be considered for the purposes of future research, including social value, novelty seeking, knowledge, and so on. Besides, value-in-use remains highly subjective and individual. Accordingly, in-depth qualitative analyses of both perceived and promised destination value-in-use are suggested for different tourist segments. Thus, next planned steps of research are to integrate the identified experience dimensions into the model of customer-based brand equity (Gartner, 2009; Chekalina 2012). Thus, by continuously monitoring unique experience dimensions, the destination management organization can control customer loyalty, upgrade and evaluate its marketing strategy, and, finally, discover the innovation potential for highly experiential tourism products.

Determinants of the Co-created Destination Experience

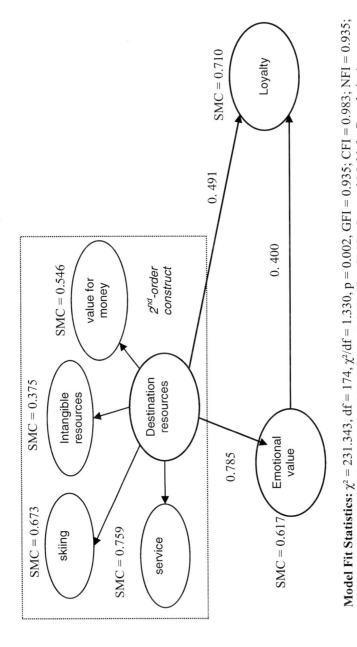

Model Fit Statistics: $\chi^2 = 231.343$, df = 174, χ^2/df = 1.330, p = 0.002, GFI = 0.935; CFI = 0.983; NFI = 0.935; RMSEA = 0.032 (LO-90 = 0.020, HI-90 = 0.042); (i.e. SMC= Squared Multiple Correlation)

Figure 2. Validation of the Structural Model: Destination resources, Emotional Value and Loyalty

Acknowledgements

This research project has been financed by the EU Structural Fund objective 2 project no. 39736 and the European Tourism Research Institute (ETOUR), Mid-Sweden University. The authors would like to thank the CEOs Lars-Börje Eriksson (Åre Destination AB), Niclas Sjögren Berg (Ski Star Åre) and Marketing Assistant Hans Ericson (Holiday Club Åre) for their excellent cooperation.

References

Abbott, L. (1955). *Quality and competition*. NY: Columbia University Press.

Alderson, W. (1957). *Marketing behaviour and executive action*. Irwin: Homewood, IL.

Arnould, E.J., & Price, L.L. (1993). River magic: Extraordinary experience and the extended service encounter. *The Journal of Consumer Research*, 20(1), 24-45.

Arnould, E.J., Price, L.L., & Tierney, P. (1998). Communicative staging of the wilderness servicescape. *The Service Industries Journal*, 18(3), 90-115.

Back, K.J., & Parks, S.C. (2003). A Brand loyalty model involving cognitive, affective and conative brand loyalty and customer satisfaction. *Journal of Hospitality and Tourism Research*, 27(4), 419-435.

Baron, S., & Harris, K. (2010). Toward and understanding of consumer perspective on experiences. *Journal of Services Marketing*, 24(7), 518-531.

Chen, C.F., & Tsai, D. (2007). How destination image and evaluative factors affect behavioral intentions? *Tourism Management*, 28(4), 1115-1122.

Chekalina, T. (2012). A value co-creation perspective on the customer-based Brand Equity Model for tourism destinations, licentiate thesis, Nr. 73, Mid-Sweden University Press, Östersund, Sweden.

Chi, C.G.Q., & Qu, H.L. (2008). Examining the structural relationships of destination image, tourist satisfaction and destination loyalty: An integrated approach. *Tourism Management*, 29(4), 624-636.

Cracolici, M.F., & Nijkamp, P. (2009). The attractiveness and competitiveness of tourist destinations: A study of Southern Italian regions. *Tourism Management*, 30(3), 336-344.

Crouch, G.I. (2011). Destination competitiveness: An analysis of determinant attributes. *Journal of Travel Research*, 50(1), 27-45.

Crompton, J.L. (1979). Motivations for pleasure vacation. *Annals of Tourism Research*, 6(4), 408-424.

del Bosque, I.R., & Martin, H.S. (2008). Tourist satisfaction - A cognitive-affective model. *Annals of Tourism Research*, 35(2), 551-573.

Echtner, C.M., & Ritchie, J.R.B. (1993). The measurement of destination image: An empirical assessment. *Journal of Travel Research*, 31 (Spring), 3–13.

Ek, R., Larsen, J., Hornskov, S.B., & Mansfeldt, O.K. (2008). A dynamic framework of tourist experiences: Space-time and performances in the Experience Economy. *Scandinavian Journal of Hospitality and Tourism*, 8(2), 122-140.

Faullant, R., Matzler, K., & Füller, J. (2008). The impact of satisfaction and image on loyalty. The case of alpine ski resorts. *Managing Service Quality*, 18(2), 163-178.

Field, A. (2005). *Discovering statistics using SPSS*. London: Sage.

Finn, M., Elliott-White, M., & Walton, M. (2000). *Tourism and leisure research methods: data collection, analysis, and interpretation.* Harlow: Longman.

Flagestad, A., & Hope, C.A. (2001). ''Scandinavian Winter'': antecedents, concepts and empirical observations underlying destination umbrella branding model. *Tourism Review*, 56(1-2), 5-12.

Fuchs, M. (2004). Strategy development in tourism destinations: A data envelopment analysis approach. *Poznan University Economics Review*, 4(1), 52-73.

Fuchs, M., & Weiermair, K. (2004). Destination benchmarking - An indicator-system's potential for exploring guest satisfaction. *Journal of Travel Research*, 42(3): 212-225.

Fuchs, M., Chekalina, T. & Lexhagen, M. (2011). Destination brand equity modelling and measurement – A summer tourism case from Sweden. In R.H., Tsiotsou, & R.E., Goldsmith, (Eds.), *Strategic Marketing in Tourism Services* (in print). UK: Emerald Publishing.

Gallarza, M.G., Saura, I.G., & Garcia, H.C. (2002). Destination image - Towards a conceptual framework. *Annals of Tourism Research*, 29(1), 56-78.

Gartner, C. (2009). Deconstructing brand equity. *Tourism Branding: Communities in Action. Bridging Tourism Theory and Practice*, 1, 51-63.

Gountas, S., Mavondo, F., Ewing, M. & Gountas, J. (2011). Exploring the effects of perceived service provider sincerity on consumers' emotional state and satisfaction during service consumption. *Tourism Analysis*, 16(4): 393-403.

Gnoth, J. (2007). The structure of destination brands: Leveraging values. *Tourism Analysis*, 12(5/6), 345–358.

Grönroos, C. (2000). *Service Management and Marketing. A customer relationship management approach.* 2nd edition. NJ: John Wiley.

—. (2006). Adopting a service logic for marketing. *Marketing Theory*, 6(3), 317-333.

—. (2008). Service logic revisited: Who creates value? And who co-creates? *European Business Review*, 20(4), 298-314.

Gupta, S., & Vajic, M. (2000). The contextual and dialectical nature of experiences. In J.A., Fitzsimmons, & M.J., Fitzsimmons, (Eds.), *New Service Development: Creating Memorable Experiences*. Thousand Oaks, CA: Sage.

Hair, J., Black, W., Babin, B., Anderson, R.E., & Tatham, R. (2006). *Multivariate data analysis.* (6th Ed.). N: Prentice Hall.

Harris, R., Harris, K., & Baron, S. (2003). Theatrical service experiences: Dramatic script development with employees. *International Journal of Service Industry Management*, 14(2), 184-99.

Helkkula, A., & Kelleher, C. (2010). Circularity of customer service experience and customer perceived value. *Journal of Customer Behaviour*, 9(1), 37-53.

Holbrook, M.B. (2006). Consumption experience, customer value, and subjective personal introspection: An illustrative photographic essay. *Journal of Business Research*, 59, 714-725.

Holbrook, M.B., & Hirschman, E.C. (1982). The experiential aspects of consumption: Consumer fantasies, feelings and fun. *Journal of Consumer Research*, 9(2), 132-40.

Hudson, S., & Shephard, G.W.H. (1998). Measuring service quality at tourist destinations: An application of importance-performance analysis to an Alpine ski resort. *Journal of Travel and Tourism Marketing*, 7(3), 61-77.

Klenoski, D.B., Gengler, C.E., & Mulvey, M.S. (1993). Understanding the factors influencing ski destination choice: A means-end analytic approach. *Journal of Leisure Research*, 25(4), 362-379.

Klenosky, D.B. (2002). The "Pull" of tourism destinations: A Means-End investigation. *Journal of Travel Research*, 40(4), 385-396.

Kline, R.B. (2005). *Principles and practice of structural equation modeling* (2nd Ed.). London: The Guilford Press.

Kneesel, E., Baloglu, S., & Millar, M. (2010). Gaming destination images: Implications for branding. *Journal of Travel Research*, 49(1), 68-78.

Komppula, R., & Laukkanen, T. (2009). Ski Destination profile based on attributes of ski destination choice. In L., Dioko, & L., Xiang, (Eds.), *3rd International Conference on Destination Branding and Marketing*, 2-4 Dec. Macau, 238-249.

Larsen, S. (2007). Aspects of a psychology of the tourist experience. *Scandinavian Journal of Hospitality and Tour*ism, 7(1), 7-18.

Moeller, S. (2010). Characteristics of services – a new approach uncovers their value. *Journal of services Marketing*, 24/5, 359-368.

Mossberg, L. (2007). A marketing approach to the tourist experience. *Scandinavian Journal of Hospitality and Tourism*, 7(1), 59-74.

Murphy, P., Pritchard, M.P., & Smith, B. (2000). The destination product and its impact on traveler perceptions. *Tourism Management*, 21, 43-52.

Nawijn, J. (2011). Determinants of daily happiness on vacation. *Journal of Travel Research*, 50(5): 559-566.

Nawijn, J., Marchand, M., Veenhoven, R. & Vingerhoets, A.J. (2010). Vacationers happier, but most not happier after a holiday. *Applied Research of Quality of Life,* 5, 35-47.

Neal, J.D., & Sirgy, M.J. (2004). Measuring the effect of tourism services on travellers' quality of life: further validation. *Social Indicators Research*, 69(3), 243–277.

Oliver, R.L. (1997). *Satisfaction: A behavioral perspective of the consumer.* NY: Irvin/McGraw-Hill.

—. (1999). Whence consumer loyalty? *The Journal of Marketing*, 63 (Special Issue), 33-44.

Palmer, A. (2010). Customer experience management: A critical review of an emerging idea. *Journal of Services Marketing*, 24/3, 196-208.

Parasuraman, A. (2002). Service quality and productivity: A synergistic perspective. *Managing Service Quality*, 12(1), 6-9.

Pettersson, R., & Getz, D. (2009). Event experiences in time and space: A study of visitors to the (2007) World Alpine Ski Championships in Åre, Sweden. *Scandinavian Journal of Hospitality and Tourism*, 9(2-3), 308-326.

Pike, S., Bianchi; C., Kerr, G., & Patti, C. (2010). Consumer-based brand equity for Australia as a long-haul tourism destination in an emerging market. *International Marketing Review*, 27(4), 434-449.

Pine, B.J., & Gilmore, J.H. (1999). *The experience economy: work is theatre and every business a stage.* Boston, Mass.: Harvard Business School.

Richards, G. (1996). Skilled consumption and UK ski holidays. *Tourism Management*, 17(1), 25-34.

Schmitt, B. (1999). *Experiential Marketing: How to Get Customers to Sense, Feel, Think, Act and Relate to Your Company and Brands.* NY: Free Press.

Seligman, M.E.P., & Csikszentmihalyi, M. (2000). Positive psychology. An introduction. *American Psychologist*, 55(1), 5-14.

Smith, S.L.J. (1994). The tourism product. *Annals of Tourism Research*, 21(3), 582-595.

Steenkamp, J.-B.E.M., & H. Baumgartner (2000). On the use of structural equation models for marketing modeling. *International Journal of Research in Marketing*, 17(2), 195-202.

Sweeney, J.C., & Soutar, G.N. (2001). Consumer perceived value: The development of a multiple item scale. *Journal of Retailing*, 77, 203-220.

Vargo, S.L., & Lusch, R.F. (2004). Evolving to a new dominant logic for marketing. *Journal of Marketing*, 68, 1-17.

—. (2006). Service-dominant logic: What it is, what it is not, what it might be. In R.F. Lusch, & S.L., Vargo, (Eds.), *The service-dominant logic of marketing: Dialog, debate, and directions* (pp: 43–56). Armonk, NY: ME Sharpe.

—. (2008). Service-dominant logic: continuing the evolution. *Journal of the Academy of Marketing Science*, 36, 1-10.

Vargo, S.L., Maglio, P.P., & Akaka, M.A. (2008). On value and value co-creation: A service systems and service logic perspective. *European Management Journal*, 26, 145-152.

Weiermair, K. & Fuchs, M. (1999). Measuring tourist judgments on service quality. *Annals of Tourism Research*, 26(4), 1004-1021.

Yoon, Y., & Uysal, M. (2005). An examination of the effects of motivation and satisfaction on destination loyalty: A structural model. *Tourism Management*, 26(1), 45-56.

Yuksel, A., Yuksel, F., & Bilim, Y. (2010). Destination attachment: Effects on customer satisfaction and cognitive, affective and conative loyalty. *Tourism management*, 31, 274-284.

Zabkar, V., Brencic, M.M., & Dmitrovic, T. (2010). Modeling perceived quality, visitor satisfaction and behavioral intentions at the destination level. *Tourism Management*, 31, 537-546.

PART 3:

SOCIAL AND ENVIRONMENTAL CONSUMPTION IN TOURISM

CHAPTER FIVE

TOURISTS' PERCEPTIONS OF TOURISM DEVELOPMENT IN NATURE AREAS

CARLA SILVA, ELISABETH KASTENHOLZ AND JOSÉ LUÍS ABRANTES

Abstract

This chapter analyzes tourists' perceptions of tourism development in nature areas. The aim is to develop a tourism impact measurement scale for assessing perceptions of tourism impacts. An extensive literature review and insights from an empirical study of 315 tourists in European Nature Destinations yield a scale with three tourism impact dimensions: (1) PSCI – Positive Social-Cultural Impacts, (2) PEI – Positive Economic Impacts and (3) NSI – Negative Social Impacts. Surprisingly, results show a focus on positive and negative socio-cultural impacts and positive economic impacts, but no significant dimension for environmental impacts was identified. The study also discusses the potential contribution of the scale to an improved understanding of tourists' sensitivity towards tourism impacts, and corresponding strategies aimed at optimizing them. **Keywords**: tourism development, nature destinations, tourism impacts, measurement scale.

1. Introduction

The acknowledgement of the potential benefits of tourism for countries, regions and local communities has led to an increased effort in developing tourism activity (Fleming & Toepper, 1990). However, these direct and indirect development impacts may be both positive and negative (Andereck, 1995; Caneday & Zeiger, 1991; George, 2010; Gursoy & Rutherford, 2004; Jackson & Inbakaran, 2006; Mathieson & Wall, 1982; Williams, 1979). The more attractive a destination, the more popular it becomes; as a consequence, it is visited and its resources are used more extensively, eventually generating negative impacts that may result in the reduction of both the quality of life of its residents and the quality of the tourist experience (Diedrich & García-Buades, 2009; Haley *et al.*, 2005; Hillery *et al.*, 2001; Zamani-Farahani & Musa, 2008). As well as inherent benefits, tourism development also brings social, cultural, economic and environmental costs (Fleming & Toepper, 1990; Mathieson & Wall, 1982). Each tourist destination is characterized by a specific level of saturation that, whenever exceeded, leads to discomfort for both tourists and residents, eventually even destroying the primary attractiveness of the place (Foster, 1985).

The impacts of tourism development have warranted increasing attention from both academia and tourism planners, given that the industry inevitably triggers both beneficial and adverse effects with a potentially significant impact on host communities (Haley *et al.*, 2005). Particularly in nature areas, which are often characterized by fragile socio-economic structures and sensitive ecosystems, tourism may lead to substantial (and not only beneficial) social, cultural, ecological and economic changes (Belsky, 1999; Butler & Hinch, 1998; Stonich, 1998, 2000). The understanding of these impacts and of tourists' awareness of them is a useful starting point for eventually controlling them, by changing attitudes and behaviours.

The perceptions of the impacts generated by tourism development have been a prominent research topic in recent decades (Andereck & Vogt, 2000). In the 1960s, these studies focused on the positive impacts of tourism, whereas in the 1970s essentially negative effects were analyzed. Since the 1980s, however, tourism impact studies have showed a more systematic approach, involving both types of impact (Andereck & Vogt, 2000; Jafari, 1986).

The intensity and magnitude of tourism development impacts may vary from destination to destination, depending on the features of the places themselves, on the activities developed there, and on the behaviour of individuals, both residents and tourists, on site (van der Duim & Caalders, 2002). In general, tourism impacts are distinguished as positive versus negative, and according to their economic, environmental or socio-cultural scope, corresponding to the three pillars of sustainability (Andereck, 1995; Caneday & Zeiger, 1991; Mathieson & Wall, 1982; Gursoy & Rutherford, 2004; Williams, 1979). We detail this further in the following sections, and complement the conceptual discussion with an empirical approach, which analyzes tourists' perceptions towards tourism development in nature areas in a holistic and multi-disciplinary manner. The aim is to develop a tourism impact measurement scale for assessing a wide range of tourism impact parameters.

This multi-dimensional scale was created with the help of an extensive literature review focused on the concept of tourism impacts, together with insights gained from an empirical study of 315 tourists in European nature destinations – the Serra da Estrela (Portugal), the Alps (France, Austria and Switzerland) and the Picos de Europa (Spain) – which determined the specific dimensions shown to be more relevant. The development of this instrument may contribute to an improved understanding of tourists' sensitivity towards the impacts of tourism activity, and thereby to the development of a means of sensitizing visitors to rural and nature destinations, as well as strategies aimed at the minimization of negative and optimization of positive impacts. Also presented are the study's limitations, as well as guidelines for future research.

2. Impacts of Tourism Development

2.1. Social impacts

The social and cultural impacts of tourism on the local community are widely recognized and have been extensively studied (Haralambopoulas & Pizam 1996). These impacts tend to occur at a slow pace over time, being sometimes neither tangible nor visible (Mathieson & Wall, 1982). However, they are typically permanent or nearly irreversible (Swarbrooke, 1999), which makes them of central importance and gives rise to the need to study them in the first place (Krippendorf, 1987).

Tourism is a phenomenon in which residents and tourists interact mutually (Gu & Wong, 2006). It is a highly involving social and cultural event both for tourists and for residents (Murphy, 1985), also constituting a phenomenon of acculturation, as pointed out by Besculides, Lee & McCormick (2002). The contact between different social groups, nationalities and cultures causes complex social interaction, the exchange of ideas (Esman, 1984) and, correspondingly, cultural exchange (Besculides *et al.*, 2002; Reisinger & Turner, 2003).

This cultural exchange, typically associated with tourism, with residents exposed to distinct cultures, may also result in increased comprehension between residents and tourists (Mathieson & Wall, 1982). As a consequence, tourism may be regarded as a unifying social force that permits a deepened understanding of other cultures and communities, thereby enhancing tolerance and respect for other societies and their ways of life, both amongst tourists and residents alike (Andereck *et al.*, 2005; Stronza, 2001;

Teye *et al.*, 2002); this is recognized by some as a contributor to peace (Goeldner & Ritchie, 2000).

Several authors claim that the tourism industry has an enormous potential to positively affect local communities in terms of quality of life (Andereck *et al.*, 2005; McCool & Martin, 1994; Perdue *et al.*, 1990). Indeed, tourism provides incentives for more active lifestyles, through additional recreational opportunities (Lankford *et al.*, 1997; Ross, 1992). Meanwhile, the simple act of revealing the local culture to visitors enhances the links between the members of the community, creating a community spirit and consequently strengthening cultural identity, confidence, pride and social cohesion (Besculides *et al.*, 2002; De Bres & Davis, 2001; Esman, 1984; Garnham, 1996; Kastenholz, 2004). Some societies even strategically use tourism as a means of strengthening their identity through what is unique to a destination and its communities (Ryan, 1991), such as local traditions (Besculides *et al.*, 2002) or festivals (De Bres & Davis, 2001). The revitalization of these communities leads to an increased interest in local culture (Esman, 1984), encouraging residents to develop and engage in cultural activities (Brunt & Courtney, 1999; De Bres & Davis, 2001; McCool & Martin, 1994).

Tourism may thereby help preserve local culture, but it may also dilute or even destroy it. While tourists visit destinations seeking the experience of the unique cultural elements of a place, residents, on the other hand, frequently initiate a process of commodification of culture, with the aim of increasing the attraction of tourists and the profitable commercialization of their cultural resources, which may lead to the creation of artificial "traditions" and tangible heritage elements that are rather inauthentic and even adapted to the tourists' taste (Besculides *et al.*, 2002). This commercialization of culture (Cohen, 1988), along with socio-cultural differences between residents and tourists, may lead to tension and even socio-cultural disruption (Reisinger, 1994; Tosun, 2002), as well as to alienation between the two populations (Ap & Crompton, 1983; McCool & Martin, 1994; Pigram & Wahab, 1997).

Other negative social impacts attributed to tourism, which are to a certain degree associated with increasing and uncontrolled tourist flows, are an increase in crime (Ap & Crompton, 1983; Haralambopoulos & Pizam, 1996), prostitution (Lindberg & Johnson, 1997) and vandalism at the destination (Liu *et al.*, 1987).

Even though irritation and conflict between tourists and residents may result, empirical evidence suggests that there are different types of resident within a community; consequently there are different attitudes towards tourism (Kuvan & Akan 2005), depending mostly on the perceived benefits associated by residents with tourism development (Ap & Crompton, 1998; Perdue *et al.*, 1987), as understandable by the social exchange paradigm. On the other hand, different types of tourists may interact distinctly with residents, depending, amongst other aspects, on "cultural proximity" (Kastenholz, 2010). Thus, by attracting those tourist segments that yield the most beneficial social interaction, i.e., by careful "management of demand", socially sustainable tourism development may be enhanced (Kastenholz, 2004).

2.2. Economic impacts

Tourism is frequently considered an economic alternative to traditional production sectors such as agriculture, especially in the less developed natural and rural regions of some countries (Fleming & Toepper, 1990; Goeldner & Ritchie, 2000; Lane, 2009). Tourism development is in this respect viewed as a fundamental tool for the economic well-being and the consequent improvement of quality of life of the residents of these areas (Nepal & Chipeniuk, 2005). Indeed, Mason (2003) suggests that the economic impacts of tourism development are the most studied in the tourism literature.

This interest is due to the potential of tourism to act as a development catalyst for the destinations in which it takes place (Gee *et al.*, 1989). Several studies show that investment in this industry may stimulate the economy, including the local destination economy, in a direct as well as indirect manner, through its connection with other activities within the economic basis (Burns *et al.*, 1986; Gelan, 2003). Economically, tourism provides destinations with the opportunity to increase income by taking advantage of local, regional and national natural and cultural resources and unique heritage elements (Crouch & Ritchie, 1999). Its development thereby leads to personal benefits for all those directly involved in tourism supply, as well as to regional benefits, mostly through the increase of residents' income (Caneday & Zeiger, 1991; Liu & Var, 1986) and the creation of new employment opportunities (Andereck *et al.*, 2005; Johnson *et al.*, 1994; Milman & Pizam, 1988; Ross, 1992), but also through the stimulation of other connected economic activities and corresponding multiplier effects (Eusébio, 2006).

Negative economic impacts may also be found, however, such as the increase in price levels (Jeong & Faulkner, 1996) and speculation (Kang, Lee, Yoon & Long, 2008), and increased substitution of local and regional produce through imported products (i.e. economic leakages) if the process is not carefully managed.

2.3. Environmental impacts

Environmental factors, landscape and nature are considered as the core elements of most forms of tourism (Crouch & Ritchie, 1999; Liu *et al.*, 1987), being particularly relevant for rural and nature tourism destinations, where they are frequently appreciated in the context of outdoor activities, especially hiking (Rodrigues & Kastenholz, 2010). Many attractions of tourist destinations are based on natural resources and heritage (Starr, 2002). A pristine natural environment, which is unpolluted and well preserved, may substantially enhance the destination's attractiveness and create an important competitive advantage (Cater, 1993).

However, although tourism is typically considered as a "clean" industry, this assumption is not always true. Tourism development may have a significant environmental impact, since it frequently takes place in environmentally attractive but fragile nature areas, whose resources may suffer from extensive, uncontrolled usage over long time periods (Vaccaro & Beltran, 2007). Tourism has the potential to disrupt, jeopardize and even destroy natural habitats (Stronza & Gordillo, 2008), leading in many cases to substantial degradation of natural heritage (Caneday & Zeiger, 1991; D'Amore, 1983), for example through air, noise or water pollution (Andereck, 1995). Still, tourism may also be understood as a means of sensitizing both visitors and residents to environmental problems, leading therefore to the preservation of the destination's natural resources (Andereck *et al.*, 2005; Cohen, 1978).

3. Methodology

All these dimensions were considered for the development of the survey instrument presented here – the questionnaire. The specific variables associated with each dimension were developed on the basis of a literature review on tourism impacts. In total, 60 studies were analyzed and pre-established scale items were integrated into the measurement instrument developed here. The initial scales were adjusted to the reality of the tourists being questioned as well as to the specificity of the mountain destination being studied.

Thirty-nine attributes were specifically used to assess tourists' perceptions of tourism from social-cultural, economic and environmental perspectives. A 5-point Likert-type scale ranging from 1 (strongly disagree) to 5 (strongly agree) was used to rate all 39 attributes. After some revisions, a sample of 30 tourists was selected to undertake a pre-test, so as to check the reliability of the scales (by using Cronbach's alpha), as well as to test the instrument's face validity, registering any misunderstanding of item wordings. Results of the pre-test were thereby used for refining the measurement instrument.

The validation of the proposed conceptual model was achieved through exploratory factor analysis (EFA), aiming at determining the relationship between the observed variables and latent variables. Having defined the variables that represent each factor and the number of acceptable factors best representing the variability within the data, a confirmatory factor analysis (CFA) was applied using the full-information maximum likelihood (FIML) estimation procedures available in LISREL (Jöreskog & Sörbom, 1993). Finally, in order to assess nomological validity, and following Churchill's recommendations on scale development and validation (Churchill, 1995), measures were tested with respect to another construct to which the tourism impacts construct is theoretically related. For this purpose, in the present study the concept "destination image" was used to test nomological validity, since it is identified as a construct related to perceptions of tourism impacts. The data processing and analysis were performed using the programs SPSS and LISREL, in their latest versions.

The tourists who visited the nature destinations of the Alps, the Picos de Europa and the Serra da Estrela are mainly from urban residential areas (80%), bachelors (49.2%), married (44.1%), and between 26 and 35 years (47.3%) or 36-45 years (23.2%) old. Most reveal a pattern of a high level of education (65.4%), with professional occupations belonging to the mid and higher levels of management (34.3%) and public administration (14.3%), with a monthly income of between €1001 and €2000 for the largest group (39.4%).

4. Data Analysis

To analyze the validity of the proposed scale, the items measuring the impact perceptions were subject to an exploratory factor analysis and later to a confirmatory factor analysis. For this purpose, the procedures used for estimating the full-information maximum likelihood model (FIML) in the LISREL 8.8 program (Joreskog & Sorbom, 1996) were applied.

The Qui squared for this model is significant (X2=306.6, df=102, p=.00). Since the Qui squared statistic is sensitive to sample size, we further analyzed additional fit indices: the Normed Fit Index (NFI), the Comparative Fit Index (CFI), the Incremental Fit Index (IFI), and the Non-Normed Fit Index (NNFI). The NFI for this model was .95, the CFI and IFI both .97 and NNFI showed a value of .96, which is satisfactory. All three constructs present levels of composed reliability (Bagozzi, 1980). Given that the fit indices may be strengthened, permitting the existence of more terms to be freely estimated, the Root Mean Square Error of Approximation (RMSEA) was also considered, which presents the mean and incorporates a penalization for lack of parsimony. A value of RMSEA above .10 indicates an inacceptable value (Steiger, 1980). The RMSEA of this measurement model is 0.080, which is acceptable.

Convergent validity is revealed by the significant and high standardized weights of each item in respect to the measured construct (the mean weight is .75). Discriminant validity between the constructs is analysed by using the Fornell and Larcker (1981) test, in which all possible construct pairs passed the test (see Table 1).

In order to assess nomological validity, measures were tested with respect to another construct to which tourism destination image constructs are theoretically related (cf. Churchill, 1979, 1995). Perceptions of tourism impacts are clearly associated with destination image, because the perceptions of the effects of tourism development in a destination influence the perception that tourists hold of it (Diedrich & García-Buades, 2009; Silva, 2011; Zamani-Farahani & Musa, 2008).

In this research work, nomological validity will be demonstrated if the scores of all three tourism impact factors are significantly correlated with destination image.

The tourists' destination image is assessed through 22 items, which are described in Table 2 and result from a literature review on destination image. All items are anchored by (1) offers very little, and (5) offers very much, with affective destination image anchored by opposite adjectives. Additionally, five image dimensions are distinguished which result from a factor analysis.

Table 3 shows the correlations between destination image dimensions and dimensions of positive socio-cultural impacts, positive economic impacts and negative social impacts. All the correlation coefficients are significant (at $p < 0.01$). Therefore, the tourism impact scale contributes to forming tourist destination image, which provides evidence for the nomological validity of the three proposed measures (cf. Cadogan, Diamantopoulos & de Mortanges, 1999; Cross & Chaffin, 1982).

Table 1 – Tourists' Perceptions of Impacts of Tourism Development

Constructs, measurement scales and reliability indices	Standardized Coefficients	T-values
PSCI - POSITIVE SOCIO-CULTURAL IMPACTS (α=0.92; $\rho_{vc(n)}$=0.57; ρ=0.93) *Tourism:*		
Results in more cultural exchange between tourists and residents	0.61	11.55
Improves educational development	0.70	13.94
Improves mutual confidence among people	0.69	13.54
Increases pride and cultural identity	0.69	13.79
Creates opportunities for using recreational facilities	0.73	14.83
Encourages development of a variety of cultural activities by the local residents	0.77	15.84
Improves tolerance of other cultures and different ways of life	0.85	18.56
Provides social interaction	0.83	17.85
Allows a better understanding of other cultures and societies	0.84	18.00
Improves quality of life in general	0.77	15.96
PEI - POSITIVE ECONOMIC IMPACTS (α=0.78; $\rho_{vc(n)}$ =0.70; ρ=0.82) *Tourism:*		
Creates more jobs /employment opportunities	0.64	1
Attracts more investment	1	14.88
NSI - NEGATIVE SOCIAL IMPACTS (α=0.81; $\rho_{vc(n)}$=0.54; ρ=0.82) *Tourism:*		
Increases crime rate	0.79	15.20
Leads to alienation between tourists and residents	0.66	12.14
Leads to prostitution	0.68	12.58
Leads to vandalism	0.75	14.25

α = Internal reliability (Cronbach, 1951); $\rho_{vc(n)}$ = Variance extracted (Fornell and Larcker, 1981);

ρ= Composite reliability (Bagozzi, 1980).

Table 2 – Tourism Destination Image Factors Held by Tourists

TDI1 – HISTORIC-CULTURAL (α=0.88)
Cultural attractions
Historic attractions
Cultural experience
TDI2 – SOCIAL AND PRESTIGE (α=0.79)
Opportunities for social interactions
Fashionable destination
Reputation and good name
Opportunities for education and new learning
TDI3 – NATURAL/ECOLOGICAL (α=0.86)
Ecological diversity
Authenticity
Water presence
Contact and proximity with Nature
Natural Park
TDI4 – LEISURE AND SPORT (α=0.79)
Opportunities for leisure and entertainment activities
Sport and recreation activities
TDI5 – AFFECTIVE (α=0.92)
Unpleasant/Pleasant
Gloomy/Exciting
Sleepy/Arousing
Distressing/Relaxing
Uninteresting/Interesting
Sad/Happy
Unimportant/Important
Bad/Good

α = Internal reliability (Cronbach, 1951)

5. Conclusion

In this study a measurement scale for assessing tourist perceptions of the effects of tourism development on nature areas was developed, regarding its socio-cultural, economic and environmental impacts, both of a positive and negative nature.

Table 3 – Correlations between Tourism Impact Dimensions and Destination Image Factors

	TDI1	TDI2	TDI3	TDI4	TDI5
PSCI	0,584**	0,639**	0,600**	0,344**	0,451**
PEI	0,344**	0,451**	0,413**	0,204**	0,280**
NSI	-0,212**	-0,330**	-0,308**	-0,261**	-0,206**

**All correlations are significant at the 0.01 level (2-tailed).

Results indicate that tourist perceptions focus on positive and negative socio-cultural impacts and positive economic impacts, but surprisingly data did not permit the inclusion of an environmental effects dimension in the LISREL model. In any case, descriptive data on the latter show that tourists tend to perceive only positive and to underestimate negative environmental impacts.

However, it must be acknowledged that tourism, frequently acting as an agent of development and innovation, may in extreme cases disrupt the relationship between man and nature (Croll & Parkin, 1992; Ingold, 1992, 1996). One of the features of modern tourism is the fact that tourist trips, particularly those involving longer distances, disrupt the sense of belonging to a specific place. The relationship between a sense of belonging to a place and the perceived impact on this place is obvious (McCool & Martin, 1994). If tourists do not feel that they belong to the place they visit, they may lose the sense of the environmental limits of human action in that place, and consequently ignore their responsibility in preserving and protecting it (Gossling, 2002; Ingold, 1993). Tourists tend to consider environmental impacts as an international problem that needs to be solved globally, implying a strengthened tendency not to assume any personal responsibility in the process. Both tourists and the tourism industry may view themselves as disconnected from the destination's environment and nature, understanding these features as a scenario for personal realization or as a given economic resource, free of any cost and concern.

Tourists seldom reveal a strong sensitivity regarding environmental impacts, implying a lack of understanding of the impacts of their own behaviour on natural areas visited (Manning, 1985; Marion & Lime,

1986). However, the success of a tourism destination depends largely on the extent of the effect of tourism on the place, so the study of tourists' perceptions of the diverse impacts of tourism reveals itself as extremely important (Zamani-Farahani & Musa, 2008). The way tourists perceive the effects of tourism on the destination will affect the entire image they develop of it, and consequently their willingness to return and recommend the visited place to other tourists (Diedrich & García-Buades, 2009).

On the other hand, tourism planning of nature areas takes place in the context of environmental change, complexity and uncertainty (McCool, 2009). It is increasingly recognized that the vulnerability of natural spaces requires the development and articulation of policies based on principles of sustainability, which is nowadays considered a fundamental approach for preserving these areas' integrity and responding to the needs, values and lifestyles of twenty-first century society. In this context, nature tourism destinations actually have a competitive advantage, which may result in an excellent opportunity for social, cultural and economic development, particularly when destinations are able to preserve their natural, social and cultural integrity.

The measurement instrument developed in this study may contribute to a better comprehension of the sensitivity of tourists regarding the impacts of tourism activity, and may thereby lead to the development of means of awareness-building amongst visitors to rural and natural areas, as well as to the definition of strategies aiming at the minimization of negative and the maximization of positive impacts.

There are, however, some limitations that must be acknowledged regarding this study. The first limitation is the assessment tool used – the questionnaire – that may have created a variance in responses that overvalues the relationship between constructs. This would have been particularly concerning if respondents had been aware of the relationship between variables. However, the items relating to the constructs were presented in a separated and randomly mixed format together with other, less relevant items, so that respondents should not have detected which of the items were really significant, and which assessed their relationship with other constructs.

Perhaps the inclusion of more items relating to environmental impacts in the scale might permit the integration of a corresponding factor into the model, making it more complete; this should be tested in future approaches.

The quantitative approach used here requires an individual to subjectively classify a set of predetermined attributes or to characterize stimuli using a standardized classification scale battery (Pike, 2007), which may be a suboptimal solution. Despite the advantages of flexibility and facility of use and codification of these structured techniques, there is the risk of omitting important constructs and of using constructs that are not the most important to respondents. Moreover, respondents are "forced" to evaluate variables in terms of the constructs specified in scales, making the consideration of additional impact aspects difficult. It should therefore be useful to apply additional methodologies, particularly of a non-structured nature, that may permit the collection of richer data sets if respondents are given the opportunity to describe freely their impressions of the effects of tourism development in nature areas.

Furthermore, it would be important to study the antecedents and consequences of the thus measured perceptions of impacts of tourism development in nature destinations. Finally, an analysis of other associated constructs, such as tourists' motivations and expectations, previous experiences with the destination, and sense of belonging to the place visited, designated in the environmental psychology literature as "place-attachment" (Kyle, Graefe, Manning, & Bacon, 2004), would also be most interesting.

References

Andereck, K. (1995). Environmental consequences of tourism: A review of recent research. *Linking Tourism, the environment, and sustainability, Annual Meeting of the National Recreation and Park Association. General Technical Report*, (pp. 77–81).

Andereck, K., & Vogt, C. (2000). The relationship between residents' attitudes toward tourism and tourism development options. *Journal of Travel Research*, 39(1), 27-36.

Andereck, K., Valentine, K., Knopf, R., & Vogt, C. (2005). Residents' perceptions of community tourism impacts. *Annals of Tourism Research,* 32(4), 1056-1076.

Ap, J., & Crompton, J. (1998). Developing and testing a tourism impact scale. *Journal of Travel Research,* 37(2), 120-130.

Bagozzi, R. (1980). *Causal models in marketing.* NY: John Wiley.

Belsky, J. (1999). Misrepresenting communities: The politics of community-based rural ecotourism in Gales Point Manatee, Belize. *Rural Sociology,* 64, 641–666.

Besculides, A., Lee, M., & McCormick, P. (2002). Residents' perception of the cultural benefits of tourism. *Annals of Tourism Research,* 29(2), 303-319.

Brunt, P., & Courtney, P. (1999). Host perceptions of socialcultural impacts. *Annals of Tourism Research,* 26(3), 493-515.

Burns, J., Hatch, J., & Mules, T. (1986). *The Adelaide Grand Prix: The impact of a special event.* Adelaide, South Australia: Centre for South Australian Economic Studies.

Butler, R., & Hinch, T. (1996). *Tourism and indigenous peoples.* London: Thompson.

Cadogan, J., Diamantopoulos, A., & Mortanges, C. (1999). A measures of export market orientation: Scale development and cross-cultural validation. *Journal of International Business Studies,* 30(4), 689-707.

Caneday, L., & Zeiger, J. (1991). The social, economic, and environmental costs of tourism to a gaming community as perceived by its residents. *Journal of Travel Research,* 30(2), 45-49.

Cater, E. (1993). Ecotourism in the third world: Problems for sustainable tourism development. *Tourism Management,* 14(2), 85-90.

Churchill, G. (1979). A paradigm for developing better measures of marketing constructs. *Journal of Marketing Research,* 16(1), 64-73.

—. (1995). *Marketing research: Methodological foundations.* Chicago: The Dryden Press.

Cohen, E. (1978). Impact of tourism on the physical environment. *Annals of Tourism Research,* 5(2), 215-237.

—. (1988). Tourism and aids in Thailand. *Annals of Tourism Research,* 15(4), 467-486.

Croll, E., & Parking, D. (1992). *Bush base: Forest farm.* London: Routledge.

Cronbach, L. (1951). Coefficient alpha and the internal structure of tests. *Psychometric,* 16, 297-334.

Cross, E., & Chaffin, W. (1982). Use the binomial theorem in interpreting results of multiple tests of significance. *Educational and Psychological Measurement,* 42, 25-34.

Crouch, G.I., & Ritchie, J.R.B. (1999). Tourism, competitiveness, and societal prosperity. *Journal of Business Research,* 44(3), 137-152.

D'Amore, J. (1983). Guidelines to planning in harmony with the host community. In P. Murphy (Ed.), *Tourism in Canada: Selected issues and options* (pp. 135-158). Victoria: University of Victoria.

De Bres, K., & Davis, J. (2001). Celebrating group and place identity: A case study of a new regional festival. *Tourism Geographies*, 3(1), 326–37.

Diedrich, A., & García-Buades, E. (2009). Local perceptions of tourism as indicators of destination decline. *Tourism Management,* 30, 512-521.

Esman, M. (1984). Tourism as ethnic preservation: The Cajuns of Louisiana. *Annals of Tourism Research,* 11(3), 451-467.

Eusébio, M. (2006). *Avaliação do impacte económico do turismo a nível regional: O caso da Região Centro de Portugal.* PhD Thesis: UA.

Fleming, W., & Toepper, L. (1990). Economic impacts studies: Relating the positive and negative impacts to tourism development. *Journal of Travel Research, 29,* 35-42.

Fornell, C., & Larcker, D. (1981). Evaluating structural equation models with unobservable variables and measurement error. *Journal of Marketing Research, 18*(1), 39-50.

Foster, D. (1985). *Travel and tourism management.* London: MacMillan.

Garnham, B. (1996). Ranfurly shield rugby: An investigation into the impacts of a sporting event on a provincial city, the case of New Plymouth, Taranaki, New Zealand. *Festival Management and Event Tourism, 4,* 145–149.

Gee, C., Choy, D., & Makens, J. (1989). *The travel industry.* NY: Van Nostrand Reinhold.

George, R. (2010). Visitor perceptions of crime-safety and attitudes towards risk: The case of Table Mountain National Park, Cape Town. *Tourism Management, 31,* 806-815.

Gelan, A. (2003). Local economic impacts: The British open. *Annals of Tourism Research, 30*(2), 406-425.

Goeldner, C., & Ritchie, B. (2000). *Tourism: Principles, practices and philosophies.* NY: John Wiley.

Gössling, S. (2002). Global environmental consequences of tourism. *Global Environmental Change, 12*(4), 283-302.

Gu, M., & Wong, P. (2006). Residents' perceptions of tourism impacts: A case study of homestay operators in Dachangshan Dao, North-East China. *Tourism Geographies, 8*(3), 253-273.

Gursoy, D., & Rutherford, D. (2004). Host attitudes toward tourism: An improved structural model. *Annals of Tourism Research, 31*(3), 495-516.

Haley, A., Snaith, T., & Miller, G. (2005). The social impacts of tourism: A case study of Bath, UK. *Annals of Tourism Research, 32*(3), 647-668.

Haralambopoulos, N., & Pizam, A. (1996). Perceived impacts of tourism: The case of Samos. *Annals of Tourism Research, 23*(3), 503–526.

Hillery, M., Nancarrow, B., Griffin, G., & Syme, G. (2001). Tourist perception of environmental impact. *Annals of Tourism Research, 28*(4), 853-867.

Ingold, T. (1996). Hunting and gathering as ways of perceiving the environnment. In R. Fukai (Ed.), *Redefining nature: Ecology, culture and domestication* (pp. 117-155). Oxford: Berg.

Jackson, M. & Inbakaran, R. (2006). Evaluating residents' attitudes and intentions to act towards tourism development in Regional Victoria, Australia. *International Journal of Tourism Research,* 8, 355-366.

Jafari, J. (1986). A systemic view of sociocultural dimensions of tourism. In *President's Commission on American Outdoors, Tourism* (pp. 33-50). Washington DC: United States Travel and Tourism Administration.

Jeong, G., & Faulkner, B. (1996). Resident perceptions of Mega event impacts: The Taejon international exposition case. *Festival Management & Event Tourism,* 4(1), 3-11.

Jonhson, J., Snepenger, D., & Akis, S. (1994). Residents' perceptions of tourism development. *Annals of Tourism Research,* 21(3), 629-642.

Joreskog, K., & Sorbom, D. (1996). *LISREL 8: User's Reference Guide.* Chicago: Scientific Software International.

Kang, S., Lee, C.-K., Yoon, Y., & Long, P. (2008). Residents perception of the impact of limited-stakes community-based casino gaming in mature gaming communities. *Tourism Management,* 29(4), 681-694.

Kastenholz, E. (2004). Management of demand as a tool in sustainable tourist destination development. *Journal of Sustainable Tourism,* 12(5), 388-408.

—. (2010). "Cultural proximity" as a determinant of destination image. *Journal of Vacation Marketing,* 16(4), 313-322.

Krippendorf, J. (1987). *The holiday makers: Understanding the impact of travel and leisure.* Oxford: Heinemann.

Kuvan, Y., & Akan, P. (2005). Residents' attitudes toward general and forest-related impacts of tourism: the case of Belek – Antalya. *Tourism Management,* 26(5), 691-706.

Kyle, G., Graefe, A., Manning, R., & Bacon, J. (2004). Effects of place attachment on users' perceptions of social and environmental conditions in a natural setting. *Journal of Environmental Psychology,* 24, 213-225.

Lane, B. (2009). Rural Tourism: An overview. In Jamal T. & Robinson M. (Eds.), *The SAGE Handbook of Tourism Studies.* London: Sage.

Lankford, S., Williams, A., & Knowles-Lankford, J. (1997). Perceptions of outdoor recreation opportunities and support for tourism development. *Journal of Travel Research,* 36(4), 65-69.

Lindberg, K., & Johnson, R. (1997). Modeling resident attitudes toward tourism. *Annals of Tourism Research,* 24(2), 402-424.

Liu, J., Sheldon, P., & Var, T. (1987). Cross-national approach to determining resident perceptions of the impact of tourism on the environment. *Annals of Tourism Research,* 14(1), 17-37.

Manning, R. (1985). Descriptive aspects of outdoor recreation: Attitudes, preferences, perceptions. In R. Manning (Ed.), *Studies in outdoor recreation: Search and research for satisfaction* (pp. 27-41). Corvalis OR : Oregon State University Press.

Marion, J., & Lime, D. (1986). Recreational resource impacts: Visitor perceptions and management responses. In D. Kulhavy, R. Conner (Eds.), *Wilderness and natural areas in the Eastern United States: A management challenge* (pp. 229–235). Austin TX: Austin State University Center for Applied Studies.

Mason, P. (2003). *Tourism impacts, planning and management.* Jordan Hill: Oxford: Butterworth-Heinemann.

Mathieson, A., & Wall, G. (1982). *Tourism: Economic, physical and social impacts.* NY: Longman.

McCool, S., & Martin, S. (1994). Community attachment and attitudes toward tourism development. *Journal of Travel Research,* 32(3), 29-34.

McCool, S. (2009). Constructing partnerships for protected area tourism planning in an era of change and messiness. *Journal of Sustainable Tourism,* 17(2), 133-148.

Milman, A., & Pizam, A. (1988). Social impacts of tourism on Central Florida. *Annals of Tourism Research,* 15(2), 191-204.

Murphy, P. (1985). *Tourism: A community approach.* London: Methuen.

Nepal, S., & Chipeniuk, R. (2005). Mountain tourism: Toward a conceptual framework. *Tourism Geographies,* 7(3), 313-333.

Perdue, P., Long, P., & Allen, L. (1987). (1987) Rural resident tourism perceptions and attitudes. *Annals of Tourism Research,* 14(3), 420-429.

Pigram, J., & Wahab, S. (1997). The challenge of sustainable tourism growth. In S. Wahab, & J. Pigram (Eds.), *Tourism, Sustainability and growth: The challenge of sustainability* (pp. 3-14). London: Routledge.

Pike, S. (2007). Repertory Grid Analysis in group settings to elicit salient destination image attributes. *Current Issues in Tourism,* 10(4), 378-392.

Reisinger, Y. (1994). The social contact between tourist and hosts of different cultural background. In A. Art, V. Seaton (Eds.), *Tourism the state of art* (pp. 743-753). Chichester: Wiley.

Reisinger, Y. & Turner, L.W. (2003). *Cross-cultural behaviour in tourism.* Oxford: Elsevier Butterworth Heinemann.

Rodrigues, A., & Kastenholz, E., (2010). Hiking as a relevant wellness activity – results of an exploratory study of hiking tourists in Portugal applied to a rural tourism project. *Journal of Vacation Marketing,* 16(4), 331-343.

Ross, G. (1992). Resident perceptions of the impact of tourism to an Australian city. *Journal of Travel Research,* 30(3), 13-17.

Ryan, C. (1991). *Recreational tourism: A social science perspective.* London: Routledge.

Silva, C. (2011). *A imagem dos destinos turísticos de montanha: Olhares de residentes e turistas.* PhD Thesis: UA.

Starr, N. (2002). *Viewpoint: An introduction to travel, tourism and hospitality.* NJ: Prentice Hall.

Stonich, S. (1998). The political ecology of tourism. *Annals of Tourism Research,* 25, 25–54.

—. (2000). *The other side of paradise: Tourism conservation and development in the Bay Islands.* Elmsford: Cognizant.

Stronza, A. (2001). Anthropology of tourism: Forging new ground of ecotourism and other alternatives. *Annual Review of Anthropology,* 30, 261-283.

Stronza, A., & Gordillo, J. (2008). Community views of ecotourism. *Annals of Tourism Research,* 35(2), 448-468.

Swarbrooke, J., & Horner, S. (1999). *Consumer behaviour in tourism.* Oxford: Butterworth Heinemann.

Teye, V., Sonmez, S., & Sirakaya, E. (2002). Residents' attitudes toward tourism development. *Annals of Tourism Research,* 29(3), 668-688.

Tosun, C. (2002). Host perceptions of impacts: A comparative study. *Annals of Tourism Research,* 29(1), 231-253.

Vaccaro, I., & Beltran, O. (2007). Consuming space, nature and culture: Patrimonial discussions in the hyper-modern era. *Tourism Geographies,* 9(3), 254-274.

van der Duim, R., & Caalders, J. (2002). Biodiversity and tourism: Impacts and interventions. *Annals of Tourism Research,* 29(3), 743-761.

Williams, T. (1979). Impact of domestic tourism in host population: The evolution of a model. *Tourist Recreation Research,* 4(1), 15-21.

Zamani-Farahami, H., & Musa, G. (2008). Residents' attitudes and perceptions toward tourism development: A case study of Masooleh, Iran. *Tourism Management,* 29(6), 1233-1236.

CHAPTER SIX

RESPONSIBILITY IN FESTIVALS AND EVENTS: A COMPETITIVE ADVANTAGE

HENRI KUOKKANEN

Abstract

Environmental sustainability and social responsibility have established themselves in most industries, and festivals and events are not immune to the trend. Competitive advantage through responsibility has been proposed by Porter and Kramer (2006), and festivals could also benefit from this strategy (Bansal & Roth, 2000; Mair & Jago, 2010). This chapter both explores the advertisement of responsibility by festival organisers in Finland and investigates whether any link between responsibility and visitor numbers can be established. The chapter concludes that use of responsibility in communication is not well adopted by most Finnish festivals. Furthermore, no connection between responsible initiatives advertised and growth in popularity was found, suggesting that the supply of responsibility by festivals does not meet demand. Therefore, the chapter calls for further research on customer expectations of responsibility in this domain. **Keywords**: Competitive advantage, CSR, events, festivals, sustainability, responsibility.

1. Introduction

Porter and Kramer (2006) make a strong case for Corporate Social Responsibility (CSR) as a potential competitive advantage. The aim of this chapter is to explore the communication of responsible and sustainable actions by festival organisers in Finland and to determine whether any link between communicated actions and change in visitor numbers can be established. Increased visitor numbers could indicate that a competitive advantage may be obtained through advertising a festival's responsibility, sometimes suggested as a motive for environmental actions (Bansal & Roth, 2000; Mair & Jago, 2010). First, the exploratory section will provide better understanding of how these actions are used and communicated by festival organisers. This chapter concentrates on actions that are clearly communicated and does not attempt to find out how many other responsible actions may exist. Second, the link between advertised actions and visitor numbers is studied in order to evaluate whether the supply of responsibility meets the demand of the intended visitors; in other words, whether the actions are something that the visitors value.

A lack of connection between visitor numbers and advertised responsibility could indicate that supply is not meeting demand, although a complete lack of interest in this area could be another reason for an absence of a link. Some evidence exists to suggest that this is not the case. A supply-side survey carried out by MVM Group (Fletcher, 2007) suggested that 30% of Australian events professionals are greatly affected by a CSR policy when choosing the type of events they organise. As for the demand, a study made for a UK advocacy group, A Greener Festival, indicated that 48% of visitors to live music festivals around Europe would pay more for a greener event and 36% found "greenery" important when deciding to buy a ticket (Buchinghamshire New University, 2008). Given such examples it would be dangerous to simply reject the notion of demand for responsibility altogether. Thus, this chapter explores the premise that some festival visitors are interested in responsibility and sustainability if offered in an appropriate way.

The tourism and events industries are increasing their emphasis on sustainability (Corporate social responsibility for EC&O Venues, 2007; Eccles, 2009). Further knowledge of the communication of responsibility and its appeal among visitors would be extremely useful for festival organisers when planning socially responsible and sustainable actions. The results will also be useful in planning communication strategies, through highlighting actions that potential visitors may or may not find interesting.

2. Definitions and Debate over Responsibility and Sustainability

The terms sustainability and responsibility are both widely used, but no single definition for them in tourism exists (Dolnicar, 2006). As the research in these fields directed specifically at events and festivals is scarce, a reference will be made to the wider field of tourism; visiting events and festivals is often combined with tourism. The distinction between sustainability regarding the natural and social environments and the sustainability of a business is also important, the latter describing the continuity and success of an event. In this chapter, sustainability refers to that of the natural and social environments.

From the World Tourism Organisation definition of sustainable tourism (UNWTO, 2010) to the definition by the Partnership for Global Sustainable Tourism Criteria (GSTC, 2009), sustainable tourism is defined by minimizing negative effects to the natural environment, enhancing the prosperity of local communities and conserving their cultural heritage. These follow closely the principles of corporate social responsibility defined by Carroll (1979); a model that he further developed into the famous pyramid of financial, legal, ethical and philanthropic responsibilities of corporations (Carroll, 1991). Furthermore, there is a clear connection between the definitions of sustainable tourism and Freeman's stakeholder theory in which businesses need to consider all groups impacted by their operations (Freeman, 1983); thus the definitions mentioned above can be considered valid guidelines.

The notion that tourism is inherently about consumption, and pessimistic views on the impossibility of sustainable tourism presented, for example, by McKercher (1993) and Sharpley (2000), are noted; however, even if their views are correct and tourism never could be entirely sustainable when it comes to the natural environment, minimising the impact on it should still be a worthy goal. Higgings-Desbiolles (2010) concludes that consumerist values prevent tourism from being sustainable and offers some insight into how sustainability might be achieved through motivating a change in values.

Lansing and De Vries (2007) and Liu (2003) all attacked sustainable tourism as a marketing ploy and green washing; among customers, these same fears create distrust and confusion in any attempted communication of responsibility. To mitigate these concerns, the development of clear standards for sustainability has been suggested by several authors (Lansing & De Vries, 2007; Liu, 2003; McCool, Moisey, & Nickelson, 2001); such agreed standards would facilitate the creation and adoption of indicators. Byrd (2007) took Freeman's stakeholder theory as a starting point for creating indicators, and other authors, including Baros and David (2007), have contributed to this area. However, practical applications of indicators are generally absent, as was observed by Blackstock, White, McCrum, Scott and Hunter (2008) in their study of Scottish National Parks. Supporting the earlier findings, Miller, Rathouse, Scarles, Holmes and Tribe (2010) investigated public understanding of sustainable tourism and concluded that the general public is not well aware of the impacts of tourism or of the alternatives available. They call for practical initiatives involving the wider public. Bergin-Seers and Mair (2008) concluded that communication of green initiatives to customers by tourism operators often remains weak; their finding partly explains those of Miller *et al.* (2010).

Francois-Lecompte and Prim-Allaz (2010) categorised French tourists and found a strong link between interest in sustainability and interest in responsibility, suggesting that people who believe in one concept generally tend to subscribe to the other. Bergin-Seers and Mair (2008) concluded that the demographics of green tourists do not differ significantly from tourists in general, but the key categories of green tourists they defined include aspects of sustainability and responsibility, again suggesting a link between the two.

3. Responsibility and Sustainability in Events and Festivals

Mair and Jago (2010) studied the drivers behind the corporate greening process in the business events sector, and found that a perceived competitive advantage significantly forwarded the greening process. Earlier Bansal and Roth (2000) concluded that a variety of reasons exist for corporations to 'go green', also implying a change towards competitive advantage. However, Mair and Jago (2010) also noted that actual gains from greening may be less than anticipated, and that demand has often been weaker than expected. Their findings coincide with the research of Bansal and Roth (2000) and Clavier-Cortes, Molina-Azorin, Pereira-Moliner and Lopez-Gamero (2007), who also identified competitive advantage as a driver for greening (though in hotels) but reported mixed results from these activities. Based on these results, companies do not seem to do well in their pursuit of additional profits through environmental actions.

Getz (2009) introduced the paradigm of sustainable and responsible events, and outlined how the Triple Bottom Line (TBL) model of Elkington (1997) could be used in festivals and events. The TBL model divides CSR into financial, social and environmental responsibilities, and building on the TBL and stakeholder theory, Karlsen and Stenbacka-Nordström (2009) studied festivals around the Barents region. They emphasized the need for a 'give and take' -relationship between the festival and its stakeholders as a prerequisite for growth and success of the event. The fundamental concepts of CSR are thus relevant also in the festivals and events industry.

Laing and Frost (2010) explored the organisation of green festivals and discussed the challenges in staging and managing green events, establishing categories of green actions and proposing further research on the supply side. As Bergin-Seers and Mair (2008) suggest, there seems to be too little research on whether consumers find green products interesting; the research should concentrate on actual purchase decisions instead of stated intentions. Thus the concrete link between greening – or responsibility towards all stakeholders – and competitive advantage in the events and festivals sector seems to remain fairly unexplored. Kasim (2006) established the link between tourism / hotels and the environment, and urged the mitigation of the resulting negative impacts. A study by Babiak and Wolfe (2006) of the NFL and especially the Super Bowl concluded that CSR would help to provide the event with a more positive image, thus suggesting benefits of CSR to this industry.

Another interesting case is a study made in Finland by Mikkonen and Ristolainen (2007) focusing on the regional impact of a rock festival that has obtained an environmental certificate. The results showed that although local inhabitants believe that the festival had improved its environmental care, the quality of the natural environment still deteriorates. Such findings can provide a basis for further development of responsibility in events and festivals.

While festivals and events as a sector have been actively studied, the author of this chapter is not aware of any research directed at establishing whether the supply of "green" initiatives – or larger responsibility – is a decision criterion for the intended visitors. This chapter aims to contribute to this knowledge. Competitive advantage is stated as one motive when justifying responsible or sustainable actions (Mair & Jago, 2010), but no evidence of this advantage exists so far. A significant link between advertised responsibility and increased visitor numbers could indicate that the supply of responsibility meets the demand of the target audience. However, this study assumes that the supply of responsibility does not meet the demand in this field, as suggested by Kuokkanen and Rios-Morales (2009) in a conceptual model and by Bergin-Seers and Mair (2008) regarding consumer interest in green actions. The following hypothesis is made:

H_1: Potential visitors do not base their decision to attend a festival on the current responsibility offering.

As the terminology has not been definitively established, the word 'responsibility' will be used to describe all actions related to minimizing negative impacts to the natural and social environments. This emphasizes the difference with sustainability often concentrating more on the natural environment only.

4. Methodology

This study focuses on the question of whether the supply of responsibility is interesting to the intended customer. Customers', or in this case festival visitors', preferences could be investigated through interviews; however, this would pose the problem of people wanting to give socially desirable answers (Dillman, 2007). This could result in claiming interest in activities that are defined as responsible, whether or not they are truly indicative of their values. To avoid this problem, this study approaches the question by looking at whether communication about responsibility seems to attract more visitors, complementing research directed at the visitor preferences, and resorts to secondary data to avoid the problem of social bias.

The study has two main goals. It explores the use of responsibility by Finnish event organisers in communicating their events. It also aims to explore whether any link between the advertisement of responsibility by festivals and actual visitor numbers can be established, testing the hypothesis stated earlier. These two goals led to a mixed method approach. A qualitative approach was used to analyse the content of festival organisers' internet pages in order to fulfil the first goal, while a quantitative analysis was used for the second goal.

This study used both primary and secondary data. The sample group was selected based on the availability of secondary data of visitors to Finnish events from 2000-2010 collected first by the Finnish Tourist Board (2000-2007) (Finnish Tourist Board, 2010); this task was taken over in 2008 by Finland Festivals, a collaborative body of festival organisers, and the data for the years 2008-2010 is from their website (Finland Festivals, 2010). The sample covered 46 music / cultural festivals with an annual total of 1.5 million visitors and a median number of annual visitors of approximately 11'000. While the majority of the sample was comprised of music festivals ranging from classical to brass to rock, various other forms of cultural expression, such as dance and poetry, were also represented. With annual visitor numbers ranging from 2'000 to 280'000, the sample could be considered representative of significant Finnish festivals.

As the visitor data had been collected by official bodies and was publicly available, it is considered reliable. However, for the transition year (2007-2008) in data collection responsibility, numbers from the two sources were compared to ensure the quality of the figures. One event was removed from the sample due to a significant discrepancy in the number of visitors between the reports of the two organisations. One further event was disqualified based on the incomparability of annual visitor numbers due to rotation of organisers and locations. One event had not joined the new organisation and collection of visitor numbers was thus interrupted. All the events have existed for a minimum of 11 years, but it should be noted that most of them have a much longer history. This increases the validity of the numbers as the majority of the festivals is very well established and has already reached their 'usual' visitor figures.

The primary data on the communication of responsible actions between 2000 and 2010 was collected using an internet archiving initiative (Archive.org). This website stores a historical log of websites over time and allows users to view these websites as they were in the past. The histories of the festival organiser websites during the study period were retrieved and searched to investigate communication of responsible actions; the data from the period leading to the festival was selected, as communication before the festival could attract potential visitors. These actions were categorised based on the major groups of actions identified. Table 1 presents this categorisation, the aim of which was to find actions related to social or environmental responsibility both on practical and conceptual levels.

Table 1 - Categorisation of Responsible Actions in Finnish Festivals

Categories of responsibility	
1	Carbon emission focus
2	Certification
3	Disabled accessibility
4	Disabled support person allowance
5	Emphasis on keeping the festival area clean
6	Emphasis on recycling
7	Emphasis on minimising waste
8	Environmental program
9	Fair trade product usage
10	Follow-up of previous year
11	Free public transportation
12	Green energy
13	Info flashes on sustainability for visitors
14	Social responsibility program
15	Support for an NGO

The categories were refined based on the variety of actions found on the websites and they also coincide with the categories used by Laing and Frost (2010). There is some conceptual difference between the categories, as some represent concrete actions (e.g. recycling, allowing a support person for a handicapped visitor to enter the festival for free) while others are very conceptual (e.g. CSR programs). Furthermore, there is some inevitable overlap between categories. For example, recycling and waste minimisation are related, but while some organisers emphasized setting up efficient recycling for visitors to use, others concentrated on reducing the amount of waste produced themselves. All of the actions were communicated on the festival websites allowing potential visitors to take them into consideration when finding information about the festival.

After categorising the actions, the data was quantified by counting the number of actions per festival each year; for example, a festival which communicated an emphasis on recycling, adopted fair trade products and used green energy, received a score of three. This database was used to explore the level of communication of responsibility by the festivals and it also reflected how the overall level of these actions has developed during the study period. It was subsequently used to analyse the link between visitor numbers and responsible actions. On a few occasions the archiving website did not contain the website's history for every year of the study period, but it is reasonable to assume that the level of communication was similar to the previous and following years, and thus these occasional gap years pose no serious risk to the reliability of the data.

In order to test the hypothesis that potential visitors do not base their decision to attend a festival on the current responsibility offering, the existence of a link was studied for three different time horizons; 10 years, 5 years and 1 year. This division was made to allow for any changes in visitor behaviour that might otherwise disappear within the longest time horizon. The average number of responsible actions advertised by the festivals overall per year was calculated, and each festival was then compared with this average, allowing for a positive or negative index figure per festival (more or fewer advertised responsible actions than the average). The annual average percentage growth in visitor numbers was calculated for each festival, and this number was compared with the average annual growth for all festivals, again allowing for a positive or a negative growth percentage (higher or lower visitor growth than festivals that year on average). The resulting percentages together with the responsibility indices were used for the analyses.

One festival directly substituting another is often not feasible. As an example, a person looking for a jazz festival would be unlikely to attend a hard rock festival simply because it is greener. In most industries a non-responsible product or service would be easier to replace by a responsible one. This was a clear limitation when interpreting the results; however, as the visitor always has at least the choice of attending or not, some link between visitors and responsibility could exist. Furthermore, many of the bigger festivals cater for a larger audience thus blurring the strict division based on, for example, genre of music.

5. Results

Although the data consisted of 46 festivals in Finland, only 22 were selected for the analysis. These were the ones with 100'000 or more visitors during the observation period. The reason for this selection was that the smaller festivals did not communicate any actions that could be categorized under the classes presented earlier. This in itself is a noteworthy finding, and it will be discussed later.

Table 2 - Responsible Actions Communicated Annually per Festival (2000-2010)

	-00	-01	-02	-03	-04	-05	-06	-07	-08	-09	-10
# of actions	0.09	0.09	0.50	0.50	0.55	0.59	0.68	0.82	1.14	1.14	1.50

The overarching finding from this analysis is how little responsibility is communicated in festivals. As Table 2 indicates, an average of more than one action communicated per festival was only reached in 2008, and even then the actions were very unevenly spread, with many festivals remaining at zero. However, an upward trend in the communication of actions is evident; in 2000 there were virtually no actions communicated (an index of 0.09) and after a steady growth, an average of 1.5 actions per festival was reached in 2010. It must be remembered that Table 2 represents only advertised actions and does not necessarily imply a complete lack of responsibility by the organisers. However, potential visitors can only take into account actions that are communicated, and only these actions can influence the success of the festival in using responsibility as a competitive advantage to attract visitors.

Due to the small number of festivals communicating responsible actions, it is hard to generalise which actions are the most popular; a further statistical analysis would thus be meaningless. Nevertheless, it is interesting to note the frequency of different responsible actions advertised during the study period, as summarized in Table 3. Initiatives related to recycling and waste minimisation were the most popular (with a total of over 50 communications), followed by allowing free entrance for someone supporting a disabled person (22 communications). Environmental initiative, including minimization of carbon emissions and free public transport, were next. Initiatives related to social stakeholders, such as CSR programs and supporting an NGO, were both mid-popular with ten occurrences. Slightly over 70% of the initiatives relate to environment. This clearly reflects the general tendency towards environmental initiatives under the banner of CSR.

Table 3 - Frequency of Responsible Actions Communicated by Category (2000-2010)

Initiatives communicated by category	
Emphasis on recycling	30
Emphasis on minimising waste	23
Disabled support person allowance	22
Carbon emission focus	18
Emphasis on keeping the festival area clean	13
Free public transportation	13
Social responsibility program	10
Support for an NGO	10
Environmental program	9
Certification	6
Fair trade product usage	4
Green energy	3
Info flashes on sustainability for visitors	3
Disabled accessibility	2
Follow-up of previous year	1
Total	167

An interesting detail is that two festivals of the sample group clearly stand out as leaders in their communication of responsibility, emphasizing, for example, a sustainability certification and a social responsibility program. Another two organisers further highlighted awards from a European festival sustainability organisation, Yourope.org, making them stand out among the sample.

As described earlier, both above/ below average communication of responsibility and above/ below average annual visitor growth were calculated for each festival. Based on the deviations from these averages, the intention was to perform linear regression analyses for time horizons of 10 years, the past five years (05-10) and the final year of the study period (09-10) to study whether communication of responsibility before the festival has had an effect on visitor growth. Examination of the data revealed that almost no correlation exists between the pairs of variables, and establishing a cause and effect –relationship using linear regression was thus impossible, as presented in Table 4.

Table 4 - Correlation Coefficients during Different Time Horizons

Variables	Comparative level of responsible communication Comparative growth in visitors	
2000-2010	Observations	211
	Correlation	0.001
2005-2010	Observations	101
	Correlation	0.095
2009-2010	Observations	18
	Correlation	0.211

There is some increase in correlation between the variables as more recent data is analysed. The sample size during the final year is too small to have meaningful results, but despite this lack of significance, the increase could imply an effect of the growing interest in responsibility during the second half of the decade. With the data used in this study it was not possible to analyse this aspect further.

To examine whether increased visitor numbers would have a link with the communication of responsibility the following year, the correlation analysis was repeated with a lag of one year. The results did not significantly change from the analysis presented above, and this suggests that organisers did not react to changes in festival size either by increasing or decreasing responsible actions.

Even without regression analysis, the almost complete lack of correlation between the two variables offers some support for the research hypothesis: festival and event visitors in Finland do not seem to base their participation decisions on the existing and communicated supply of responsibility. However, the low number of communicated responsible actions creates a clear limitation for the interpretation of the results.

6. Discussion

This study clearly illustrates how little festival organisers in Finland communicate about responsibility. Without interviewing the organisers themselves it is impossible to know how much these topics are actually incorporated in the planning process, but the aim of this study was to concentrate on what is being communicated. This lack of advertising does not match with the notion of searching for competitive advantage (Bansal & Roth, 2000; Clavier-Cortés *et al.,* 2007; Mair & Jago, 2010), as it is challenging to create an advantage without letting the customers know about the actions. Thus the first question raised by the results is why more communication on responsibility does not exist. One reason could be that the organisers are afraid of being accused of green washing (Lansing & De Vries, 2007; Liu, 2003), and thus are reluctant to communicate implemented actions. This result would support the need for indicators, as called for by Byrd (2007) and Baros and David (2007). Obviously another reason for minimal communication could be the lack of responsible actions, but this seems less likely considering the greening trends in festivals presented by Laing and Frost (2010). The growth in communication observed throughout the study period suggests that the use of responsibility is increasing, but whether the driver behind this growth is the search for competitive advantage should be studied further.

The finding that small festivals (under 100'000 visitors during the study period did not communicate any responsible actions could be due to the limited resources smaller festivals have at their disposal. This does not necessarily suggest that the smaller organisers are less responsible; it could simply indicate that scarce resources must be carefully focused where they are most needed. As the visitors do not seem to be interested in these actions, no effort of communication is made. The topic should be studied further to understand the real drivers behind it.

Most of the actions communicated within the sample were related to the natural environment and can be qualified as greening initiatives. This seems logical; often problems related to waste management and transportation are the most visible during major festivals and events. A clear similarity can be found with the greening practices discussed by Laing and Frost (2010). Allowing support persons for disabled people to enter for free is a borderline responsible action; it could also be described as general humanity. More interesting are the organisers who have broadened their understanding of responsibility to include social stakeholders. Claiming to have a CSR program and supporting an NGO are both halfway down the list with ten organisers naming them on their websites. These actions indicate a clear enlargement of the traditional environmental approach to responsibility, and demonstrate a connection with the TBL model of Elkington (1997). This could further indicate an effort to gain competitive advantage, and the motivations behind these emerging responsible actions should be researched further. Despite the general lack of advertised responsibility, it seems that a few festivals are willing to invest more in the idea.

The two forerunner festivals mentioned earlier both concentrate on music. However, one is a jazz festival while the other attracts fans of rock music; thus it is not possible to make any conclusions based on the genre of music. Furthermore, while the jazz festival is the second largest of the festivals in terms of visitors, the rock festival is mid-sized and again no evident explanation for the two being forerunners stands out. Further study could reveal, for example, whether the persons responsible for managing these festivals are personally oriented towards responsibility.

Bergin-Seers and Mair (2008) pointed out the absence of research into whether potential customers actually find green products interesting. The results of this study seem to suggest that the offering of responsibility by festival organisers in Finland is not interesting to customers, as no relationship between communicated responsible initiatives and visitor numbers could be established. The question raised is thus whether the lack of connection indicates that visitors are not interested in responsibility as part of a festival or an event.

The results from Babiak and Wolfe (2006) suggested that CSR would be beneficial in the NFL, and keeping in mind the stated customer interest in green festivals (Buchinghamshire New University, 2008) it would be dangerous to write off responsibility in the events and festivals industry altogether. The concept is new to both organisers and visitors, and thus it is more likely that supply is not currently meeting demand, as argued by Kuokkanen and Rios-Morales (2009). The question comes down to first verifying whether demand exists, and in case of positive findings, defining its nature. Whether the assumed demand would exist for some other forms of responsibility, or for better communication and measurement of the actions taken, should be studied further.

These results do not invalidate the efforts made by some of the organisers to make their festivals responsible; it merely shows that visitors do not make a real difference between 'responsible' and 'non-responsible' festivals. It must be noted, however, that festivals can be poor substitutes for each other, and responsibility can hardly be a major decision criteria for a potential visitor. Even so, the right combination of responsible actions and communication could attract new first-time visitors, who could later become regular attendees.

7. Conclusion

This chapter had two major objectives. The first was to explore the level of communication of responsible actions by festivals in Finland, and to determine which types of actions are communicated. The results clearly illustrate that during the period of 2000-2010, festivals in Finland were not very active in communication regarding responsibility, though a few forerunners did emerge. This lack of communication could be due to an absence of initiatives, but the reasons could also lie in the deep-rooted fears of green washing allegations when clear indicators are not available. In either case, this area requires further research. Unexplored questions include finding out how many responsible initiatives remain uncommunicated, and why festivals do not advertise responsibility more actively to gain competitive advantage. The lack of communication by smaller festivals should also be studied further.

The second objective of this chapter was to contribute to the research on whether consumers find the supply of responsibility interesting, and to test the hypothesis that visitors do not use it as a decision criterion. The results did not indicate any significant link between visitor numbers and communicated responsibility. This could mean a general lack of interest in the topic, or a dislocation between supply and demand of responsibility; however, the difficulty of one festival substituting for another one must also be taken into account. There is evidence of consumer interest in responsibility and green initiatives in general, and current supply not meeting the demand could well play a role in the observed lack of connection. The nature of demand for responsibility, and whether meeting it would create a competitive advantage, are two key topics for further research. For practitioners these results should offer new insights; studying consumer preferences is standard practise before the launch of a new service, and the same should be true for consumers' preferences towards responsibility.

References

Babiak, K., & Wolfe, R. (2006). More than just a game? corporate social responsibility and super bowl XL. *Sport Marketing Quarterly*, 15, 214-222.

Bansal, P., & Roth, K. (2000). Why companies go green: A model of ecological responsiveness. *Academy of Management Journal*, 43(4), 717-737.

Baros, Z., & Lorant, D. (2007). A possible use of indicators for sustainable development in tourism. *Anatolia,* 18(2), 350-356.

Bergin-Seers, S., & Mair, J. (2008). *Sustainability practices, awards and accreditation programs in the tourism industry: Impacts on consumer purchasing behaviour.* Gold Coast, Australia: CRC for Sustainable Tourism.

Blackstock, K.L., White, V., McCrum, G., Scott, A., & Hunter, C. (2008). Measuring responsibility: An appraisal of a Scottish National Park's sustainable tourism indicators. *Journal of Sustainable Tourism*, 16(3), 276-297.

Buckinghamshire New University. (2008). Summary of Research. Retrieved December 2010, from: http://www.agreenerfestival.com/

Byrd, E.T., Cardenas, D.A., & Greenwood, J.B. (2008). Factors of stakeholder understanding of tourism: The case of Eastern North Carolina. *Tourism and Hospitality Research*, 8(3), 192-204.

Carroll, A.B. (1979). A three-dimensional conceptual model of corporate performance. *Academy of Management Review,* 4(4), 497-505.

—. (1991). The pyramid of corporate social responsibility: Toward the moral management of organizational stakeholders. *Business Horizons*, 34(4), 39-48.

Clavier-Cortés, E., Molina-Azorin, J.F., Pereira-Moliner, J., & Lopez-Gamero, M. D. (2007). Environmental strategies and their impact on hotel performance. *Journal of Sustainable Tourism*, 15(6), 663-679.

Corporate social responsibility for EC&O Venues. (2007). Conference & Exhibition Fact Finder, 22(9), 4.

Dillman, D.A. (2007). *Mail and internet surveys: The tailored design method* (2nd Ed.). Hoboken, NJ: Wiley.

Dolnicar, S. (2006). Nature-conserving tourists: The need for a broader perspective. *Anatolia*, 17(2), 197-210.

Eccles, R. (2009). Green consulting - standard operating procedure. *Corporate Meetings and Incentives*, 28(9), 20-21.

Elkington, J.B. (1997). *Cannibals with forks: The triple bottom line of 21st century business.* Oxford: Capstone Publishing.

Finland Festivals. (2010). Tilastotietoa. Retrieved December 2010, from: http://www.festivals.fi/tilastotietoa/?/fin/

Finnish Tourist Board. (2010). Matkailukohteiden kävijämäärätutkimukset. Retrieved September 2010, from: http://www.mek.fi/w5/mekfi/index.nsf/(pages)/Kävijämäärätutkimukset

Fletcher, M. (2007). Survey says CSR will surge in importance. *Event, 5.*

François-Lecompte, A., & Prim-Allaz, I. (2010). Les Français et le tourisme durable proposition d'une typologie. *Revue Management et Avenir,* 29, 308-326.

Freeman, R.E., & Reed, D.L. (1983). Stockholders and stakeholders: A new perspective on corporate governance. *California Management Review*, 25(3), 88-106.

Getz, D. (2009). Policy for sustainable and responsible festivals and events: Institutionalization of a new paradigm. *Journal of Policy Research in Tourism, Leisure and Events*, 1(1), 61-78.

GSTC. (2009). About the Criteria. Retrieved January 2011, from: http://www.sustainabletourismcriteria.org

Higgins-Desbiolles, F. (2010). The elusiveness of sustainability in tourism: The culture–ideology of consumerism and its implications. *Tourism & Hospitality Research*, 10(2), 116-129.

Karlsen, S., & Stenbacka Nordström, C. (2009). Festivals in the Barents Region: Exploring festival-stakeholder cooperation. *Scandinavian Journal of Hospitality and Tourism*, 9(2-3), 130-145.

Kasim, A. (2006). The need for business environmental and social responsibility in the tourism industry. *International Journal of Hospitality and Tourism Administration*, 7(1), 1-22.

Kuokkanen, H., & Rios-Morales, R. (2009). Conceptual Design of a Financial Approach to Developing Competitive Advantage through Responsible Tourism (pp. 921-93). Cyprus: EuroMed Press.

Laing, J., & Frost, W. (2010). How green was my festival: Exploring challenges and opportunities associated with staging green events. *International Journal of Hospitality Management*, 29, 261-267.

Lansing, P., & De Vries, P. (2007). Sustainable tourism: Ethical alternative or marketing ploy. *Journal of Business Ethics*, 72(1), 77-85.

Liu, Z. (2003). Sustainable tourism development: A critique. *Journal of Sustainable Tourism,* 11(6), 459-475.

Mair, J., & Jago, L. (2010). The development of a conceptual model of greening in the business events tourism sector. *Journal of Sustainable Tourism*, 18(1), 77-94.

McCool, S.F., Moisey, R., & Nickelson, N.P. (2001). What should tourism
sustain? The disconnect with industry perceptions of useful indicators.
Journal of Travel Research, 40(2), 124-131.

McKercher, B. (1993). Some fundamental truths about tourism:
Understanding tourism's social and environmental impacts. *Journal of
Sustainable Tourism,* 1(1), 6-16.

Mikkonen, J., & Ristolainen, K. (2007). *Selvitys Ilosaarirockin
alueellisesta vaikuttavuudesta.* Joensuu: University of Joensuu.

Miller, G., Rathouse, K., Scarles, C., Holmes, K., & Tribe, J. (2010).
Public understanding of sustainable tourism. *Annals of Tourism
Research*, 37(3), 627-645.

Porter, M.E., & Kramer, M.R. (2006). Strategy and society: The link
between competitive advantage and corporate social responsibility.
Harvard Business Review, 84, 78-92.

Sharpley, R. (2000). Tourism and sustainable development: Exploring the
theoretical divide. *Journal of Sustainable Tourism*, 8(1), 1-15.

UNWTO (2010). Mission statement. Retrieved from:
http://www.unwto.org/sdt/index.php

CHAPTER SEVEN

HEY LOOK, I'M A GREEN CONSUMER: ONLINE SOCIAL VISIBILITY AND THE WILLINGNESS TO PAY FOR CARBON OFFSETTING SCHEMES

FRANÇOIS J. DESSART, LUISA ANDREU, ENRIQUE BIGNÉ AND ALAIN DECROP

Abstract

In this chapter, we investigate whether giving potential consumers the possibility of social visibility through online social networks might make green tourist services more attractive. Focusing on carbon offsetting schemes in aviation, we additionally test the predicting power of three determinants of general pro-environmental consumption—environmental knowledge, perceived efficacy and environmental concern—for the willingness to pay for this specific green product. We use a hypothetical scenario to build an experimental approach, and a subsequent survey to measure the independent variables. In line with costly signalling theory and impression management theory, results suggest that online social visibility raises the willingness to pay for green products. **Keywords:** green consumption, carbon offset, costly signalling, visibility.

1. Introduction

Are all tourists, and consumers in general, who choose green alternatives mainly driven by their concern for the environment? For instance, do tourists who choose eco-certified hotels do so, above all, because they care about the state of the earth? Two recent examples seem to indicate that this is not always the case. First, the typical German user of solar thermal systems—a highly visible green product—is actually *not* very environmentally orientated, and is more likely than those who have not installed such a system in their home to consider that "environmental problems are exaggerated by environmentalists" (Welsch & Kühling, 2009). Second, marketers now offer green alternatives to regular products, ostentatiously labelled as such—e.g. organic t-shirts displaying wide "green" printings such as Vivienne Westwood's "Tree-shirt" in the frame of UN Environment Programme's GreenUp initiative (UNEP, 2011)—leading us to think that these may be used as an identity signal. In short, it seems that some consumers choose green products like these in order to showcase their eco-friendliness rather than to lower their environmental impact.

The aim of this chapter is to explain the factors that influence the consumption of a pro-environmental tourist service, namely carbon offsetting schemes. Specifically, we analyze the role of visibility of consumption as well as other traditional determinants of pro-environmental consumption. It is posited that, if tourists wish to showcase their eco-friendly buying behaviour, they need their consumption to be somehow visible to their peers. Visibility of consumption can take two forms (Reingen, Foster, Johnson Brown, & Seidman, 1984): either it is visible because of its sheer physicality, or because of verbal communication. The former type of consumption visibility has been proven to favour the attractiveness of products' green alternatives (Griskevicius, Tybur, & Van den Bergh, 2010). This chapter proposes to investigate the role of the latter type of consumption visibility in the attractiveness of pro-environmental services in tourism within the framework of online social networks. More precisely, we address the following research question: does visibility of consumption through online peer-to-peer communication lead to a higher willingness to pay for carbon offsetting schemes?

As a secondary objective, this research tests the stability of three determinants of general pro-environmental consumption, namely environmental knowledge, environmental concern and perceived efficacy. The importance of including these determinants is to use a holistic model and to contribute to the debate in the literature regarding the level of specificity that should be used for such factors.

The present research focuses on individual voluntary carbon offsetting schemes (COS) in air transport as the pro-environmental product under study. This service, proposed by a number of airlines, such as Easyjet, Continental Airlines, Scandinavian Airlines, British Airways, and Qantas, offers "to 'neutralize' emissions caused by consumption in one sector" (here, aviation) "through compensation in another sector, for instance by investing in renewable energy, energy efficiency, or forestry projects"

(Gössling, Haglund, Källgren, & Hultman, 2009, p. 3). Although still small, the market for voluntary carbon offsetting schemes has grown rapidly between 1997 and 2006, with an increase in the number of providers from 4 to 40 organizations (Gössling et al., 2007).

COS are considered as one of the options available to reduce the environmental impact of tourism and travel. Although they constitute a curative rather than a preventive way of lowering this impact, we consider that they can be useful when no alternative to air travel is available. According to the World Tourism Organization (2009), global tourism and travel is a vector of climate change, accounting for approximately 5% of global carbon dioxide emissions, which could increase by 130% by 2035 under a business as usual scenario. The present research aims at understanding how offsetting schemes can be made more attractive.

Motivations for this research are threefold. First, the growth of the environmentally orientated segments of tourism (Dodds & Joppe, 2005) suggests the necessity for uncovering what's driving it. Second, carbon offsetting schemes as such are little explored (Gössling *et al.*, 2007), making them an interesting ground for study (MacKerron, Egerton, Gaskell, Parpia, & Mourato, 2009). Third, there is a strong call for research contributing to the sustainability of tourism originating from practitioners (IATA, 2010), governments (Spanish Presidency of the European Union, 2010), and from the academic world (Bigné, Andreu, Sánchez, & Alvarado, 2008; Fayos-Solá & Jafari, 2010).

2. Literature Review

2.1. Visibility of consumption

The consumption of pro-environmental products and services, such as sustainable tourism and transport services, has recently been explained, in some cases, in the light of costly signalling theory.

Costly signalling theory (Zahavi, 1975) applied to human psychology suggests that individuals often engage in behaviour that is very costly as a way of signalling honest information about themselves (MacAndrew, 2002). Applied to altruism, it states that public philanthropy and, more generally, altruistic acts are a communicative signal that allows for higher social status because they demonstrate both one's willingness and one's ability to incur the costs of self-sacrifice for public welfare (Griskevicius, Tybur, Sundie, Cialdini, Miller, & Kenrick, 2007). According to Smith and Bird (2000), four conditions are necessary for an act to be a costly signal. First, the act must be costly to the signaller, in the sense that it must consume some of his or her resources, be they time, energy, money or risk. Second, the act must be easily visible, observable by others. Third, it must increase the probability that the signaller will gain some material or social advantage. Fourth, the act must be an indicator of some potentially important traits, such as the access to resources, a prosocial orientation, or the signaller's courage, health or intelligence.

Griskevicius *et al.* (2010) consider that pro-environmental consumption (PEC), when blatant to others, can be considered as a public act of philanthropy and act thus as a costly signal, since green products usually cost more, offer less quality and benefit the environment for everyone, as compared with regular products. Using an experimental approach, they find that activating status motives increases the desire for green products when shopping in public (but not private), and when products cost more (but not less) than non-green products. Of special importance to the present research is the role of shopping visibility: when asked to choose between a more luxurious non-green option and a less luxurious green option of three different products (a backpack, batteries and a table lamp), respondents were more likely to choose the green option when they were asked to imagine they were shopping at a store than when imagining that they were shopping online. These findings are in line with costly signalling theory, according to which status motives lead people to forgo luxury, and desire prosocial environmental products, only when it is clear that such choices can be observed, and enhance one's reputation.

Visibility of pro-environmental consumption (PEC) seems thus to be fundamental. In an influential paper, Bourne (1957, p. 218) proposed a framework of public vs. private consumption. In his view, publicly consumed products are those that are "seen by others, […] which other people are aware you possess and use", whereas privately consumed products are "not seen by others, […] which one uses at home or in private at some location". Any product can be placed on a continuum of the degree to which consumption is witnessed by others. Later, Reingen et al. (1984) proved that not only the location of consumption was significant for determining its public or private character, but also social relationships, as the latter may channel opportunities for *observation* of consumption through *verbal communication*. In this sense, social relations may make consumption behaviour visible even for "private" products as defined by Bourne (1957).

Visibility of consumption can thus take two forms: either physical visibility or visibility through verbal communication (Reingen et al., 1984). In the above-mentioned research by Griskevicius *et al.* (2010), the effect of physical visibility of the act of purchase on PEC is assessed.

Although hypothesized by some authors (Welsch & Kühling, 2009), the effect of the second form visibility on PEC has not yet been investigated: the present research aims at shedding some light on this issue. Empirical evidence proves that, from a social dilemma and social identity perspective, when a person had the opportunity to discuss (i.e. through verbal communication) his or her choice of prosocial behaviour with his or her in-group (i.e. the group with which he or she identifies), he or she was more likely to choose the prosocial option of self-sacrifice (Dawes, 1980). We argue that the same effect can be expected for PEC, since it can be considered as an altruistic act.

Following along the same lines, within the theory of impression management (Schlenker, 1980), i.e. the "process of controlling how one is perceived by other people" (Leary, 1996, p.2), it was suggested that the publicity (i.e. visibility) of one's behaviour determines the degree to which people will be motivated to regulate their self-presentation (Schlenker & Weigold, 1992). Prosocial behaviour is considered by Leary (1996) as one of the tactics used by individuals for impression management, since this type of behaviour would actually be motivated by self-interest, because it helps them to make a good impression and to get social approval. We consider the consumption of pro-environmental goods as a form of prosocial behaviour that may help consumers for their impression management.

Specifically, we consider online peer-to-peer communication through social networking websites as the channel to make the consumption of green services visible to significant others. Impression management is a major motive for actively participating in social networking sites, since these provide more control over self-presentation behaviour than face-to-face communication (Krämer & Winter, 2008). Hence, we posit that:

H1: A higher level of perceived consumption visibility through online peer-to-peer communication yields a higher willingness to pay for voluntary carbon offsetting schemes in aviation

2.2. Traditional determinants of pro-environmental consumption

Determinants of pro-environmental consumption (PEC) typically include socio-demographic, psychographic, cognitive and affective factors.

Regarding the *socio-demographic and psychographic* factors of PEC, it was found, for instance, that female consumers were more likely to choose green alternatives than males (see for example Laroche, Bergeron,

& Barbaro-Forleo, 2001 and Diamantopoulos, Schlegelmilch, Sinkovics, & Bohlen, 2003). Specifically regarding carbon offsetting schemes (COS), the only study that studied the determinants of their purchase concluded that neither individual income nor the presence or absence of children discriminated between buyers and non-buyers of such green services (MacKerron *et al.*, 2009).

Extant research on the *cognitive and affective* factors influencing PEC is very rich. Overall, there is a consensus that attitudinal variables are better predictors of PEC than demographic factors (Cleveland, Kalamas, & Laroche, 2005). Environmental concern, environmental knowledge, and perceived efficacy are the most popular factors investigated in the literature. *Environmental concern* is the degree of emotionality related to pollution-environment issues (Maloney, Ward, & Braught, 1975): most studies find a positive relationship between this construct and PEC (e.g. Fraj Andrés & Martínez Salinas, 2007), usually mediated by an intentional construct (Chan, 2001; Kaiser, Wolfing, & Fuhrer, 1999), in line with the theory of reasoned action (Ajzen & Fishbein, 1980).

Nevertheless, there are some counter-arguments in the literature regarding the role of environmental concern (Gupta & Ogden, 2009). Unclear conclusions are also found regarding the possible correlation between *environmental knowledge* (the cognitive element referring to the extent to which consumers are aware of the causes, the consequences and the severity of environmental damage (Maloney *et al.*, 1975)), and PEC. While some studies find a (low) positive relationship between environmental knowledge and PEC (Barreiro *et al.*, 2002; Laroche, Toffoli, Kim, & Muller, 1996), others suggest that environmental knowledge is rather a moderating variable of the relationship between environmental concern and PEC (Martin & Simintiras, 1995). Finally, *perceived efficacy*—i.e. the "extent to which one believes that his or her own contributions help to achieve the collective goals" (van Lange, Liebrand, Messick, & Wilke, 1992, p. 18)—was found to be positively related to PEC (Gupta & Ogden, 2009).

It is noteworthy that there is a major debate in the literature regarding the different levels of specificity in the measurement of PEC (Gupta & Ogden, 2009): should researchers consider *general* pro-environmental behaviour or focus instead on *specific* pro-environmental consumptions when relating them to explanatory factors? Most researchers (Fraj Andrés & Martínez Salinas, 2007; Kaiser *et al.*, 1999) consider that it is better to talk about broad ecological behaviour rather than specific environmental actions or behaviour. The same question can be asked regarding the level of specificity of the predictors. Some authors consider that consumers' own general beliefs and values will determine their specific attitude of global rejection of any action that would hurt the environment, so that their pro-environmental behaviour would be generally coherent (Dietz, Stern, & Guagnano, 1998; Mainieri, Barnett, Valdero, Unipan, & Oskamp, 1997; Vinson, Scott & Lamont, 1977). Through this research, we wish to contribute to this debate by testing as a secondary objective the stability of three *general* affective and cognitive determinants of PEC extensively studied in the above-mentioned literature (environmental knowledge, perceived efficacy and environmental concern), for a *specific* form of PEC, namely the consumption of voluntary COS in aviation. Hence, we propose that:

H2: The level of environmental knowledge positively influences consumers' willingness to pay for voluntary carbon offsetting schemes in aviation.

H3: The level of perceived efficacy positively influences consumers' willingness to pay for voluntary carbon offsetting schemes in aviation.

H4: The level of environmental concern positively influences consumers' willingness to pay for voluntary carbon offsetting schemes in aviation.

3. Methodology

In line with Griskevicius *et al.*'s research (2010), we chose to build on an experimental task approach to measure the willingness to adopt the pro-environmental service under study. This is justified by the desire to counter the disadvantage of stated behavioural commitment, often dissonant with actual behaviour in PEC (Gupta & Ogden, 2009), and to provide realistic and actionable management implications. For the same (latter) reason, this approach was therefore made as realistic as possible, using prices and logos actually all retrieved from the website of a major airline.

3.1. Population and recruitment

The study's population consisted of students in different universities in Valencia, Spain, who were users of the online social network Facebook. In order to avoid self-selection bias, respondents were randomly selected from the university campuses, without informing them of the actual purpose of the study.

3.2. Research design

An online realistic purchase situation and a subsequent survey—both self-completed—were developed. In order to decrease potential suspicion, the cover story used consisted in the booking simulation of a round-trip intra-European medium-haul flight (Valencia-London Gatwick) on the internet, as part of a 3 to 5-day leisure trip. Specifically, respondents were told on the screen:

> *Imagine you have to book a flight ticket in order to visit a friend temporarily living in Gatwick (England). You would like to be there for his/her birthday, which is on October 16. From Valencia, there's only one airline flying to Gatwick, which is [airline name]. On the next screen you will find a [airline name] booking simulator on which we ask you to choose a flight.*

The Internet was chosen as it is a realistic and increasingly popular channel for booking flights (United Nations World Tourism Organization, 2010), and as it presents low social desirability bias (Kreuter, Presser, & Tourangeau, 2009). The choice of an intra-European medium-haul flight (more than 1,500 km) was justified by the need to consider routes where no other modes of transport were economically or time competitive, so that no plausible alternative to a plane was available, given the length of the stay. We also focused on flights within Europe so that respondents were more likely to have some previous experience. A leisure holiday was preferred as it is a "major market for individual voluntary carbon offsets consumption, and it is easily understood as a discrete offsetting scenario" (MacKerron *et al.,* 2009, p. 1373).

Just as it is the case on the real booking system of the major airline's website used, several options were available to the tourist, including luggage, travel insurance and COS (in this case, a UN certified compensation project). We used actual prices as retrieved from the same major airline's website (€3.41 in the case of COS). Respondents had to indicate the level of probability that they would purchase each option on a seven-point Likert scale with 1 = would definitely not buy, and 7 = would definitely buy. The only option we were interested in was the one related to COS; however in order not to raise respondents' attention, we chose to let them answer the question for all three options. Willingness to pay measured as a likelihood was preferred to more realistic binary purchase/no purchase options, because the willingness to pay for COS was expected to be rather low within the target population, and would thus have most likely resulted in an insufficient number of COS purchasers for our model. This is also in line with Gupta and Ogden's (2009) methodology and Kaiser *et al.*'s (1999) recommendation to use probability of behaviour in order to take into account the influences beyond people's actual control.

Social visibility of purchase through online peer-to-peer communication was manipulated as follows: for 75% of the respondents, next to the COS option, a Facebook "share" button was placed, allowing the participant, if he or she wished to do so, to supposedly directly publish the following sentence on his Facebook wall (along with a link to the airline's carbon compensation information page and the picture of wind turbines):

> *I've just offset the environmental impact of my [airline name] flight. I have reduced the carbon emissions impact of my [airline name] flight through UN certified compensation projects.*

The remaining 25% did not have a Facebook publishing option. Facebook is the most popular online social networking platform, with 500 million users worldwide (Expansión, 2010) and more than 8 million users in Spain, half of them viewing the website on a daily basis (Moreno, 2010).

3.3. Variables

After the flight booking simulator, respondents were first asked how frequently they used Facebook. Non-users were excluded from the rest of the survey and, hence, from the sample used to test the hypothesis. They were then asked to answer a short survey containing questions in order to operationalize the possible explanatory factors of PEC in the specific case of COS (see Table 1). The order in which the items presented within each block were randomized. Respondents were further required to give some classification details, including age category, gender, education currently being completed (type and level), the university where they were enrolled and their flying frequency.

Table 1 – Variables

Construct	Items	Author(s)	Reliability (α)
Willingness to pay for COS	How likely is it that you would choose this option?	Custom	n/a
Environmental knowledge (EK)	Score on 5 to a multiple-choice questionnaire: (variable = number of correct answers) - What is ecology? - What is the company "Ecoembalajes"s business ? - What is normally the cause of the earth's pollution? - What is the main cause of pollution in cities? - What is "Ecovidrio"?	Fraj and Martínez (2007) (removing two irrelevant questions)	n/a
Perceived efficacy (PE)	There is not much that any one individual can do about energy conservation (REVERSE CODED) The energy conservation efforts of one person are useless as long as other people refuse to conserve (REVERSE CODED)	Ellen *et al.* (1991)	.70
Environmental concern (EC)	I am afraid that the food I eat may be contaminated with pesticides. It makes me furious to think that the government does nothing to control the environment pollution. I get irritated when I think of the damage caused by pollution to plants and animal life. I get depressed on days with pollution (fog, smoke, stink). When I think of how industries pollute, I get very angry	Maloney *et al.*'s (1975) "affect" component of their Ecology Scale, as revised and adapted by Fraj and Martínez (2007)	.74
Visibility through peer-to-peer communication (VI)	Whether I've offset the carbon emissions of this flight or not will be something… V1: my friends will know about V2: public for my friends V3: noticed by my friends	Fisher & Ackerman (1998), Griskevicius *et al.* (2007)	.81

4. Results

After a pretest with 10 participants, a total of 132 students answered the survey entirely. We present a summary of the descriptive variables used in the survey. The sample was quite balanced regarding gender, age and university where enrolled. Almost 7 out of 10 respondents (67.4%) had taken at least one return flight during the 12 months prior to the survey, and a slightly lower proportion (63.7%) said that they logged on to Facebook "every day" or "almost every day". For any of these variables, no significant difference appeared between the group of respondents who had the opportunity to publish their action on Facebook and the ones who did not.

4.1. Manipulation of visibility

Perceived visibility was manipulated successfully (measured as the average of the 3 variables of this construct), as it was significantly higher among the group who could publish their action on Facebook than among the group who could not $(3.15 - 2.69, p = .1)$.

4.2. Hypotheses testing

The dependent variable, i.e. the willingness to pay for carbon offsetting schemes, was measured as mentioned before, using an experimental approach. The four exogenous variables are environmental knowledge, perceived efficacy, environmental concern and perceived visibility. Environmental knowledge was measured as the score on 5 to a multiple-choice questionnaire, whereas we used the average score of the different indicators for each of the three other independent variables. The internal consistencies of the constructs were assessed using Cronbach's alpha. Cronbach's alphas of .8 or above are considered as desirable (Hair, Anderson, Tatham, & Black, 1998). As shown in Table 1, the three constructs have Cronbach's alphas ranging from .70 to .81, which we consider as satisfactory.

In order to check the hypotheses, we used multiple regression analysis (SPSS software). Using Mahalonobis and Cook's distances, we detected, prior to the formal analysis, the presence of 4 outliers which were eliminated for further analysis.

Before testing the hypotheses, we first checked the three main model assumptions of regression analysis: (1) the homoscedasticity (constant variance) of the errors (residuals); (2) the normality of the error distribution;

and (3) the absence of multicollinearity between the independent variables. Homoscedasticity of the residuals was checked by observing the *residuals versus predicted value* scatterplot, which revealed no serious violation of this assumption, as residuals plot was approximately the same width for all values of the predicted dependent variable. The normality of the residuals was checked by the observation of the normal probability plot of the residuals, which fall very close to the diagonal line. Further, formal support for this assumption was provided by the Kolmogorov-Smirnov normal distribution test on the standardized residuals (K-S Z = 1.124; p = .160). Eventually, the absence of multicollinearity between the independent variables was confirmed by the absence of significant Pearson correlations (see Table 2) and tolerance statistics all above .90 (see Table 4)

Table 2 - Correlations between the Independent Variables

Variable	EK	PE	EC	VI
Environmental knowledge (EK)	1.000			
Perceived efficacy (PE)	.029	1.000		
Environmental concern (EC)	-.050	.021	1.000	
Perceived visibility (VI)	-.106	-.004	.143	1.000

* $p < .05$

Basic descriptive statistics for all the variables in the model are provided in Table 3. Overall, the willingness to pay for carbon offsetting schemes is average (M = 3.3281 – scale: 1-7).

Table 3 - Basic Descriptive Statistics

Variable	Range of value	M	SD
Willingness to pay for Carbon Offsetting Schemes (WP)	1-7	3.3281	2.0083
Environmental knowledge (EK)	0-5	1.8516	.09646
Perceived efficacy (PE)	1-7	4.0547	1.8371
Environmental concern (EC)	1-7	4.4391	1.2115
Perceived visibility (VI)	1-7	2.8649	1.5358

The regression model of the four independent variables on the willingness to pay for COS was significant and of average quality (R = .318, R^2 = .101) with the vector of the regression coefficients significantly different from the null vector ($F(4, 123) = 3.471$, $p = .01$).

Table 4 - Regression Coefficients

	Coefficients			Collinearity stats.	
	Stand. Coef. β	t	Sig	Tolerance	VIF
Environmental knowledge (EK)	.020	.237	.81	.987	1.013
Perceived efficacy (PE)	.129	1.503	.13	.999	1.001
Environmental concern (EC)	.165	1.911	.05	.978	1.023
Perceived visibility (VI)	.218	2.508	.01	.970	1.031

The standardized regression coefficients shown in Table 4 were significant for environmental concern and perceived visibility, but insignificant for environmental knowledge and perceived efficacy. Thus we can confirm H1 and H3, and must reject H2 and H4.

5. Discussion

Results from the study suggest that the level of perceived visibility through online peer-to-peer communication is significant in predicting the level of willingness to pay for carbon offsetting schemes. Specifically, when consumers were given the opportunity to let their friends find out that they had purchased carbon offsetting schemes (COS), they were more likely to be willing to buy them than when they thought this would remain unnoticed by their friends. The level of visibility was successfully manipulated by giving the possibility to part of the sample to publish their green action on their Facebook profile, whereas the other part was not given this possibility.

This result is in line with various studies and concepts. First, it is mainly connected to costly signalling theory (Griskevicius *et al.,* 2007), according to which altruistic acts (including pro-environmental consumption - PEC) are used to demonstrate one's willingness and one's ability to support the (time, resource, or physical) costs of self-sacrifice for public welfare, which enables one to acquire higher social status. For an altruistic act to constitute a costly signal, it must be observable by others (Smith & Bird, 2000): by "sharing" their purchase action on their online social network, consumers were given the opportunity to use this consumption as a costly signal. Second, impression management theory suggests that the visibility of one's behaviour determines the degree to which people will be motivated to regulate their self-presentation (Schlenker & Weigold, 1992).

Furthermore, it has been proved within the framework of social dilemma theory that allowing people to discuss with each other makes them more likely to sacrifice their self-interest for the general good (Dawes, 1980). In our case, communication through online social networks provides a tool for such discussion, leading to higher visibility of the purchase of COS, an invisible, immaterial purchase. Eventually, the effect of perceived visibility can also be explained by its documented effects on consumption patterns: a higher level of perceived consumption visibility causes a higher expectation of normative outcomes, i.e. social rewards or punishment from referent others (Fischer & Price, 1992). Talking about their consumption of a sustainable tourist service on their social network profile leads to higher visibility and can thus provide some sort of recognition in the sense of Fisher and Ackerman (1998). Thus, this first finding suggests that the search for social rewards, an egotistic motivation, can drive pro-environmental consumption, therefore contributing to the debate on the relative role of altruistic vs. egotistic motivations of prosocial behaviour (Batson & Powell, 2003).

As a secondary finding, the results of this study suggest that traditional affective and cognitive determinants of *general* pro-environmental consumption (PEC) are usually not significant in predicting the willingness to pay for a specific green product, here COS. Specifically, neither *general* environmental knowledge nor *general* perceived efficacy (although almost significant for this latter factor) significantly explained the willingness to pay for this sustainable tourist service. However, general environmental concern did significantly predict the willingness to offset the carbon emissions of a flight. These three factors have usually been used to predict general or composite PEC, often mediated by an intentional factor in line with the theory of reasoned action (Ajzen & Fishbein, 1980). The non-significance of two of these factors echoes the well-known inconsistency between attitudes and behaviour in PEC.

We argue that specific knowledge of aviation-related environmental problems (e.g. knowledge about the actual emissions of a flight as compared to the emissions of a train, or to the annual emissions of heating a normal household) and specific perceived efficacy of COS (e.g. perceived efficacy of the offsetting schemes proposed—planting trees or building wind turbines, for instance), or maybe a combination of such specific measures with general considerations, might be more appropriate in determining the level of willingness to pay. Possible explanations for the non-significance of perceived efficacy and environmental knowledge stem from the assumptions that "pro-environmental behaviours, like most behaviours, are to a large extent, situation-specific" (Cleveland *et al.,*

2005, p. 200) and that "those consumers who recycle plastic may not be the consumers who would pay more for low-phosphate detergent" (Laroche et al., 2001, p. 515). The significant relationship between *general* environmental concern and the propensity to purchase carbon offsetting schemes (COS) challenges the current vision in the literature that environmental concern is a weak predictor of pro-environmental behaviour because of the primacy of economic considerations and the multifaceted nature of environmental concern (Cleveland *et al.,* 2005).

6. Conclusion

The main goal of this chapter was to explain how the consumption of voluntary carbon offsetting schemes (COS) was determined by the visibility of such consumption through online peer-to-peer communication. Specifically, it aimed at proving that higher levels of perceived visibility of consumption thanks to verbal communication on online social networks about the consumption of COS could enhance the attractiveness of such services. Furthermore, this chapter sought to contribute to the debate regarding the level of specificity of the measurement of pro-environmental consumption (PEC), by assessing the stability of three of its widely investigated determinants at a global level (environmental concern, environmental knowledge and perceived efficacy) to the level of the consumption of a specific sustainable tourist service. We focused on carbon offsetting schemes (COS) in aviation as the pro-environmental services under study. The attractiveness of such services was measured using an experimental approach, rather than a declarative approach as is usually the case in the literature on PEC. Multiple regression analysis was used to test the hypotheses.

This chapter contributes to the understanding of the determinants of PEC, and specifically of the consumption of carbon offsetting schemes, in two ways.

First, findings suggest that verbal communication through online social networks contributes to making the consumption of carbon offsetting schemes (COS) in air transport—an invisible, immaterial action—visible by others, and consequently makes it a costly signal, thanks to which consumers may hope to gain social status. Such online social visibility also makes consumers more likely to manage the impression they make on others.

Second, results lead us to argue that *general* affective and cognitive determinants of PEC are usually not useful in explaining why consumers choose a *specific* green product or service, such as COS. A notable exception to this pattern is the level of *general* environmental concern, which did predict the willingness to pay for COS, i.e. a *specific* green product. Results thus suggest the need to measure environmental attitudes at the same level of specificity as the pro-environmental behaviour under study.

The effect of perceived visibility on the consumption of sustainable tourist services has some important managerial implications. Although somewhat disturbing for environmentalists, this study confirms the importance of social rewards (i.e. egotistic motives) in pro-environmental consumption. Specifically, this study implies that promoting visibility through online communication among consumers raises the attractiveness of sustainable tourist services. This might be especially useful for goods and services that are not very visible, invisible or even totally immaterial, such as eco-labelled accommodation, carbon offsetting schemes, or ecotourism, etc. We focused on conversation through online social networks, but other channels may be more adapted to certain types of consumers. Fostering conversation between consumers can also be realized by targeting consumers when they are in group rather than alone, for example at conventions or group travel.

This study contains a number of limitations which open avenue for further research. First, hypothetical bias (Murphy, Allen, Stevens, & Weatherhead, 2005) might be a concern, as the realistic choice task did not involve real costs. Second, we manipulated the *possibility* of consumers making their purchase visible instead of its actual visibility. However it is arguable that merely making it possible for consumers to publish their actions on their online social network primes *per se* the perception of a higher visibility. Finally, a major concern of the present research is external validity. The population of this study was made out of university students (who are in their virtual entirety below 30 years old) who were users of Facebook. Considering that younger people have higher identity and status concerns than average (Helson & Soto, 2005), the effects may be weaker among older consumers. Additionally, this study focused on a specific pro-environmental service, i.e. carbon offsetting schemes. Other green products, or more broadly other forms of prosocial consumption, should be investigated in order to generalize our results.

Focusing now on possible future research, the actual social recognition linked to PEC may be interesting grounds for investigation. Does higher visibility through personal communication about PEC actually allow social recognition, and thus higher social status, or does it conversely lead to the image of an boastful sender? Additionally, it would be interesting to compare the discriminating power of the two types of visibility. This study only took into account visibility through personal communication, not physical visibility. Some marketers are now considering putting on the market COS sold along with t-shirts making such consumption physically visible to others, thanks to the display of carbon offsetting slogans (Earth Patrol, 2011). Research that would determine which type of visibility is therefore most effective in enhancing the attractiveness of pro-environmental products would be valuable.

Acknowledgement

The authors would like to thank Joaquín Aldas (Universitat de València, Spain) for his thoughtful comments and suggestions.

References

Ajzen, I., & Fishbein, M. (1980). *Understanding Attitudes and Predicting Social Behavior.* Englewood Cliffs, NJ: Prentice Hall.

Barreiro, J.M., Lopez, M.A., Losada, F., & Ruzo, E. (2002). Análisis de las dimensiones cognoscitiva y afectiva del comportamiento ecológico del consumidor. *Revista Galega de Economía , 11*(2), 1-21.

Batson, C.D., & Powell, A.A. (2003). Altruism and Prosocial Behavior. In I. B. Weiner, *Handbook of Psychology* (pp. 463-484). Hoboken, NJ: John Wiley.

Bigné, J.E., Andreu, L., Sánchez, I., & Alvarado, A. (2008). Investigación internacional en marketing turístico: análisis de contenido sobre temas y metodologías. *PASOS. Revista de Turismo y Patrimonio Cultural, 6* (3), 391-398.

Bourne, F.S. (1957). Group Influence in Marketing and Public Relations. In R. Likert, & S.P. Hayes (Eds.), *Some Applications of Behavioral Research.* Basil, Switzerland: UNESCO.

Chan, R.Y. (2001). Determinants of Chinese consumers' green purchase behavior. *Psychology and Marketing, 18*(4), 389-413.

Cleveland, M., Kalamas, M., & Laroche, M. (2005). Shades of green: linking environmental locus of control and pro-environmental behaviors. *Journal of Consumer Marketing, 22*(4), 198-212.

Dawes, R.M. (1980). Social dilemnas. *Annual Review of Psychology , 31*, 169-193.

Diamantopoulos, A., Schlegelmilch, B.B., Sinkovics, R.R., & Bohlen, G.M. (2003). Can socio-demographics still play a role in profiling green consumers? A review of the evidence and an empirical investigation. *Journal of Business Research, 56*, 465-480.

Dietz, T., Stern, P.C., & Guagnano, G.A. (1998). Social structural and
    social psychological bases of environmental concern. *Environment and
    Behavior, 30*(4), 450-471
Dodds, R., & Joppe, M. (2005). *CSR in the Tourism Industry? The Status
    of and Potential for Certification, Codes, of Conduct and Guidelines.*
    Working Paper, World Bank, CSR Practice Foreign Investment
    Advisory Service - Investment Climate Department, Washington.
Earth Patrol. (2011). *Offset your carbon footprint for a year.* Retrieved
    May 10, 2011, from http://www.earthpatrol.co.za/carbon-solutions/
    offsetting-your-footprint.html
Ellen, P.S., Weiner, J.L., & Cobb-Walgren, C. (1991). The role of
    perceived consumer effectiveness in motivating environmentally
    conscious behaviors. *Journal of Public Policy and Marketing, 10*(2),
    102-117.
Expansión. (2010, July 22). *Facebook ya tiene 500 millones de usuarios.*
    Retrieved July 29, 2010, from Expansion.com:
    http://www.expansion.com/2010/07/22/empresas/digitech/1279788625
    .html
Fayos-Solá, E., & Jafari, J. (2010). *Cambio climático y turismo: realidad y
    ficción.* Valencia: Universitat de València.
Fischer, R.J., & Ackerman, D. (1998). The effects of recognition and
    group need on volunteerism: A social norm perspective. *Journal of
    Consumer Research, 1998*(December), 262-275.
Fischer, R., & Price, L.L. (1992). An investigation into the social context
    of early adoption behavior. *Journal of Consumer Research,
    19*(December), 477-486.
Fraj Andrés, E., & Martínez Salinas, E. (2007). Impact of environmental
    knowledge on ecological consumer behaviour: An empirical analysis.
    Journal of International Consumer Marketing, 19 (3), 73-102.
Gössling, S., Broderick, J., Upham, P., Ceron, J.-P., Dubois, G., Peeters,
    P., & Strasdas, W. (2007). Voluntary carbon offsetting schemes for
    aviation: Efficiency, credibility and sustainable tourism. *Journal of
    Sustainable Tourism, 15*(3), 223-248.
Gössling, S., Haglund, L., Källgren, H., & Hultman, J. (2009). Swedish air
    travellers and voluntary carbon offsets: Towards the co-creation of
    environmental value? *Current Issues in Tourism, 12*(1), 1-19.
Griskevicius, V., Tybur, J.M., & Van den Bergh, B. (2010). Going green
    to be seen: Status, reputation, and conspicuous conservation. *Journal
    of Personality and Social Psychology, 98*(3), 392-404.
Griskevicius, V., Tybur, J.M., Sundie, J.M., Cialdini, R.B., Miller, G.F., &
    Kenrick, D.T. (2007). Blatant benevolence and conspicuous consumption:

When romantic motives elicit strategic costly signals. *Journal of Personality and Social Psychology, 93*(1), 85-102.

Gupta, S., & Ogden, D.T. (2009). To buy or not to buy? A social dilemna perspective on green buying. *Journal of Consumer Marketing*, 376-391.

Hair, J.F., Anderson, R.E., Tatham, R.L., & Black, W.C. (1998). *Multivariate data analysis with readings* (5th ed.). Englewood Cliffs, NJ: Prentice-Hall.

Helson, R., & Soto, C. J. (2005). Up and down in middle age: Monotonic and nonmonotonic changes in roles, status, and personality. *Journal of Personality and Social Psychology, 89* (2), 194–204.

IATA. (2010). *IATA - Environment.* Retrieved from IATA: http://www.iata.org/whatwedo/environment/Pages/index.asp

Johnson, R.A., & Wichern, D.W. (1998). *Applied Multivariate Statistical Analysis.* Englewood Cliffs, NJ: Prentice-Hall.

Kaiser, F.G., Wolfing, S., & Fuhrer, U. (1999). Environmental attitude and ecological behaviour. *Journal of Environmental Psychology, 19*, 1-19.

Krämer, N.C., & Winter, S. (2008). Impression management 2.0. The relationship of self-esteem, extraversion, self-efficacy, and self-presentation within social networking sites. *Journal of Media Psychology, 20*(3), 106-116.

Kreuter, F., Presser, S., & Tourangeau, R. (2009). Social desirability bias in CATI, IVR, and web surveys. The effects of mode and question sensitivity. *Public Opinion Quarterly, 72*(5), 847-865.

Laroche, M., Bergeron, J., & Barbaro-Forleo, G. (2001). Targeting consumers who are willing to pay more for environmentally friendly products. *Journal of Consumer Marketing, 18*(6), 503–520.

Laroche, M., Toffoli, R., Kim, C., & Muller, T. (1996). The influence of culture on pro-environmental knowledge, attitudes and behaviour: A Canadian perspective. *Advances in Consumer Research, 23*, 196-202.

Leary, M.R. (1996). *Self-Presentation: Impression Management and Interpersonal Behavior.* Madison, WI: Brown & Benchmark Publishers.

MacAndrew, F.T. (2002). New evolutionary perspective on altruism: Multilevel-selection and costly-signaling theories. *Current Directions in Psychological Science, 11*, 79-82.

MacKerron, G. J., Egerton, C., Gaskell, C., Parpia, A., & Mourato, S. (2009). Willingness to pay for carbon offset certification and co-benefits among (high-)flying young adults in the UK. *Energy Policy, 37*, 1372-1381.

Mainieri, T., Barnett, E.G., Valdero, T.R., Unipan, J.B., & Oskamp, S. (1997). Green buying: The influence of environmental concern on consumer behavior. *The Journal of Social Psychology, 137*(2), 189-204.

Maloney, M.P., Ward, M.P., & Braught, G.N. (1975). A revised scale for the measurement of ecological attitudes and knowledge. *Psychology in Action, July*, 787-790.

Martin, B., & Simintiras, A.C. (1995). The impact of green product lines on the environment: Does what they know affect what they feel? *Marketing Intelligence and Planning, 13*(4), 16-23.

Moreno, M. (2010, February 1). *Facebook ya tiene en España más habitantes que Andalucía.* Retrieved August 12, 2010, from Trecebits.com: http://www.trecebits.com/2010/02/01/facebook-ya-tiene-en-espana-mas-habitantes-que-andalucia/

Murphy, J.J., Allen, P.G., Stevens, T.H., & Weatherhead, D. (2005). A meta-analysis of hypothetical bias in stated preference valuation. *Environmental and Resource Economics, 30*, 313-325.

Reingen, P.H., Foster, B.L., Johnson Brown, J., & Seidman, S.B. (1984). Brand congruence in interpersonal relations: A social network analysis. *Journal of Consumer Research, 11*(3), 771-783.

Schlenker, B.R. (1980). *Impression management: the self-concept, social identity and interpersonal relations.* Monterey, CA: Brooks Cole.

Schlenker, B.R., & Weigold, M.F. (1992). Interpersonal processes involving impression regulation and management. *Annual review of psychology, 43*, 133-168.

Smith, E.A., & Bird, R.L. (2000). Turtle hunting and tombstone opening: public generosity as costly signaling. *Evolution and Human Behavior, 21*, 245-261.

Spanish Presidency of the European Union. (2010, 04 15). *Declaration of Madrid within the scope of the informal ministerial meeting for tourism.* Retrieved 06 05, 2010, from www.2010.eu

Steven, J. (1992). *Applied Multivariate Statistics of the Social Sciences.* Hillsdale, NJ: Lawrence Erlbaum Associates.

UNEP. (2011, October 11). *Buy a Westwood Tree-shirt to GreenUp! Europe.* Retrieved January 18, 2012, from United Nations Environment Programme (UNEP): http://www.unep.org/newscentre/default.aspx?DocumentID=2656&ArticleID=8893&l=en

United Nations World Tourism Organization. (2010, 06 29). *International Tourism: Recovery Confirmed, but Growth Remains Uneven.* Retrieved 07 06, 2010, from World Tourism Organization (UNWTO): www.unwto.org/media/news/en/press_det.php?id=6241&idioma=E

van Lange, P.A., Liebrand, W.B., Messick, D.M., & Wilke, H.A. (1992). Social dilemmas: the state-of-the-art - Introduction and Literature Review. In W.B. Liebrand, D.M. Messick, & H.A. Wilke, *Social Dilemmas: Theoretical Issues and Research Findings* (pp. 3-28). Oxford: Pergamon Press.

Vinson, D.E., Scott, J.E., & Lamont, L.M. (1977). The role of personal values in marketing and consumer behavior. *Journal of Marketing*, *41*(2), 44-50

Welsch, H., & Kühling, J. (2009). Determinants of pro-environmental consumption: the role of reference groups and routine behavior. *Ecological behavior, 69*, 166-176.

World Tourism Organization. (2009). *From Davos to Copenhagen and Beyond: Advancing Tourism's Response to Climate Change.* Retrieved from World Tourism Organization:
http://www.unwto.org/pdf/From_Davos_to%20Copenhagen_beyond_UNWTOPaper_ElectronicVersion.pdf

Zahavi, A. (1975). Mate selection: Selection for a handicap. *Journal of Theoretical Biology, 53*, 205-214.

PART 4:

INFORMATION AND COMMUNICATION TECHNOLOGIES IN TOURISM

CHAPTER EIGHT

IMPROVING THE TOURISM EXPERIENCE BY EMPOWERING VISITORS

JOÃO V. ESTÊVÃO, MARIA JOÃO CARNEIRO AND LEONOR TEIXEIRA

Abstract

Although Destination Management Systems (DMSs) are intrinsically innovative due both to their technological pre-requisites and to the cohesion that they require amongst a destination's components, it is pertinent to ask how these broad and complex networks give visitors a more active role in planning their travel experiences. This chapter empirically analyzes and evaluates how advanced DMSs are enabling visitors to play a more active role in building their experiences through the implementation of Web 2.0 functionalities. Most of the research conducted in the area of DMSs focuses on destination-based stakeholders rather than on their customers and on the increasingly dynamic role they tend to have in most areas of e-tourism. **Keywords**: Destination management systems, Web 2.0, information and communication technologies.

1. Introduction

In recent years, an increasing number of destinations compete to obtain, or at least maintain, considerable tourism flows (Dwyer, Edwards, Mistilis, Roman, & Scott, 2009). One of the major tasks for destinations seeking to improve competitiveness is achieving high levels of cooperation and coordination between stakeholders (Wang, 2008). However, tourism destinations are often composed of a mix of many kinds of stakeholders, with sometimes overlapping or opposing interests, which can lead to fragmentation and an undermining of cooperation between them (Elbe, Hallén, & Axelsson, 2009). Thus, designated Destination Management

Organizations (DMOs) should strive to bring destination actors together and to mobilize resources to produce a coordinated destination development, rather than limiting themselves to undertaking marketing efforts (Gretzel, Fesenmaier, Formica, & O'Leary, 2006).

In the meantime, travelers are progressively seeking more flexibility in their travel arrangements and demanding an effective provision of destination information (Chen & Sheldon, 1997). This has led to a more active role for DMOs, not only in fostering cooperation between destination stakeholders and conducting marketing efforts (Hall, 2000), but also, as predicted by the World Tourism Organization (WTO) in 1999, in acting as a kind of intermediary between suppliers and consumers (World Tourism Organization Business Council, 1999).

In parallel, the internet is now the most relevant and influential source of travel information for tourists (Fu Tsang, Lai, & Law, 2010; Jani, Jang, & Hwang, 2011). The rapid development of information and communications technology (ICT) has dramatically changed the tourism sector, and destinations have not been immune to this process (Fu Tsang *et al.*, 2010). Thus, nowadays, the competitiveness of destinations is largely determined by their capacity to satisfy the information needs of local actors and visitors through ICT-based applications (Buhalis & Law, 2008; Höpken, Fuchs, Keil, & Lexhagen, 2011).

One of the most important advances in the use of ICT by DMOs since the 1990s has been the emergence of Destination Management Systems (DMSs) (Buhalis & Spada, 2000). DMSs are, first and foremost, web-based internal networks established between DMOs and the destination's tourism system, aimed at optimizing coordination amongst them by enhancing information flows. However, they also enable destinations to implement consumer-facing websites that are capable of a much higher degree of interaction with visitors in comparison to traditional destination websites (Buhalis, 2003; Buhalis & Spada, 2000; Pollock, 1995). Thus, DMSs usually include a set of functionalities that allow an enhanced and broader interaction between official destination websites and future visitors.

Regarding the optimization of interaction levels between web applications and correspondent users, perhaps one of the most relevant paradigm shifts regarding the internet has been the implementation of Web 2.0 tools that support user-generated content (UGC), also referred to as consumer-generated media (CGM), allowing users to play an active part in creating the contents of websites (Casaló, Flavián, & Guinalíu, 2011; Cox, Burgess, Sellitto, & Buultjens, 2009; Parra-López, Bulchand-Gidumal, Gutierrez-Taño, & Díaz-Armas, 2011; Sigala, 2011; Yoo & Gretzel,

2011). Thus, Web 2.0 and consequent UGC creation has fostered a dynamic relationship between consumers in the process of value creation and communication, distinct from the traditional perspective under which this process occurs solely between firms and customers. In fact, by enabling mass collaboration and communication, Web 2.0 tools and their consequent UGC empower users by giving them further chances to socially collaborate, network and learn (Sigala, 2011). The tourism sector's web applications are among those that registered the most considerable growth concerning UGC (Sigala, 2011; Yoo & Gretzel, 2011).

Regarding the research that has been conducted around the theme of UGC applications in tourism, most studies seem to focus on the benefits of these applications for tourists and tourism businesses (Ascaniis & Morasso, 2011; Sigala, 2010; Xiang & Gretzel, 2010; Ye, Law, Gu, &, Chen, 2011), on the trustworthiness of the information that tourists and businesses obtain through Web 2.0 (Chiappa, 2011; Cox et al., 2009; Kyung Hyan Yoo & Gretzel, 2010), and on the influence of personality in consumers' behavior towards UGC (Casaló et al., 2011; Xiang & Gretzel, 2010; Yoo & Gretzel, 2011). Although there are some exceptions, scarce research has been conducted to assess the current extent of the use that different tourism suppliers and intermediaries make of Web 2.0.

As official destination websites such as DMSs seek to establish closer and broader interaction flows with current and potential visitors, and UGC applications foster proximity and interactions between customers and businesses, it seems appropriate to take a relational approach to UGC and DMSs. One objective of this chapter is to analyze the relevance that researchers have given to the implementation of Web 2.0 functionalities, particularly UGC applications, in DMSs. This chapter also aims to analyze whether DMSs have Web 2.0 functionalities and which of these functionalities have been implemented in DMS applications.

2. DMSs vs. Traditional Official Destination Web Applications

Regarding the relevance of ICTs and of the internet, in particular to promote and distribute information and services relating to a specific destination, Buhalis (2003) suggests that visitors are becoming more sophisticated and demanding, seeking one-stop-only online platforms which allow users the possibility of searching for information about several tourism services on offer at a destination, and making reservations in one integrated platform.

However, as research findings suggest (Ndou & Petti, 2007; Sigala, 2009), most DMOs have still only developed brochure websites which only allow tourists to receive promotional messages and general information about a destination.

Egger and Buhalis (2008) define the DMS as a collection of computerized information about a destination that is accessible in an interactive way, and argue that DMSs usually include information about attractions and services, incorporating the possibility of making reservations. Regarding their ownership and management, Buhalis (2003, p. 282) states that "DMSs are usually managed by Destination Management Organizations, which can be public, private or public-private organizations". One of the first approaches to the concept of the DMS was made by Pollock (1995), defining it as the ICT infrastructure used by a DMO to gather, store, manipulate and distribute information through various means. However, perhaps the most relevant and innovative aspect of Pollock's definition is that DMSs also allow transactions, bookings and other commercial activities. In the early studies concerning the concept of the DMS, much relevance is given to their role as a marketing tool directed towards consumers. Primarily, a DMS is a marketing tool that promotes the tourism products of a specific destination, whether it is a country, region, town or a place of other geographical scope (Sussmann & Baker, 1996). DMSs can have up to three components (Sussman & Baker, 1996, p. 102):

- a product database (of attractions, accommodation, travel information, etc.);
- a customer database (of those using, or who have used, the database);
- a booking and reservation system.

There is evidence that the ability to handle bookings, either via the DMS's reservation system or establishments' reservation systems, transforms any destination portal from a computerized brochure into something significantly more powerful. When compared with the traditional tourism distribution channels previously mentioned (intermediaries – tour operators and travel agencies – and direct distribution done by each service provider), DMSs bring clear advantages to destinations as a whole and to small and medium-sized enterprises (SMEs) in particular (Matloka & Buhalis, 2010; Sigala, 2009), by satisfying the needs of more sophisticated and autonomous consumers.

Among the most frequently mentioned advantages of DMSs for both suppliers and visitors of a destination (Buhalis, 2003; Buhalis & Spada, 2000; Egger & Buhalis, 2008, Sigala, 2009) are the following:

- enhanced coordination of destinations' promotion and distribution efforts by optimizing cohesion and interaction levels amongst suppliers that share an official marketing and eCommerce web-based application;
- improved visibility of SMEs globally, allowing them a more autonomous distribution as well as diminishing their dependency on intermediaries;
- optimized presence of destinations as a whole in the global market;
- more reliable, comfortable (one-stop-only), flexible (that enable dynamic packaging) and independent means of searching, planning and booking the whole array of a destination's offerings through a single web-based application;
- improved direct interaction between past and potential future visitors and the destination.

3. The Web 2.0 in Tourism

Ever since the advent of the World Wide Web, an increasing number of travelers have been using the internet for travel planning (Law, Qi, & Buhalis, 2010). However, until recently, most websites were built under a Web 1.0 perspective, in which the vast majority of users were only able to act as consumers of content (Cormode & Krishnamurthy, 2008). More recently, the advent of Web 2.0 introduced a different and original philosophy which allowed any user to become a content creator, thus democratizing online content creation (Cormode & Krishnamurthy, 2008).

Some authors suggest that although Web 2.0 as a concept is still unclear and relatively vague, leading to harsh criticism of the concept itself (Egger, 2010), it nonetheless represents a "collective expression comprising both the technical but above all the social and societal advances in the internet" (Egger, 2010, p. 126).

Sigala (2011, p. 608) is one of the various authors to take a conceptual approach to Web 2.0, defining it as a set of tools of "mass collaboration, as they enable and empower internet users to actively and simultaneously collaborate with others for producing, consuming and diffusing internet-based information and applications".

Most researchers agree that Web 2.0 has brought considerable benefits to organizations and to the general public. Benefits include users being more reliable information sources and, at the same time, allowing users a more interactive and flexible participation regarding content creation (Chiang, Huang, & Huang, 2009). In addition, Web 2.0 also enables richer user experiences and improved content through usage (Chiang *et al.*, 2009).

According to Sigala (2011), Web 2.0 gave rise to two major features – user-generated content (UGC) and social networks – which have dramatically transformed the way users search, distribute, share and create information. Yoo & Gretzel (2011, p. 610) argue that consumer-generated media (as UGC is also known) constitute "a new form of word-of-mouth that serve informational needs by offering non-commercial, detailed, experimental and up-to-date information with an access beyond the boundaries of one's immediate social circle".

Regarding the recent development of UGC, there is evidence that the development and sharing of UGC made possible by Web 2.0 applications is continuously increasing (Casaló *et al.,* 2011; Sigala, 2008, Yoo & Gretzel, 2008). In some countries, such as the US, a substantial majority of consumers search for fellow consumers' product reviews online and most of these reported that they had a more decisive role on their decision-making processes than reviews posted by professionals (Casaló *et al.,* 2011).

Nowadays, Web 2.0 is changing the way that consumers engage with information presented via the internet (Chiappa, 2011; Davies, 2008), and has major implications for the way companies relate to their customers. It provides the opportunity to exchange, systematize and evaluate information via users (collective intelligence), and the possibility of obtaining feedback and recording user behavior in order to systematically adapt and enhance offerings (perpetual beta), among other features (Egger, 2010).

Web 2.0 applications available to consumers can be used in two different ways: a more passive use of Web 2.0 material includes searching and reading other users' content, while a more active use, usually designated as Web 2.0 authorship, involves the edition and insertion of content by users (Gray, Thompson, Clerehan, Sheard, & Hamilton, 2011; Yoo & Gretzel, 2008).

According to Yoo and Gretzel (2011), the main Web 2.0 applications that empower UGC are online communities and discussion forums, blogs, online reviews, and video and photo sharing.

Blogs are a sort of personal journalism, presenting important opportunities to communicate information beyond the dominant narratives of tourism marketers (Pudliner, 2007). Reviews from past visitors are one of the most relevant forms of travel-related UGC (Yoo & Gretzel, 2008). Contrary to other forms of Web 2.0, *travel reviews* are often very structured and are not aimed at documenting a personal experience, but rather are directed at other potential visitors. Unlike all other functionalities, *user rating* (of a website's contents) focuses on the opinions of users about websites themselves rather than on the correspondent destinations. According to Yoo and Gretzel (2011, p. 610), online travel communities and forums "have the longest tradition as online venues for travelers to engage in travel storytelling or share information and support travel planning". *Photo and video sharing* have not been the subject of academic analysis with regard to their relevance for tourism businesses and destinations (Tussyadiah & Fesenmaier, 2009). However, a study conducted by Yoo & Gretzel (2010) about the use of Web 2.0 tools by American internet users empirically demonstrated that the most common Web 2.0 activity was looking at other users' travel photos (67% of the sample), and the third most common was watching videos from previous visitors (56.7% of the sample). The empirical analysis to be described later on will focus only on these tools, as they are the most relevant functionalities for stimulating UGC.

As information is the lifeblood of the tourism industry, the use and spread of Web 2.0 has had an extensive impact on both tourism suppliers and visitors (Sigala, 2011). Because of the experiential nature of tourism products, Web 2.0 is particularly relevant for tourists because they often rely on other tourists' feedback when planning their trips (Yoo & Gretzel, 2010). With the rise of Web 2.0, travelers are able to more actively interact with their peers in creating, consuming and sharing data through the web, thus assisting them in their decision-making processes (Yoo & Gretzel, 2011).

Regarding the advantages that Web 2.0 and consequent UGC might bring to tourism businesses, a close cause-effect relationship has been empirically proved between the use of Web 2.0 by hotels and their online sales of rooms: Ye, Law, Gu & Chen (2011) demonstrated that a 10% increase in the ratings of user reviews could boost online bookings.

Although commercial websites adopting Web 2.0 are rapidly emerging within the tourism industry, they are mostly developed by individual businesses or tourism intermediaries (Casaló *et al.*, 2011). The use of Web 2.0 by destinations and their respective official web applications seems to be only in its infancy, since it is still a virtually unexplored area in terms of research.

Taking into consideration the role of Web 2.0 and resulting UGC in official destination websites from a B2C perspective, it seems relevant to refer to a study on the trustworthiness of travel-related UGC, which revealed that official tourism bureau websites would greatly benefit from supporting a venue for UGC, because the content proved more trustworthy when featured in official bureau websites (Yoo, Lee, Gretzel, & Fesenmaier, 2009).

Concerning the potential benefits of Web 2.0 applications for destinations from a B2B perspective, the implementation of Web 2.0 by official destination bureaus also allows suppliers themselves to share and spread information through the destination's extranet. This can be useful in supporting the DMO's role of maximizing interaction flows among internal destination suppliers, and can be valuable in enhancing the pivotal role of DMOs towards a more collaborative destination management (Sigala & Marianidis, 2010).

Most studies that examine Web 2.0 in tourism tend either to focus on consumer trust and behavior towards UGC (Casaló et al., 2011; Chiappa, 2011; Casaló et al., 2011; Yoo & Gretzel, 2011; Yoo et al., 2009), or explore the advantages Web 2.0 brings to visitors and to particular businesses or subsectors within the tourism industry (Sigala, 2011; Ye et al., 2011). However, the analysis of the implementation of these applications by destination websites, namely DMSs, seems to be relatively unexplored in the literature.

There is evidence that both advanced destination web applications, such as DMSs, and Web 2.0 as a philosophy and a set of functionalities, have in common the fact that they foster a more direct, close and flexible relationship between entities (such as destinations) and their respective publics. Thus, it seems pertinent and relevant to investigate how and to what extent destination web applications have implemented Web 2.0.

This chapter aims to be a first step in filling the above-mentioned gap. First it will explore the importance that case studies in the literature on DMSs have given to their use of Web 2.0. Second, the Web 2.0 functionalities that actually exist in the DMSs examined in those case studies will be analyzed. Furthermore, it is also considered as a relevant original approach to explore whether there is any correlation between the actual Web 2.0 tools implemented by DMSs and the references made to these tools in literary sources.

The sole fact that, according to Yoo et al. (2009), official tourism bureau websites were proven to be the most reliable vehicle of UGC, is reason enough for assessing the current state of UGC usage by the type of official destination portal widely considered most effectively to interact with past and potential visitors – DMSs.

4. Methodology

This study seeks to evaluate the use of Web 2.0 applications by DMSs, in particular the specific UGC-enabler tools they convey, through a content analysis of Web 2.0 functionalities.

Since the concept of a DMS is rather diffuse (Buhalis, 2003), choosing specific DMSs to analyze was not an easy task; simply analyzing the consumer-facing area of a tourism destination's website is not enough to determine whether a web application is a DMS or just a brochure website. At first glance, the existence of transactional functionalities in an official destination web application might be an indicator that it is a DMS. However, it is not possible for an ordinary user to ascertain whether a particular destination website is a network that connects suppliers and DMOs, enhancing a destination's coordination, which is also a pre-requisite for a web application to be considered a DMS.

Taking this fact into consideration, it seemed a more cautious and objective approach for the present research to analyze twelve destination web applications that were previously identified as DMSs in the literature, in order to identify the Web 2.0 tools that they convey. The selected DMSs were *Australia.com*, the national Australian DMS (referred by Buhalis, 2003); *BonjourQuebec.com*, the DMS from the Canadian province of Québec (Bédard & Louillet, 2008); *Feratel.com*, a DMS provider for fourteen European countries (Schröcksnadel, 2008); *Gulliver.ie*, the national Irish DMS (European eBusiness Market Watch, 2005); *Holland.com*, the Dutch official DMS (Buhalis, 2003); *Jersey.com*, the DMS of the island of Jersey, UK (Buhalis, 2003); *Tiscover.com*, an Austrian-based DMS provider for various central European countries which specializes in the Alps (Kärcher & Alford, 2008); *Visitbath.co.uk*, the local DMS for the historic spa city of Bath (Inversini & Cantoni, 2009); *VisitBritain.com*, the national British DMS (Guthrie, 2008); and *VisitFinland.com*, the Finnish official DMS (Buhalis, 2003).

Based on the Web 2.0 applications that Yoo and Gretzel (2011) considered those that empower UGC, this study only took into account Web 2.0 applications that were detected at least once in the literature review or in the content analysis of the DMSs. Some more technical Web 2.0 tools that most websites already have, such as content syndication or social tagging, were not also taken into consideration; instead, emphasis was placed on those applications that foster the participation of users in the creation of DMS content. Thus, the travel Web 2.0 functionalities that were analyzed were: blogs, photo sharing, rating of tourism products, rating of the website, reviews, and video sharing.

In order to better grasp all those possible applications, it was considered necessary to register as a user at each website, since some feedback and Web 2.0 applications might only be available for registered users. The website content analysis of the DMS functionalities was undertaken between May and July 2011.

5. Results

The content analysis of the DMS functionalities revealed that some Web 2.0 functionalities are to be found in several DMSs analyzed, and that there is also a considerable diversity in terms of the types of Web 2.0 applications used (Figure 1).

One of the primary and most noteworthy results of the empirical analysis is that only half of the DMSs analyzed integrate Web 2.0 functionalities into the DMSs themselves. This was the case of *Australia.com*, *BonjourQuebec.com*, *Feratel.com*, *Gulliver.ie*, *Tiscover.com* and *Visitbritain.com*. None of the other six DMSs analyzed support Web 2.0 tools internally, which does not mean that the respective DMOs do not take them into consideration in their *eTourism* strategies. In fact, although the remaining DMSs do not include Web 2.0 tools, all of them have links to their official channels/pages in major Web 2.0 platforms such as *Facebook*, *YouTube* or *Flickr*.

Regarding the six websites that support Web 2.0 tools and display UGC, Figure 1 summarizes the findings in terms of the functionalities they offer.

Figure 1- Travel 2.0 applications found in the analyzed DMSs

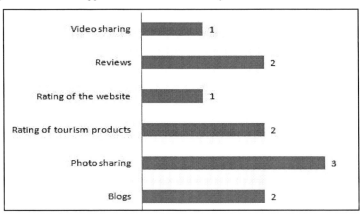

Although most of the Web 2.0 applications identified can be found in the DMS websites themselves, there were three cases in which users' shared comments, photos and videos feature in another website attached to the main destination portal. This was the case of *Australia.com* and *Bounjourquebec.com*, which implemented aggregated websites aimed at having Web 2.0 functionalities and presenting UGC to all users (namely *Nothinglikeaustralia.com* and *Destinationquebec.com*) and *Gulliver.ie*, the national Irish DMS. Although *Gulliver.ie* includes some more commercially oriented Web 2.0 functionalities, such as service reviews and ratings, it is only possible to find an official travel *blog* in the more information-oriented Irish official website *Goireland.com*. However, since all these websites are aggregated to their main destination portals, they were considered as part of the correspondent DMSs.

As shown in Figure 1, *photo sharing* functionalities are the most frequently implemented Web 2.0 tool, existing in three of the analyzed DMSs. In contrast, only one of the tested DMSs integrates *video sharing* and *ratings of the website*, evaluating particular content of the DMS. Regarding the possibility of sharing comments through *blogging*, only *Gulliver.ie* and *Feratel* have *blogs*. As previously mentioned, *Gulliver.ie*'s *blog* can only be found at *Goireland.com* and includes articles on more than twenty categories (e.g. Irish food and drink, Christmas in Ireland, festivals in Ireland, etc.) which can be commented on by any user after inserting name, e-mail and, optionally, website. *Feratel* also has a *blog* which is divided into eight categories, such as events, sports and news. Most of the articles and corresponding comments, which can also be easily submitted after stating name and e-mail, are written in the German language. *Visitlondon.com*, which is a local-level partner website of *Visitbritain.com*, incorporates a *blog* that allows all users to comment on articles on that local destination, as well as to make remarks on other users' comments. However, *Visitbritain.com* itself does not have a *blog* for the national destination.

Regarding both *reviews* and *rating of tourism products*, only *Gulliver.ie* and *Tiscover* support these functionalities. In both cases, it is only possible to attribute ratings and insert reviews on accommodation units, and it is not possible to rate or review general features of the destination or other types of tourism businesses. In the case of *Gulliver.ie*, the website clearly states that only customers who have made reservations through the DMS's booking engine and who have already stayed at a certain accommodation unit are allowed to rate and review that same unit. Every user who searches for accommodation can easily find past visitors' ratings and reviews, and there is no need to register and log on to access them. The average customer rating appears immediately next to the name of an accommodation unit and ranges from one to ten. In order to read textual reviews and consult individual and more detailed information, one simply has to click on *reviews* below the name of the hotel. Ratings from one to ten are divided into eight categories, namely rooms, staff/service, restaurant, value for money, check-in cleanliness, recommend to a friend, and bar.

Past customers can also insert textual reviews about a particular hotel, which any user can easily access. In the ratings/reviews area, the Irish DMS also provides users with information on the types of travelers that rated and/or reviewed a specific business. Here, the categories are young couple, mature couple, business traveler, family with kids, tour group, and other. The case of *Tiscover* is very similar to that of *Gulliver.ie*, since ratings and reviews are also easily accessible from the moment the results of an accommodation search appear on screen. The rating scale ranges from one to five but is much more detailed than *Gulliver.ie*'s since it includes decimals. Ratings are divided into only five categories, including facilities, value for money, catering, offers (such as sports and leisure activities and wellness, among others), and service/support (friendliness, helpful staff). It seems evident that, amongst the six analyzed DMSs, *Gulliver.ie* and *Tiscover* are the ones that are more committed to developing more commercially-oriented Web 2.0 tools such as customer ratings and reviews. This might be a result of the fact that they are partly owned and managed by private companies, which tend to have a more commercial approach to the market.

From the twelve analyzed DMSs, only Québec's supports ratings of the website that also include short text reviews about the contents of the website itself. In the website's homepage, the option *share* gives access to an aggregated website designated *Destinationquebec.com*, including photos, videos and comments from Québec's past visitors. To insert comments and ratings (ranging from one to five) on other users' photos and videos it is also necessary to register and log on.

Québec's DMS is also the only one that allows video sharing. In order to upload photos or videos of Québec, it is required to log on or create an account at *Destinationquebec.com*. This website presents more than 13,000 photo and video sharing contributions, illustrating 22 tourist regions and 23 categories, such as architecture and scenery, events and festivals, hunting, restaurants and gastronomy, among others.

The photo sharing functionalities implemented by three of the analyzed DMSs have considerable differences which seem relevant to address. In the case of *Australia.com*, there are two elements which make its Web 2.0

applications quite particular. Firstly, the website *Nothinglikeaustralia.com* was purposely implemented to hold Web 2.0 applications, such as comments and photo sharing. Secondly, this sharing is not a systematic, ongoing practice, but rather the result of a short-term contest during which, for less than a month, visitors from various countries could upload one photo and a text of up to 25 words illustrating their experiences when visiting the country. Although every user could access the uploaded photos and comments through *Nothinglikeaustralia.com* up to the date that this chapter was conceived, this initiative was isolated, being integrated in the 2011 Tourism Australia promotional campaign. *Bonjourquebec*'s photo sharing functionalities are available at *Destinationquebec.com* and, as previously mentioned, are the subject of other users' comments and ratings. The third DMS that supports photo sharing is *Visitbritain.com*, which allows registered users to upload photos directly to the website through *Flickr*.

As regards the six DMSs that do not support Web 2.0 functionalities inside the DMSs themselves, *YourSingapore.com* and *VisitFinland.com* in particular give access to a considerable number of third-party websites conveying a wide range of Web 2.0 tools and extensively publicize them in their websites. In the case of *VisitFinland.com*, one of the options of the consumer-facing website's menu is *Interact and Share*, which consists of a sort of a gateway to third-party Web 2.0 sites on Finland, where users can directly connect to *YouTube's* official channel of *VisitFinland*.com to see videos, to read and share comments and media on *VisitFinland.com*'s *Facebook* page, and see or share photos of Finland on *Flickr*. In the case of *YourSingapore*.com, the B2C interface of the DMS gives access to all the types of Web 2.0 tools, but not on the official website itself. In fact, *YourSingapore.com* offers links to *YouTube*, *Flickr*, *Facebook*, and *Twitter* for video, photo and comment sharing. Additionally, it has an area named *YourSingapore News,* which gives access to blogs and travel websites that incorporate Web 2.0 such as *CNNGo*, in which users can share and rate other users' comments. A further example of the importance that the Singapore national DMO gives to Web 2.0 tools, although it doesn't integrate them in its official website, is the fact that *YourSingapore.com* invites users to check the Tourism Singapore area of *TripAdvisor* where they can not only find ratings and comments regarding specific tourism services, but are also able to create their own reviews and ratings. From all the twelve analyzed DMSs, only *Jersey.com* also has a link to the Jersey's area in *Tripadvisor*. *Jersey.com* also has links to major Web 2.0 platforms such as *YouTube* or *Facebook*.

All the other three websites that do not integrate Web 2.0 themselves are also linked to their respective areas/pages on the most prominent media and comment sharing websites.

6. Conclusion

The chief conclusion that can be taken from this chapter's empirical content analysis of the selected DMSs is that they use Web 2.0 tools in considerably different ways. While some DMSs, such as *Gulliver.ie*, use most of the Web 2.0 tools enabling UGC, others, such as *Australia.com*, only use a few and in an ephemeral manner. On the other hand, whereas other tourism agents, such as private *infomediaries* (e.g. *Tripadvisor* or *Holidaycheck*), have a more homogeneous use of commercially-oriented Web 2.0 tools, focusing on consumer ratings and reviews of concrete products, destination portals tend to have a considerably heterogeneous approach to UGC, sometimes neglecting the potential advantages of Web 2.0. Thus, while *Australia.com* integrates Web 2.0, for instance, in ephemeral promotional campaigns for the destination which have a more limited and instrumental scope, others, such as *Gulliver.ie* and *Tiscover*, emphasize a more systematic, ongoing commercial facet of Web 2.0, highlighting customer ratings and reviews on particular businesses. Another example of the differences between the use of Web 2.0 among analyzed DMSs relates to the insertion or visualization of UGC. While some DMSs limit access to Web 2.0 tools to registered users – especially for content insertion – others do not require registration to users wishing to access Web 2.0 functionalities.

The empirical analysis shows that DMOs are not reluctant to let users judge their destinations' characteristics and quality, as one might conclude by only analyzing the corresponding case studies. Although only six of the analyzed DMSs support Web 2.0 functionalities, the remaining six do not appear to disregard UGC in their promotional efforts, but rather seem to prefer a different approach to Web 2.0 that privileges third-party websites that have global visibility (e.g. the links of *Jersey.com* and *Yoursingapore.com* directly to their pages in *Tripadvisor*).

However, it is also noteworthy that only two of the analyzed DMSs – *Gulliver.ie* and *Tiscover* – focus on a commercially oriented Web 2.0 approach that gives users the opportunity to rate and review individual, clearly identified businesses. The fact that both *Gulliver.ie* and *Tiscover* are managed by private-sector entities might be a reason for their different approach to Web 2.0. The other four DMSs only use Web 2.0 for promotional purposes, fostering UGC on general features of the destination, and not allowing the evaluation of particular services and infrastructure. Thus, in future research on this subject, it would be useful to analyze whether the complexity of destinations, stemming from the variety of actors that comprise them, as well as the fact that DMOs must play the role of the impartial official body, representing and promoting destinations as a whole, are inhibitors to the implementation of Web 2.0 by official destination websites such as DMSs.

References

Ascaniis, S.D., & Morasso, S.G. (2011). *When tourists give their reasons on the Web: the argumentative significance of tourism related UGC.* Paper presented at the Information and Communication Technologies in Tourism 2011 (pp.125-138). Wien-NY: Springer.

Bédard, F., & Louillet, M.C. (2008). BonjourQuebec.com: A vision, a strategy, a brand. In R. Egger and D. Buhalis (2008). *eTourism – Case Studies*, 200-212. Ed. Butterworth Heinemann, Oxford.

Buhalis, D. (2003). *eTourism: information technologies for strategic tourism management.* Harlow: Pearson Higher Education.

Buhalis, D., & Law, R. (2008). Progress in information technology and tourism management: 20 years on and 10 years after the Internet—The state of eTourism research. *Tourism Management, 29*(4), 609-623.

Buhalis, D., & Spada, A. (2000). DMS: criteria for success – an exploratory research. . *Information Technology and Tourism, 3*(1), 41-58.

Casaló, L.V., Flavián, C., & Guinalíu, M. (2011). Understanding the intention to follow the advice obtained in an online travel community. *Computers in Human Behavior, 27,* 622-633.

Chen, H.-M., & Sheldon, P.J. (1997). Destination information systems: design issues and directions. *Journal of Management Information Systems, 14*(2), 151-176.

Chiang, I.P., Huang, C.-Y., & Huang, C.-W. (2009). Characterizing Web users' degree of Web 2.0-ness. *Journal of the American Society for Information Science and Technology, 60*(7), 1349-1357.

Chiappa, G.D. (2011). Trustworthiness of Web 2.0 applications and their influence on tourist behavior: an empirical investigation in Italy. In R. Law, M. Fuchs, F. Ricci, (Eds.). *Information and Communication Technologies in Tourism 2011* (pp. 331 – 342). Wien-NY: Springer.

Cormode, G., & Krishnamurthy, B. (2008). Key differences between Web 1.0 and Web 2.0. *First Monday,* 13(6).

Cox, C., Burgess, S., Sellitto, C., & Buultjens, J. (2009). The role of user-generated content in tourists' travel planning behavior. *Journal of Hospitality Marketing & Management,* 18(8), 743-764.

Davies, G. (2008). Web 2.0 Arrives. *Travel Trade Gazette UK & Ireland,* (January), 49-50.

Dwyer, L., Edwards, D., Mistilis, N., Roman, C., & Scott, N. (2009). Destination and enterprise management for a tourism future. *Tourism Management,* 30(1), 63-74.

Egger, R. (2010). Theorizing Web 2.0 phenomena in tourism: A sociological signpost. *Information Technology & Tourism,* 12(2), 125-137.

Egger, R., & Buhalis, D. (2008). *eTourism: Case studies.* Oxford: Butterworth Heinemann - Elsevier.

Elbe, J., Hallén, L., & Axelsson, B. (2009). The destination management organisation and the integrative destination-marketing process. *International Journal of Tourism Research,* 11(3), 283–296.

Fu Tsang, N., Lai, M., & Law, R. (2010). Measuring e-service quality for online travel agencies. *Journal of Travel & Tourism Marketing,* 27(3), 306-323.

Gray, K., Thompson, C., Clerehan, R., Sheard, J., & Hamilton, M. (2011). Web 2.0 authorship: Issues of referencing and citation for academic integrity. *Internet and Higher Education,* 11(2), 112-118.

Gretzel, U., Fesenmaier, D. R., Formica, S., & O'Leary, J. T. (2006). Searching for the future: challenges faced by destination marketing organizations. *Journal of Travel Research,* 45(2), 116-126.

Guthrie, C. (2008). VisitBritain: Satisfying the online market dynamics. In R. Egger and D. Buhalis (Eds.), *eTourism: Case Studies* (pp. 181-189). Oxford: Butterworth Heinemann - Elsevier.

Hall, C.M. (2000). *Tourism planning: policies, processes and relationships.* Harlow: Pearson Education.

Höpken, M., Fuchs, M., Keil, D., & Lexhagen, M. (2011). The knowledge destination – a customer information-based destination management information system. In R. Law, M. Fuchs and F. Ricci (Eds.). *Information and Communication Technologies in Tourism 2011* (pp. 587-598). Wien-NY: Springer.

Inversini, A. & Cantoni, L. (2009) Cultural destination usability: The case of Visit Bath. In W. Höpken, U. Gretzel & R. Law (Eds.). *Information and Communication Technologies in Tourism 2009* (pp. 319-331). Wien-NY: Springer.

Jani, D., Jang, J.H., & Hwang, Y.H. (2011). Personality and tourists' internet behaviour, In R. Law, M. Fuchs, F. Ricci (Eds.). *Information and Communication Technologies in Tourism 2011* (pp. 587-598). Wien-NY: Springer.

Kärcher, K. & Alford, P. (2008). Tiscover: Destination management system pioneer. In R. Egger and D. Buhalis (Eds.), *eTourism: Case Studies* (pp. 233-242). Oxford: Butterworth Heinemann - Elsevier.

Law, R., Qi, S., & Buhalis, D. (2010). Progress in tourism management: A review of website evaluation in tourism research. *Tourism Management,* 31(3), 297-313.

Matloka, J. & Buhalis, D. (2010) Destination marketing through User Personalised Content (UPC). In U. Gretzel, R. Law & M. Fuchs (Eds.) *Information and Communication Technologies in Tourism 2010* (pp. 519-530). Wien-NY: Springer.

Ndou, V., & Petti, C. (2007). DMS business models design and destination configurations: choice and implementation issues. *Information Technology & Tourism,* 9, 3-14.

Parra-López, E., Bulchand-Gidumal, J., Gutierrez-Taño, D., & Díaz-Armas, R. (2011). Intentions to use social media in organizing and taking vacation trips. *Computers in Human Behavior,* 27, 640-654.

Pollock, A. (1995). The impact of information technology on destination marketing. *Travel and Tourism Analyst,* 3, 66-83.

Pudliner, B. A. (2007). Alternative literature and tourist experience: Travel and tourist weblogs. *Journal of Tourism and Cultural Change,* 5(1), 46-59.

Schröcksnadel, M. (2008). Feratel media technologies: Providing DMS technology. In R. Egger & D. Buhalis (Eds.), *eTourism: Case Studies,* 243-251. Oxford: Butterworth Heinemann.

Sigala, M. (2009) Destination Management Systems (DMS): A reality check in the Greek tourism industry. In W. Höpken, U. Gretzel & R. Law (Eds.). *Information and Communication Technologies in Tourism 2009* (pp. 319-331). Wien-NY: Springer.

—. (2010). Web 2.0, social marketing strategies and distribution channels for city destinations: enhancing the participatory role of travelers and exploiting their collective intelligence. In A. E. In Tatnall (Ed.), *Web Technologies: Concepts, Methodologies, Tools, and Applications* 4,1249-1273.

—. (2011). Preface – special issue on Web 2.0 in travel and tourism: empowering and changing the role of travelers. *Computers in Human Behavior* 27, 607-608.

Sigala, M., & Marianidis, D. (2010). DMOs, e-democracy and collaborative destination management: An implementation framework. In U. Gretzel, R. Law and M. Fuchs (Eds.). *Information and*

Communication Technologies in Tourism 2010 (pp. 235-246). Wien-NY: Springer.

Sussmann, S., & Baker, M. (1996). Responding to the electronic marketplace: Lessons from destination management systems. *International Journal of Hospitality Management,* 15(2), 99-112.

The European e-Business Market Watch. (2005). Case study: The online Destination Management System of Gulliver, Ireland. *ICT and Electronic Business in the Tourism Industry. ICT Adoption and e-Business Activity in* 2005, 45-52. European Commission, Brussels.

Tussyadiah, I., & Fesenmaier, D. (2009). Mediating tourist experiences: Access to places via shared videos. *Annals of Tourism Research,* 36(1), 24-40.

Wang, Y. (2008). Collaborative destination marketing: Understanding the dynamic process. *Journal of Travel Research,* 47(2), 151-166.

World Tourism Organization Business Council. (1999). Chapter *1: Introduction. In: Marketing Tourism Destinations Online: Strategies for the Information Age*, Madrid: World Tourism Organization.

Xiang, Z., & Gretzel, U. (2010). Role of social media in online travel information search. *Tourism Management,* 31, 179–188).

Ye, Q., Law, R., Gu, B., & Chen, W. (2011). The influence of user-generated content on traveler behavior: An empirical investigation on the effects of e-word-of-mouth to hotel online bookings. *Computers in Human Behavior,* 27(2), 634-639.

Yoo, K.-H., & Gretzel, U. (2008). Understanding differences between online travel review writers and non-writers. In T. Hara (Ed.). *Proceedings of the 13th Annual Graduate Education and Student Research,*, 21-29. Conference in Hospitality and Tourism, Orlando, FL, January 23-25, 2008.

—. (2010). Antecedents and impacts of trust in travel-related consumer-generated media. *Information Technology & Tourism,* 12(2), 139-152.

—. (2011). Influence of personality on travel-related consumer-generated media creation. *Computers in Human Behavior,* 27, 609-621.

Yoo, K.H., Lee, Y., Gretzel, U., & Fesenmaier, D.R. (2009). Trust in travel-related consumer generated media. In W. Höpken, U. Gretzel and R. Law (Eds.) *Information and Communication Technlogies in Tourism 2009* (pp. 49-59). Wien-NY: Springer.

CHAPTER NINE

MODELING INFORMATION ASYMMETRIES IN TOURISM

RODOLFO BAGGIO AND JACOPO A. BAGGIO

Abstract

Tourism has long been described as an information asymmetric market where consumers are unable to fully assess the quality of the products offered. A recognized consequence of this situation is that the space available for high quality products is greatly reduced. The diffusion of information through the World Wide Web may have modified this asymmetry. Indeed, it is possible to envisage circumstances where consumers are better informed than suppliers about the real quality and value of the offerings. Using a set of agent-based numerical simulations, this chapter compares two possible asymmetric conditions. The results are discussed with respect to possible strategies to be adopted by both buyers and sellers in order to re-balance satisfaction (customers) and earnings (suppliers). **Keywords**: information asymmetry, tourism experience, agent-based modeling, numerical simulations.

1. Introduction

It is well known that providing *experience* (from a consumer point of view) is an important factor influencing the growth (or even the survival) of a firm. This is even more important in markets where information, more than tangible objects, plays a vital role. Information flows are central to many economic activities and represent a major factor for the stability and efficiency of markets. Many of these are characterized by imperfect information and, in particular, by *asymmetric information* where sellers of a product know its true characteristics and value while potential buyers are not so well informed. In his *The market for "Lemons"*, Akerlof (1970) highlights how such a situation could spoil the proper functioning of a market by preventing profitable transactions from taking place and thus generating inefficiencies in the market. In extreme cases, a consumer's inability to assess the real quality and value of goods could lead to a significant reduction in their perceived quality and eventually to the collapse of the market.

Tourism has long been recognized to be a market characterized by asymmetric information (Cohen, 1979; Smeral, 1993). On the basis of information made available by providers and intermediaries before their trip, travelers are able to assess only partially the quality of features of the package they are considering. The advent of the Internet suggests that this asymmetry may be reduced by providing consumers with more opportunities to collect details about their travel destinations and the products and services being considered (Schwabe *et al.*, 2008; Sirgy *et al.,* 2006; Werthner & Klein, 1999).

In practice, this asymmetry has not decreased significantly; due in part to new online intermediaries that have replaced 'bricks and mortar' travel agents (Chen & Schwartz, 2006; Fernández-Barcala *et al.,* 2010). The promise of a reduction in uncertainty due to the spread of easy-to-use information technologies has not appeared and some authors argue that, in the case of online markets (Lin *et al.*, 2010, p. 2):

> despite the rapid growth of these markets that bring together atomistic buyers and sellers, the 'virtual' nature of these markets further exacerbates issues of information asymmetry and the likelihood of opportunistic behaviors.

The Web 2.0 environment has modified this scenario by making readily available an immense quantity of information on practically any aspect of human life. In the past the number of other people that an individual could meaningfully connect with in order to share experiences and information about products and services was limited to a small number of close friends or relatives. These people are likely to have similar experiences and knowledge and the probability of engaging with someone who had knowledge about an unknown travel experience was low.

Web 2.0 environments have generated the possibility to consult a massive number of sources where tourism destinations, providers, products and services are discussed, compared, commented and evaluated. These sources have rapidly changed the way individuals face the problem of gathering information about trips, make choices or anticipate experience (Inversini *et al.,* 2009; Jones & Yu, 2010; Xiang & Gretzel, 2010; Zehrer *et al.*, 2010; Zhang *et al.*, 2009). Web 2.0 services and functions greatly facilitate this opportunity by significantly widening the concept of friendship, thus multiplying the number of information sources available to any single individual.

In the Web 2.0 environment, it is thus possible to envisage a situation in which information asymmetry is still present but the buyer is more informed than the seller. A recent paper names this a *market for gems* (Dari-Mattiacci *et al.,* 2010). In this work, the authors describe the consequences of an *inverse adverse selection mechanism* (the mirror image of Akerlof's *lemons* model). Despite the symmetry between the two models, the authors find that the two problems generate asymmetric consequences for real-life markets where different solutions and different strategic approaches are required. While for the lemons problem, signaling and screening appear to be the best practical solutions, for the gems problem auctions seem to be the way to go, the authors conclude.

The main objective of this exploratory chapter is to provide a model that is able to represent these two market configurations (i.e. market for lemons and the market for gems) in a tourism setting. With such a model we look at how different levels and types of asymmetries influence the functioning of the tourism market. This may allow guidelines to be derived for the strategies a tourism operator (or a destination) may use in order to improve profitability while not decreasing the satisfaction of the tourists with regard to their experience. Mathematical methods used to address such problems are complicated and, oftentimes, not fully solvable, therefore a numerical simulation approach was taken and an agent-based model was implemented.

The rest of this chapter is organized as follows. The next section briefly describes the information asymmetry issue, then we describe the methods used and present the results of the simulations performed. Finally we interpret these outcomes deriving the implications for the tourism sector.

2. Information Asymmetry: Lemons and Gems

The ideal world studied by classical economic theories is a world in which the different actors behave in a rational way having full information on the products and the market in which they are embedded. This perfect market involves a configuration of production and exchange in which optimal outcomes are realized efficiently without the need for intervention by external (nonmarket) actors. As George Soros states (1987: 12):

Economic theory [...] introduces the assumption of rational behavior. People are assumed to act by choosing the best of the alternatives, but somehow the distinction between perceived alternatives and facts is assumed away. The result is a theoretical construction of great elegance that resembles natural science but does not resemble reality. It relates to an ideal world in which participants act on the basis of perfect knowledge and it produces a theoretical equilibrium in which the allocation of resources is at an optimum.

Today, an increasing awareness of the complexity of economic systems, with the associated nonlinearities, emergent and self-organizing features and their extreme sensitivity to certain classes of events, has modified (at least under certain conditions) the dream of a system evolving towards equilibrium and stability (Arthur, 1999; Foster, 2005). From this dream, at least regarding the perfect knowledge, economists were awakened by three American scholars in the early 1970s. Akerlof, Spence and Stiglitz used different approaches to analyze a more realistic economic market: one in which information about the different products is not evenly distributed and either the supply or demand side lack some knowledge about the quality of the products in relation to the price at which they are offered (Akerlof, 1970; Rothschild & Stiglitz, 1976; Spence, 1973).

Let us describe a simple case such as the one discussed by Akerlof (see for example Varian, 1992). Assume that in a market a number of suppliers offer a range of products (Akerlof refers to used cars, but the argument is obviously valid for any product) whose quality can be expressed by a quantity q, with $q \in [0,1]$. If q is uniformly distributed over $[0,1]$, then its expected value is $E(q)=0.5$. A number of buyers are willing to pay a price kq $(k \geq 1)$, and a number of sellers are willing to accept some price: $p(q) \in (kq, q)$. If the consumers cannot fully assess the quality, the consumers would estimate it as having the average quality $\langle q \rangle$ among the products offered on the market, therefore they will be willing to pay a price $p=k\langle q \rangle$. In this situation only sellers whose products are of quality $q \leq p$ will offer them for sale (for the other sellers p is less than their minimum price q). Since quality is uniformly distributed in $[0,p]$, the average quality is $q=p/2<0.5$. Buyers, then, are only prepared to pay $kq=k(p/2)=(k/2)p<p$. Thus, no products will be sold at price p. Since p is chosen arbitrarily, no product is sold at any price $p>0$, and the equilibrium price is $p=0$. In other words demand and supply are zero. Asymmetric information thus destroys the market for the products considered.

The consequences and the possible remedies for this issue have been extensively analyzed by the economic literature (Kirmani & Rao, 2000), and tourism studies are no exception (Calveras & Orfila, 2007; Crase & Jackson, 2000). Less well analyzed, however, is the symmetric but opposite problem: the one in which sellers have less information than buyers. The situation is described by the work of Dari-Mattiacci *et al.* (2010). The authors find that also in this *inverse adverse-selection* setting the market tends to disappear, but it disappears *from the bottom* rather than from the top. In other words, the high-value products (termed *gems*) remain on the market longer than the low-value ones (Akerlof's *lemons*). Table 1 provides a comparison between the two conditions.

Table 1 - Dualities in Information Asymmetric Markets

	Adverse selection (lemons market)	Inverse adverse selection (gems market)
Buyer	Uninformed	Informed
Seller	Informed	Uninformed
Market	Disappears for high-value goods	Disappears for low-value goods
Goods on market	Low-value goods (lemons)	High-value goods (gems)
Buyer's surplus	Zero	Positive
Seller's surplus	Positive	Zero

Source: Adapted from Dari-Mattiacci *et al.*, 2010.

Besides the obvious symmetry, the two problems have different consequences for a market. The main difference, highlighted by the authors, is the fact that while informed sellers could be easily detected: buyers accumulate experience with time and they can try to force sellers to release more information or find ways to protect themselves (for example by asking for warranties), better informed buyers are difficult to identify because their knowledge is private. It is built upon personal experience and it is not possible to force disclosures or to enforce legal protections. In summary, uninformed sellers are at disadvantage with respect to buyers and can be in conditions in which they may never understand they are selling at prices that are too low.

In the lemons case possible circumventions are known: signaling (forcing the seller to communicate the real quality), screening (filtering incorrect information) or legal protections (warranties). In the gems case Dari-Mattiacci *et al.* (2010) find that the only feasible way is to auction the product, leaving competition between buyers to improve the quality/price ratio.

3. Methodology

Agent-based modeling (ABM) is used in this work to simulate the various configurations of a market. Sellers and buyers are characterized by a parameter defining their informational content level. In this way both the classical lemons and the new gems markets can be simulated. The ABM approach allows exploring the structural and dynamic characteristics of systems which may prove difficult to handle with analytical methods, and let the researcher to define even a large set of parameters and vary them with more ease that in the case of analytical methods.

The importance of an agent based model lies in its ability to advance the comprehension of phenomena that are difficult or impossible to handle with analytical methods. Agent based models explain, rather than predict, enhancing a qualitative understanding of the fundamental processes of the system under study (in our case, asymmetric information in tourism systems). As Henrickson and McKelvey (2002, p. 7295) state:

> Future, significant, social science contributions will emerge more quickly if science-based beliefs are based the joint results of both ABMs and subsequent empirical corroboration.

The model presented here is, to the best of our knowledge, a reasonable and valid representation of the information asymmetries existing in the tourism market. Following Taber and Timpone (1996) the model replicates processes well established in the literature concerning information asymmetries (Wen, 2010). The model has been thoroughly tested so as to avoid coding errors and to ensure a good correspondence between the code and the conceptual model (i.e. ensure that the model's behavior is what we, as the modelers, really intend it to be).

From a methodological point of view the results obtained are sound and reliable since care has been taken to consider all the issues related to the use of ABM in the study of social and economic systems, and the software tools employed are stable and verified (Galán *et al.,* 2009; Garson, 2009; Mollona, 2008). The model is built according to the most important methodological specifications and guidelines, [for a discussion on ABM in tourism see Baggio, (2011)].

The model considers N_d suppliers (destinations) and N_t consumers (travelers). At each time-step a traveler chooses his destination based on his expected quality given by the information the traveler has been able to gather and the price set by the destination.

More precisely, a traveler will assess the decision to travel to a specific destination if and only if the price offered by the destination (p_d) is lower than the price a traveler is willing to pay for that specific destination (p_t).

Table 2 - Model parameters

Symbol	Variable Name	Values
N_d	Number of destinations	10
N_t	Number of travelers	100
q_d	Quality of destinations	random uniform $\in [0, 1]$
i_d	Level of information destinations have on themselves	[0, 0.25, 0.5, 0.75, 1]
i_t	Level of information travelers have on destinations	[0, 0.25, 0.5, 0.75, 1]

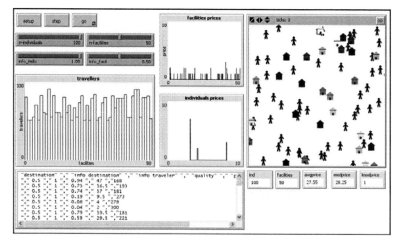

Figure 1. NetLogo model implementation

Prices are computed by weighting the quality by the information available to both destinations and travelers. The quality of the N_d facilities (q_d) is determined at the beginning of every simulation and is randomly distributed in the interval *[0, 1]* (uniformly). The price set by a destination p_d is given by the quality of the destination, weighted by the destination's information level: $p_d = q_d * i_d$, while the price a traveler is willing to pay depends on the perceived quality: $p_t = q_d * i_t$.

At each time-step an individual looks for those destinations that comply with the rule outlined above ($p_d \leq p_t$) and chooses randomly between the suitable destinations. Table 2 summarizes symbols, variables, and parameter values used in the simulation.

Two series of runs were performed. The first one simulates the lemon problem: destinations have complete information about themselves ($i_d = 1$), while travelers' knowledge is limited ($i_t \in [0, 0.25, 0.5, 0.75, 1]$). The second series reverses the situation: travelers have full information while destinations suffer from information asymmetry ($i_t = 1$ and $i_d \in [0, 0.25, 0.5, 0.75, 1]$). Every run (with the same set of controlling parameters) was simulated 100 times for 100 time-steps. At the end the prices and the cumulative number of travelers that chose the different destinations were recorded. The model (Figure 1) was implemented by using the NetLogo simulation environment (Wilensky, 1999). A detailed description of the model is provided in the ODD (Overview, Design concepts, and Details) protocol available as appendix to this chapter. The ODD protocol is a standard tool for describing individual and agent based models (Grimm et al., 2006) implemented with the objective of allowing a deeper understanding of the model and to facilitate replication.

4. Results

The main results of the simulations are depicted in Figure 2. For the two cases examined (lemons and gems) the boxplots represent the cumulative number of travelers who have chosen the different destinations with respect to the real quality levels.

As can be seen, when the information asymmetry affects travelers (lemons), the market shrinks towards low-quality destinations, while the opposite happens when the level of information travelers have on destinations is higher than that destinations have on themselves (gems).

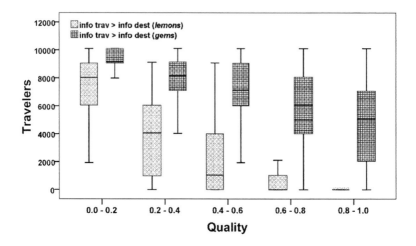

Figure 2. Cumulative number of travelers vs. destination quality for the two cases examined (outliers have been removed for clarity)

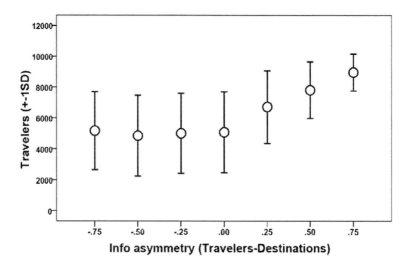

Figure 3. Cumulative number of travelers vs. information asymmetry: i_t - i_d (error bars represent 1 SD)

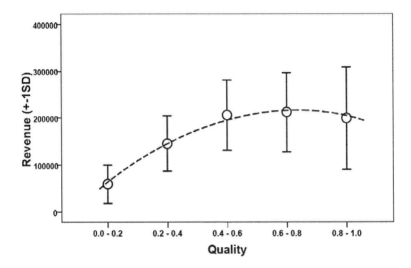

Figure 4. Revenue vs. Quality when travelers are more informed than destinations (error bars represent 1 SD; the dotted line is only intended to guide the eye)

This result is in agreement with the theoretical predictions and testifies to the validity of the model implementation. It is interesting to note then that the difference in information levels significantly affects the size of the market along with the direction of the asymmetry. In fact (Figure 3) as long as the difference in information levels is negative (travelers know less than destinations) the number of travelers is rather constant and starts increasing when travelers begin to be more informed. Furthermore, the dispersion decreases, thus reinforcing the effect.

Considering the price a traveler is willing to pay it is possible to calculate potential revenue for the different destinations when travelers are more informed ($i_t - i_d > 0$). As Figure 4 shows (the dotted line is only intended to guide the eye and does not represent a fit), increasing quality generates growing revenue, but at higher values the growth flattens clearly indicating that destinations are missing out on their capabilities to generate economic revenues.

In conclusion: a negative information asymmetry (travelers less informed) shrinks the marked towards low-quality offers, creating a distortion and, in the long term, risks eliminating all suppliers of high-quality products. On the other hand, positive information asymmetry (travelers are more informed) generates a distortion in the market, with the result that suppliers offering high-quality products cannot fully exploit their capabilities.

The agent-based model presented here is the initial step of a line of research which, in the future, will explore more deeply this phenomenon by better defining (and widening) the set of parameters used, for example by increasing the heterogeneity of agents, modifying the rules for making the rules for making decisions or by adding different types of social structures to the market considered. As Izquierdo and Izquierdo (2007) have shown, in fact, the topology of the set of relationships existing in the social group formed by the buyers can strongly affect the efficiency and the functioning of a market.

Information asymmetries are a natural feature of many markets, tourism included. While in the case of the asymmetries affecting consumers the literature offers a range of possible remedies such as those briefly recalled previously (signaling, screening or legal protections), the reverse case is more difficult to handle. The only *practical* solution seems to be the one of Dari-Mattiacci *et al.* (2010) concerning auctions. However, besides the technical and theoretical peculiarities (Krishna, 2009), this path does not seem to have attracted much of the tourism industry. The few examples known use auctions mainly as a marketing and promotional instrument to raise awareness in case of new products or services.

The real solution to this issue rests in improving the efforts directed to obtain a better and deeper knowledge of the market and the customers' preferences, beliefs and behaviors. Under certain conditions, a buyer can achieve better results by dealing with an individual seller rather than turning to some kind of mass procurement (Manelli & Vincent, 1995). In a sense, this is what happens today when buyers make extensive use of online sources in order to choose the better offer for a specific product or service.

A number of applications are available today that allow tracking of the *sentiment* travelers express on practically every aspect of their journeys providing a wealth of information about features, characteristics, equipments, services offered (e.g. Klout, klout.com; Twitalyzer, www. twitalyzer.com; Radian6, www.radian6.com). These tools can provide an assessment of the perceived value of a product when this is compared to other similar offers in a destination, even beyond the *intrinsic* value of the product itself. Use of these tools, then, seems to be the only practical option for destinations, companies or organization to better communicate with their customers, to make them better aware of the peculiar values of their proposals and to increase the perception of value by the travelers.

Although difficult and still developing, the complex issue of monetizing promotional activities on online social networks has begun to provide some initial guidelines (Clemons, 2009). The literature shows that a good appreciation of the quality of the products offered allows producers to position their products on the market correctly (i.e. with the right price). Low information levels lead to less knowledgeable subjects who, as Rob and Sieben (1992) demonstrate have systematically lower price limits. The clarity of the information provided, and thus an improvement of a continuous bidirectional communication may prove critical for high quality destinations. Thus, as Hu et al. (2000) point out, tourist destinations should not only focus on improving the satisfaction of existing customers, but also on improving the customer's perception of their overall quality. This allows a correct positioning of the destination, especially when increasing information on high quality offers has negligible costs (Daughety & Reinganum, 2008).

5. Conclusion

Information plays a crucial role in any economic matter and we may state that the dynamic laws of an economy stem from some perturbation of the information equilibrium (Hawkins *et al.,* 2010). In particular, when some form of asymmetric information exists, the economic system cannot be explained in terms of rational behavior which should guide the actions of the agents involved in the system. In cases when a difference exists between the information consumers and suppliers have of the products offered on the market, economic agents do not act any more on the basis of a *perfect knowledge* and the theoretical equilibrium in which the allocation of resources is at an optimum is lost.

Tourism has long been characterized as an information asymmetric market in which tourists have lower level of information that their suppliers. However, with the advent of modern technologies, and especially with the wide diffusion of the participative Web 2.0 functionalities, it is not difficult to envisage situations where the information asymmetry is reversed and a traveler is more able to fully value the product offered than the supplier. The phenomenon, in this form, has been rarely addressed by the literature, but can have important consequences for the functioning of the tourism economic system.

In this chapter, we have presented an agent-based model for the study of tourism markets in which information on the products is not evenly distributed between the supply and the demand side. The results presented here have a dual interest. On one side, they demonstrated how a simple agent-based model can describe the classic Akerlof-type market for lemons and show that a relative ignorance of the quality of the products shrinks the market towards low quality offerings.

On the other hand, when consumers, as happens today, have available vast and trusted information about all aspects of the products and services offered, high quality suppliers (destinations, organizations or companies) risk loss of revenues through their inability to fully understand the market value of their offer. Their *gems* are undervalued, more consumers may acquire the products, but the total revenue is lower than the one we could expect in a perfect equilibrium case.

The literature has provided remedies for both configurations. In the lemons case, widely studied, signaling or legal protections are possible solutions. In the gems case a solution is to put in place some auction mechanisms. However, with some exceptions (Fuchs et al., 2011), these have not become a successful practice in tourism. Thus, the only possible practical antidote seems consist of conceiving actions for improving suppliers' ability to effectively communicate their quality to travelers through an efficient and effective use of today's advanced technological capabilities in order to see recognized their efforts with an even pricing.

This work is a first step towards a full valuation of the economic role of information in the tourism sector. Future work will improve the model presented in this chapter by exploring wider and more complex parameter spaces and assessing how different social structures may influence the outcomes discussed here.

Acknowledgements

The authors wish to thank Noel Scott and Michael Schoon for their help while preparing this chapter.

References

Akerlof, G.A. (1970). The market for "Lemons": Quality uncertainty and the market mechanism. *The Quarterly Journal of Economics,* 84(3), 488-500.

Arthur, W.B. (1999). Complexity and the economy. *Science,* 284(5411), 107-109.

Baggio, J. A. (2011). Agent-based modeling and simulations. In R. Baggio & J. Klobas (Eds.), *Quantitative Methods in Tourism: A Handbook* (pp. 199-219). Bristol: Channel View.

Calveras, A., & Orfila, F. (2007). *Intermediaries and Quality Uncertainty: Evidence from the Hotel Industry*. Palma de Mallorca, Spain: Universitat de les Illes Balears. Retrieved February, 2011, from http://ssrn.com/abstract=1009647.

Chen, C.-C., & Schwartz, Z. (2006). The importance of information asymmetry in customers' booking decisions: A cautionary tale from the internet. *Cornell Hospitality Quarterly,* 47(3), 272-285.

Clemons, E.K. (2009). The complex problem of monetizing virtual electronic social networks. *Decision Support Systems,* 48, 46-56.

Cohen, E. (1979). Rethinking the sociology of tourism. *Annals of Tourism Research,* 6(1), 18-35.

Crase, L., & Jackson, J. (2000). Assessing the effects of information asymmetry in tourism destinations. *Tourism Economics,* 6(4), 321-334.

Dari-Mattiacci, G., Onderstal, S., & Parisi, F. (2010). *Inverse Adverse Selection: The Market for Gems*: Amsterdam Center for Law & Economics Working Paper No. 2010-04; Minnesota Legal Studies Research Paper No. 10-47. Retrieved August, 2010, from http://ssrn.com/abstract=1661090.

Daughety, A.F., & Reinganum, J.F. (2008). Communicating quality: a unified model of disclosure and signalling. *RAND Journal of Economics,* 39(4), 973-989.

Fernández-Barcala, M., González-Díaz, M., & Prieto-Rodríguez, J. (2010). Hotel quality appraisal on the Internet: a market for lemons? *Tourism Economics,* 16(2), 345-360.

Foster, J. (2005). From simplistic to complex systems in economics. *Cambridge Journal of Economics,* 29(6), 873-892.

Fuchs, M., Eybl, A., & Höpken, W. (2011). Successfully selling accommodation packages at online auctions – The case of eBay Austria. *Tourism Management*, 32(5), 1166-1175,

Galán, J.M., Izquierdo, L.R., Izquierdo, S.S., Santos, J.I., del Olmo, R., López-Paredes, A., & Edmonds, B. (2009). Errors and Artefacts in Agent-Based Modelling. *Journal of Artificial Societies and Social Simulation,* 12(1), 1.

Garson, G.D. (2009). Computerized simulation in the social sciences: A survey and evaluation. *Simulation and Gaming,* 40(2), 267-279.

Grimm, V., Berger, U., Bastiansen, F., Eliassen, S., Ginot, V., Giske, J., Goss-Custard, J., Grand, T., Heinz, S. K., Huse, G., Huth, A., Jepsen, J. U, Jørgensen, C., Mooij, W. M., Müller, B., Pe'er, G., Piou, C., Railsback, S. F., Robbins, A. M., Robbins, M. M., Rossmanith, E., Rüger, N., Strand, E., Souissi, S., Stillman, R. A., Vabø, R., Visser, U., & DeAngelis, D. L. (2006). A standard protocol for describing individual-based and agent-based models. *Ecological Modeling,* 198(1-2), 115-126.

Hawkins, R.J., Aoki, M., & Frieden, B.R. (2010). Asymmetric information and macroeconomic dynamics. *Physica A,* 389(17), 3565-3571.

Henrickson, L., & McKelvey, B. (2002). Foundations of "new" social science: Institutional legitimacy from philosophy, complexity science, postmodernism, and agent-based modeling. *Proceedings of the Academy of Sciences of the USA, 99*(Suppl 3), 7288-7295.

Hu, (Sunny) H.-H., Kandampully, J., & Juwaheer, T.D. (2009). Relationships and impacts of service quality, perceived value, customer satisfaction, and image: an empirical study'. *The Service Industries Journal,* 29(2), 111-125.

Inversini, A., Cantoni, L., & Buhalis, D. (2009). Destinations' information competition and web reputation. *Information Technology & Tourism,* 11(3), 221-234.

Izquierdo, S.S., & Izquierdo, L.R. (2007). The impact of quality uncertainty without asymmetric information on market efficiency. *Journal of Business Research,* 60(8), 858-867.

Jones, C., & Yu, R. (2010). Travel industry uses Facebook and Twitter to reach customers. *USA Today* (7 July 2010). Retrieved July, 2010, from http://www.usatoday.com/tech/news/2010-09-07-travelsocialmedia07_CV_N.htm.

Kirmani, A., & Rao, A.R. (2000). No pain, no gain: A critical review of the literature on signaling unobservable product quality. *Journal of Marketing,* 64(2), 66-79.

Krishna, V. (2009), *Auction Theory* (2nd Ed.). NY: Academic Press.

Lin, M., Viswanathan, S., & Agarwal, R. (2010). *An Empirical Study of Contractual Relations in Online Software Outsourcing* (Working Paper #10-22). NY: NET Institute, Stern School of Business. Retrieved from http://www.netinst.org/Lin_Viswanathan_Agarwal_10-22.pdf.

Manelli, A.M., & Vincent, D.R. (1995). Optimal procurement mechanisms. *Econometrica*, 63, 591-620.

Mollona, E. (2008). Computer simulation in social sciences. *Journal of Management & Governance,* 12, 205-211.

Rothschild, M., & Stiglitz, J.E. (1976). Equilibrium in competitive insurance markets: An essay on the economics of imperfect information. *The Quarterly Journal of Economics,* 90(4), 629-649.

Schwabe, G., Novak, J., & Aggeler, M. (2008). *Designing the Tourist Agency of the Future.* Paper presented at the 21st Bled eConference, Bled, Slovenia, 15-18 June. Retrieved June, 2010 from http://aisel.aisnet.org/bled2008/42/.

Sirgy, M., Lee, D.-J., & Bae, J. (2006). Developing a measure of Internet well-being: Nomological (predictive) validation. *Social Indicators Research,* 78(2), 205-249.

Smeral, E. (1993). Aspects to justify public tourism promotion: An economic perspective. *Tourism Review,* 61(3), 6-14.

Soros, G. (1987). *The Alchemy of Finance: Reading the Mind of the Market.* NY: Wiley.

Spence, M. (1973). Job market signaling. *The Quarterly Journal of Economics,* 87(3), 355-374.

Rao, A.R., & Sieben, W.A. (1992). The effect of prior knowledge on price acceptability and the type of information examined. *The Journal of Consumer Research,* 19(2), 256-270.

Taber, C.S., & Timpone, R.J. (1996). *Computational Modeling.* London: Sage.

Varian, H.R. (1992). *Microeconomic Analysis* (3rd Ed.). NY: W.W. Norton.

Wen, J. (2010). *Essays on Adverse Selection and Moral Hazard in Insurance Market.* Risk Management and Insurance Dissertations, Paper 25 (http://digitalarchive.gsu.edu/rmi_diss/25). Atlanta: Georgia State University

Werthner, H., & Klein, S. (1999). *Information technology and tourism - a challenging relationship.* Wien: Springer.

Wilensky, U. (1999). NetLogo. http://ccl.northwestern.edu/netlogo. Evanston, IL: Center for Connected Learning and Computer-Based Modeling. Northwestern University.

Xiang, Z., & Gretzel, U. (2010). Role of social media in online travel information search. *Tourism Management,* 31(2), 179-188.

Zehrer, A., Crotts, J.C., & Magnini, V.P. (2010). The perceived usefulness of blog postings: An extension of the expectancy-disconfirmation paradigm. *Tourism Management,* (in press).

Zhang, L., Pan, B., Smith, W., & Li, X. (2009). Travelers' use of online reviews and recommendations: A qualitative study. *Information Technology and Tourism,* 11(2), 157-167.

Appendix: ODD Protocol

Purpose

To explore the effects of asymmetric information regarding the tourism system. Here two main cases are examined: one in which sellers have more information than buyers (the classic market for lemon of Akerloff, 1970), and one in which buyers have more information than the sellers (the market for gems described in Dari-Mattiacci et al., 2010).

State Variables and Scale

The model comprises $N_d = 10$ suppliers (i.e. tourist destinations) and $N_t = 100$ consumers (travelers). Each destination is able to provide a determined quality q_d and to set a price given the information i_d she has about herself. Each traveler expects a determined quality given the information i_t she has about a destination and is willing to pay a certain price for a specific level of expected quality. Both, destinations and travelers use the amount of information they have in order to make more (or less) informed decisions regarding, respectively, prices and willingness to pay.

Process, Overview and Scheduling

Each traveler has a specific amount of information on the different destinations (all travelers are able to gather the same amount of information), and given the information available, each traveler expects a certain quality from a destination. Each destination has information on herself and sets the price according to this information and her quality. At each time-step, travelers decide to travel to a destination if and only if the price they are willing to pay is lower or equal to the price set by the destination. Quality of destinations are randomly assigned according to a random-uniform distribution $\in[0, 1]$. Figure A1 represents diagrammatically the process described.

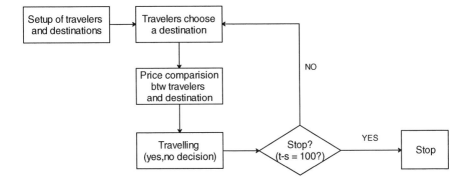

Figure A1 Diagram representing the model process

Design Concepts
Emergence: Number of travelers per destination.

Interaction: Travelers and destinations interactions are based on information and consequently on expected quality, actual quality and prices.

Stochasticity: Quality of destination is random-uniformly distributed. Travelers chose randomly a potential destination at every time-step.

Output: At the end of each run, the following output is.
- Quality of the destinations
- Level of traveler information
- Level of destination information
- Number of travelers per destination (computed as the sum of travelers to a specific destination during the simulation run)

Initialization
Two different initialization procedures are set. In the first one, representing the market for lemons, travelers and destinations are initialized according to variables and values reported in Table A1. However, $i_d = 1$ (destinations have perfect information) while i_t varies as reported in Table A1. In the second initialization, representing the market for gems, $i_t = 1$ (travelers have perfect information) while t_d varies according as reported in Table A1. Every initialization (run) is repeated 100 times. Each run lasts 100 time-steps.

Input

Table A1 Input data: symbols, variable descriptions and values used

Symbol	Variable Name	Values
N_d	Number of destinations	10
N_t	Number of travelers	100
q_d	Quality of destinations	random uniform $\in [0, 1]$
i_d	Level of information destinations have on themselves	[0, 0.25, 0.5, 0.75, 1]
i_t	Level of information travelers have on destinations	[0, 0.25, 0.5, 0.75, 1]

Submodels

Price determination:
Prices are computed by weighting the quality of the destination by the information available to travelers and destinations:

$p_{di} = q_{di} * i_d$
$p_{ti,dj} = q_{dj} * i_t$

where:
p_{di} = price of destination i; q_{di} = quality of destination i; i_d = information level of destinations, and $p_{ti,dj}$ = price traveler i is willing to pay to visit destination j; q_{dj} = quality of destination j; i_t = information level of travelers

Travel choice:
Traveler i will actually travel to destination j if and only if the price the traveler is willing to pay is smaller or equal to the price set by the chosen destination:

$p_{dj} \leq p_{ti,dj}$

Implementation
Netlogo 4.1.3 (Code available upon request from the authors and online at: www.OpenAbm.org)

CHAPTER TEN

MAINTAINING THE REPUTATION OF REVIEW SITES IN TRAVEL AND TOURISM

BRITA SCHEMMANN AND ERIC HORSTER

Abstract

Consumer generated reviews of travel and tourism products are an important source of information within the consumer's decision-making process as they help to reduce uncertainty before purchasing a tourism product. The impact of online reviews in travel and tourism has been widely assessed in the last few years, but not much attention has been paid to the control mechanisms used by the review sites. Based on the source of control, this chapter describes four different types, and two sub-types, of travel and tourism-related review sites which are derived from an analysis of 59 German language websites containing travel and tourism-related consumer reviews. In addition, three different control mechanisms used by these sites to avoid fake entries—and therefore maintain the reputation of the sites—are described and analysed. **Keywords:** Online reputation management (ORM), eWOM, word of mouth marketing, social media, consumer-generated reviews.

1. Introduction

According to the 2009 Nielsen Global Online Consumer Survey involving over 25,000 respondents from 50 different countries, seven out of every ten Internet users trust consumer opinions and peer recommendations posted online (The Nielsen Company, 2009). Recent studies from Germany provide further insights into the travel and tourism sector. A study carried out in 2008 in different German cities showed that 60 per cent of all respondents have experience of reading online consumer reviews. The survey also discovered that online reviews on holiday accommodation was the most frequently used source of information, followed by travel guides, travel agents' recommendations, and hotel rating systems (Sidali, Schulze, & Spiller, 2009). This seems to be in line with the results of a survey carried out by Trivago (2009), an online travel platform, which shows that for German consumers online peer reviews of hotels are among the most common reasons for making a booking decision. On the other hand, the German hotel industry has begun to respond to this trend: more than 50 per cent of German hotels already monitor what customers write online about their services (Regele, 2009).

These studies underline the increasing importance of online consumer communication and take word-of-mouth communication (WOM) to a new era. Consumer WOM can be defined as follows:

> […] informal communications directed at other consumers about the ownership, usage, or characteristics of particular goods and services and/or their sellers (Westbrook, 1987, p.261).

The positive effects of WOM on marketing and distribution have been widely assessed (Bayus, 1985; Beck, 2007; Hogan, Lemon, & Libai, 2004). The Internet and so-called Web 2.0 applications in particular enable users to produce or receive electronic word of mouth (eWOM). This leads to the following assumption:

> Customer comments articulated via the Internet are available to a vast number of customers, and therefore can be expected to have a significant impact on the success of goods and services (Hennig-Thurau & Walsh, 2004, p. 51).

Due to the nature of the Internet, such consumer comments and reviews are archived and therefore available to other (potential) consumers for a long period of time, and can also be accessed globally (Kilian, Walsh, & Zenz, 2008). Tourism-related consumer review sites, such as Tripadvisor or Holidaycheck, very much depend on their reputation—based on the reliability of eWOM. This reliability has recently suffered some negative publicity (Spielberger, Schöpe, & Chehimi, 2009; Stiftung Warentest, 2010). Stiftung Warentest, a credible and popular product testing institution in Germany, tested 13 different travel review sites and discovered that only two of them identified the manipulated entries made by the testing institution. In addition to the survey, incidents have been published about customers who tried to blackmail hotels by threatening the staff that they would write negative online reviews if they did not receive a discount or additional services (Dube, 2009). This can eventually lead to these review platforms' loss of reputation. Tourism-related review sites must therefore implement a sustainable and effective control system to protect themselves from fake entries. Only when consumers see a review platform as trustworthy can the platform maintain its own reputation and relevance to both the tourism industry and the customer. However, the reputation management and different forms of control used by these review sites have not received much scientific attention so far.

2. Measuring and Managing Reputation

Regarding the conceptualization, definition and measurement of reputation, there is considerable dissent among the various scientific disciplines. Fombrun (2007) identifies a total of 183 research approaches in 38 countries to measure reputation (Fombrun, 2007). What reputation measurement methods have in common is that they cover *who* (in this case the customer) credits *whom* (in this case a tourism company) with *which* kind of reputation (Liehr, Peters, & Zerfaß, 2009).

The new networking possibilities of the Internet have an impact on the information flow in the tourist business and run parallel to changes in media utilisation (Buhalis & Egger, 2006). The reputation of the providers of tourism products has been particularly affected by this development. Across the different disciplines, reputation has been acknowledged to be the result of communication processes. Reputation will not necessarily derive from direct experience, but it will additionally be influenced through social interaction. At its core, reputation is thus the diffusion of information exchanged by actors within a social network (Einwiller & Schmid, 2003). Accordingly, reputation-making includes the dissemination and acknowledgement of user-generated reviews. It is important to keep in mind that reputation may be a conveyed, second-hand acknowledgement, which thus transcends personal contact networks (Eisenegger, 2005). Reputation has a public application area and is the result of interaction processes. It is therefore created within the dialogue between customers and highly related to word-of-mouth communication. Through this exchange the individual attitudes of the users are negotiated. Service providers thus have to face the potential and ubiquitous danger of losing their good reputation through negative reviews (Einwiller & Schmid, 2003).

Within the context of the Social Web, reputation management in tourism means determining who will influence the reputation of the service providers, in which areas, and through which factors. In order to maintain the reputation of being a credible source of information, the control of entries is important. Depending on the source of control,

Hennig-Thurau (2004) divided online consumer articulation into three types: consumer, company and third-party controlled types:

Consumer-controlled consumer articulation: Here, the consumers publish their personal opinions and product reviews on a website entirely controlled by the consumers themselves. This type of consumer articulation can often be found in so-called boycott-sites, where consumers express their negative experiences with certain companies, products, and services, such as the blog ihatedell.net that deals with quality and service problems of the computer company DELL (Steinmann & Ramseier, 2008), and on the other hand, so-called fan-sites, where consumers articulate their extreme satisfaction with a product, service, or company (Hennig-Thurau, 2004).

Company-controlled consumer articulation: In this case, a company offers its customers an online platform to articulate their opinions and reviews on the company's products and services. Often consumer chats, virtual guest books, or discussion forums are used to encourage customers to express their opinions and give feedback. The company itself controls the way consumer articulation is made public (ibid.). Many companies invested in developing company-owned blogs and virtual communities in order to offer consumers a platform to network with the company and other consumers and to articulate themselves. Successful examples of company-controlled consumer articulation have been created by the service industry (such as Southwest Airlines) and producers of consumer products (such as Frosta) alike.

Third-party controlled consumer articulation: According to Hennig-Thurau and Walsh (2004), this third type of consumer articulation is published on platforms neither controlled by the consumers, nor by the company. Instead, a third party offers a *virtual opinion platform*—sometimes also called *consumer portals*—where consumers can articulate their opinions on a wide variety of products and services. Examples for widely used virtual opinion platforms in Germany are ciao.de and dooyoo.de. Such platforms enable consumers to interact with each other and publish opinions regarding companies and products (Gay, Charlesworth, & Esen, 2007).

This leads to the research questions of this paper: Does the classification of Hennig-Thurau also apply to travel and tourism-related review sites? How can sites which contain tourism-related reviews be classified regarding their source of control? In addition, we need to ask what these sites do in order to keep their reputation for containing credible and trustworthy information about travel and tourism products, such as hotels, airlines, cruises, or holiday homes.

3. An Analysis from a German Consumer Perspective

International tourism revenues reached US$852 billion (€611 billion) in 2009. The ranking by international tourism spenders is led by Germany, followed by the USA and the UK (World Tourism Organization, 2010). Due to the impact of German travellers and tourists on the international tourism industry, an analysis of German-language Web 2.0 sources containing consumer-generated reviews dealing with travel and tourism services was carried out in March and April 2010. Google.de, currently the most commonly used search engine in Germany (Kolokythas, 2010), was used to search the Web with five frequently used keywords with regard to travel and tourism services: *Hotels* (hotels), *Pauschalreisen* (package holidays), *Reisen* (travel), *Ferienhäuser* (holiday homes) and *Kreuzfahrten* (cruises). In addition, the word *Bewertung* (review) was combined with ten common travel and tourism service keywords: *Hotelbewertungen* (hotel reviews), *Reisebewertungen* (travel reviews), *Bewertungen Airlines* (airline reviews), *Bewertungen Ferienwohnungen* (holiday homes reviews), *Bewertungen Fluggesellschaften* (air carrier reviews), *Bewertungen Hotels* (hotel reviews), *Kreuzfahrten Bewertungen* (cruise reviews), *Reiseveranstalter Bewertungen* (tour operator reviews), *Schiffsbewertungen* (ship reviews), *Bewertungsportale Reisen* (travel review platforms). For each of the keywords or keyword combinations, the top ten findings were used for further analysis.

Out of the 150 findings in total, 108 offered some kind of consumer-generated reviews on a travel and tourism service, such as hotels, cruises, holiday homes, or airline services. As many of the sources were not only found once but appeared several times under different keywords, 59 websites containing consumer reviews were extracted. The amount of sources found indicates that German consumers are therefore very likely to be confronted with consumer reviews when searching the Internet for information about travel and tourism services, or when specifically looking for reviews and evaluations. This outcome is in line with the findings of Xiang and Gretzel (2010) who recently examined the role of social media, including consumer review sites, in online information search. The 59 findings containing reviews were further analysed with regard to the types of control and control mechanisms used.

4. Types of Control in Travel and Tourism-related Consumer Articulation

All three types of control can be found within the 59 findings, and an additional type of consumer articulation can be defined. At first sight, this *consumer articulation controlled by booking platforms* seems to be similar to the *third-party controlled consumer articulation* as described by Hennig-Thurau and Walsh (2004). But the purpose of such platforms is different from *consumer portals*, so they cannot therefore be included. In travel and tourism, consumers often do not book the services needed (such as flights, hotel rooms, holiday homes, cruises) directly with the service provider (such as airline, hotel, holiday home operator, and cruise company). Instead, booking and reservation platforms act as an intermediator between the consumer and the actual service provider. These booking platforms, which can increasingly be seen as an integral part of today's tourism sales processes (Sonntag & Aderhold, 2010), also encourage their customers to articulate themselves regarding the services (i.e. hotels, holiday homes, cruises) booked via their platform. In contrast to the independent third-party controlled virtual opinion platforms mentioned in the model above, these booking platforms have a strong connection to the products and services evaluated by consumers, although they are not the ones who supply these services. The service providers (such as hotels, airlines, and cruise companies) cannot, however, control consumer articulation on these platforms. Here, the difference with company-controlled consumer articulation becomes apparent. Based on the 59 findings, the following four different types, including two sub-types, are suggested for travel and tourism-related review sites:

Consumer-controlled consumer articulation (one finding): independent, consumer-controlled, consumer review platform with a clear focus on independent reviews and no apparent commercial use or benefits.

Company-controlled consumer articulation (five findings): company websites containing consumer reviews on the company's own products and services.

Third-party controlled consumer articulation: virtual opinion platforms with a clear focus on consumer reviews and evaluation—distribution of products and services is a subordinate aim, if at all.

- Virtual opinion platforms specialised in travel and tourism-related services (22 findings).

- Virtual opinion platforms offering reviews dealing with a wide range of goods and services, including travel and tourism-related services (three findings).

Consumer articulations on travel and tourism-related booking/reservation platforms (28 findings): the main focus lies on sales and distribution. Consumer-related recommendations are more of a side-product of these platforms—some booking or reservation platforms distribute the services of one provider, other platforms distribute the services of several providers.

The majority of sources found during the Web search are virtual opinion platforms (25 sources) and booking platforms (28 sources). The majority of consumer articulation is thus not controlled by the ones responsible for the development, production, or operation of the service (i.e. hotels, cruise companies, airlines). Instead, it is controlled by a third party who is often directly involved in the distribution process. On the one hand, such platforms have an interest in attracting large numbers of consumer-generated reviews, and on the other hand, their reputation is directly linked to the trustworthiness of the reviews and reviewers.

5. Control Mechanisms to Maintain Credibility of Entries

To prevent fake or false entries and therefore maintain their reputation, the sources analysed make use of very different control mechanisms, which can be described as follows.

Only registered users can write reviews. Users who want to write a review have to either register or identify themselves with a valid email address. This is a fairly limited control mechanism as a valid email address does not say much about the reviewer. There is no proof that the reviewer has really used the service evaluated. On the other hand, this might be a barrier for some genuine reviewers who could be put off from writing a review as they fear junk mail or other consequences from mentioning their email address.

Only actual customers of the respective service can write reviews. Users who want to write a review need to be customers of the relevant platform and can only write reviews about the services they have booked. Usually, customers receive an email after they stayed at the hotel. This email contains a link which customers can use in order to write a review. This control mechanism is fairly sophisticated and makes it much harder to publish fake reviews. Such a control mechanism can, however, only be used for services that include some kind of previous booking processes (i.e. hotel or airline booking). It is hard to imagine how such a control mechanism could be extended to other services, such as restaurants, which do not require the same high-level booking services. In addition, such a mechanism is only an option for platforms offering some kind of booking or reservation service.

Reviews are checked with regard to their credibility before they are published. Some platforms mention that reviews will be verified regarding their credibility before they are published. Bearing in mind the large number of reviews added every day (some platforms receive several hundred per day), it is questionable how such inspections can be carried out in an efficient, and yet effective, manner. The results of the tests mentioned above show that most platforms are not very successful in discovering fake reviews. In addition, censorship is a very sensitive topic in social media. There is a risk of putting review writers off, as they might fear that such approval systems prior to publication could be misused for censorship.

In addition to the mechanisms mentioned above, it is very likely that these review sites will also use technical control mechanisms such as checking IP addresses to avoid double entries for one product, or monitoring abnormal numbers or entries to avoid spam or semantic analysis of content (Brauck, 2010). Holidaycheck, for example, recently introduced a 'manipulation seal' that punishes hotels which tried to produce fake entries (Horster, 2011). As such mechanisms cannot be detected by the method used in this analysis, this is a topic for future research.

6. Conclusion

Based on the different types of online consumer articulation described by Hennig-Thurau (2004), this chapter presented an analysis of 59 travel and tourism-related review sites. With reference to the sources of control four different types, including two sub-types, were suggested and described. Three different control mechanisms to avoid fake entries were analysed and described. The first two of the three mechanisms focus on identifying the reviewer as an attempt to prevent anonymous hate or praise reviews. Based on the assumption that "anonymity may help people to speak the truth, but it doesn't help me to trust them" (Levine, 2009, p. 29), these control mechanisms hope to generate trustworthy reviews and therefore maintain the reputation of the site.

However, both of the two mechanisms have their limitations. The first one only leads to a questionable form of identification as a valid email address is not a reliable source of identification. The second control mechanism described can only be used for services that include some kind of previous booking process. It is therefore only an option for sites which act as an intermediator and have a large number of customers. As both of these mechanisms have severe limitations, review sites must find alternative ways to link entries and identities. There are different possible and feasible solutions to this problem which are interesting themes for future research. Recent innovations, such as Facebook Connect or Twitter Connect, can solve the issue of the missing link between the identity of the author and the generated content. Many websites already take advantage of the possibility of connecting their own site with a social network (such as Facebook). This leads to a login process via Facebook or Twitter Connect. In this way, each review is directly linked to the respective Facebook or Twitter account—a simple but effective control mechanism which could even be an option for small and medium-sized companies. This solution enables the reader to see a review in context, as the review is also linked to the personal data of the reviewer. In addition, the identity of the review writer is traceable, which could reduce the number of attempts to submit fake entries.

A recent development by Google is likely to have an impact on review sites: Google changed its search algorithm in November 2010 and by default now shows local providers (Local Search) at the top of their result page when the search term has a regional reference. In addition, reviews can be written directly on the Google Places Profiles of the service providers. In this case, the review writer must be registered with a Google ID. In addition Google recently launched its own hotel finder. At the same time, reviews from other review sites such as TripAdvisor are no longer integrated in the Google Places profiles. As these profiles receive top ranking positions, this could reduce the importance of specialised review sites unless these sites manage to offer additional benefits to the user. If these technologies become "state of the art", review sites offering anonymous entries could be under pressure—regardless of the control mechanisms they use.

In addition, there are community-building trends within recommendation sites. Tripadvisor and Facebook have launched a new feature called "Trip Friends". This social plug-in allows sharing recommendations on travel destinations with friends on Facebook (Bly, 2010). Therefore, reviews and recommendations will no longer come from strangers, but from friends and people one knows. Further research will have to analyse the diffusion and effects of these developments and innovations, the adoption by the users as well as the impact on reviews and review sites.

References

Bayus, B. L. (1985). Word of mouth: The indirect effect of marketing efforts. *Journal of Advertising Research, 25*(3), 31-39.

Beck, J. (2007). The sales effect of word of mouth: A model for creative goods and estimates for novels. *Journal of Cultural Economics, 31*(1), 5-23.

Bly, L. (2010). *Tripadvisor lets users tap Facebook friends for advice.* USA Today Travel. Retrieved May 2011 from: http://travel.usatoday.com/destinations/dispatches/post/2010/06/tripadv isor-taps-facebook-friends-for-advice/96568/1

Brauck, M. (2010). *Die kritische Masse.* Der Spiegel. Retrieved May 2011 from: http://www.spiegel.de/spiegel/print/d-74184603.html

Buhalis, D., & Egger, R. (2006). Informations- und Kommunikations-technologien als Mittel zur Prozess- und Produktinnovation für den Unternehmer. In B. Pikkemaat, M. Peters, K. Weiermair (Eds.), *Innovationen im Tourismus. Wettbewerbsvorteile durch neue Ideen und Angebote* (pp. 163-176). Berlin: Erich Schmidt.

Dube, J. (2009). *Gute Noten nur gegen Rabatt.* Der Spiegel. Retrieved April 2011 from: http://www.spiegel.de/reise/aktuell/0,1518,610738,00.html

Einwiller, S., & Schmid, B. (2003). *Vertrauen durch Reputation im elektronischen Handel.* Berlin: Gabler.

Eisenegger, M. (2005): *Reputation in der Mediengesellschaft. Konstitution, Issues Monitoring, Issues Management* (Diss.). Wiesbaden: Verlag für Sozialwissenschaften.

Fombrun, C.J. (2007). List of lists. A compilation of international corporate reputation ratings. *Corporate Reputation Review, 10*(2), 144-153.

Gay, R., Charlesworth, A., & Esen, R. (2007). *Online marketing—a customer-led approach.* NY: Oxford University Press.

Hennig-Thurau, T. (2004). Motive des Lesens von Kundenartikulationen im Internet: Theoretische und empirische Analyse. In G. Walsh (Ed.), *Konsumentenverhalten im Internet: Konzepte, Erfahrungen, Methoden* (pp. 171-193). Wiesbaden: Gabler.

Hennig-Thurau, T., & Walsh, G. (2004). Electronic word-of-mouth: Motives for and consequences of reading customer articulations on the internet. *International Journal of Electronic Commerce, 8*(2), 51-74.

Hogan, J. E., Lemon, K. N., & Libai, B. (2004). Quantifying the ripple: Word-of-mouth and advertising effectiveness. *Journal of Advertising Research, 44*(3), 271-280.

Horster, E. (2011). *Die Reputation der Reputation: Holidaycheck geht gegen gefälschte Bewertungen vor.* Retrieved January 2012, from: http://www.eric-horster.de/2011/11/die-reputation-der-reputation-holidaycheck-geht-gegen-gefalschte-bewertungen-vor/

Kilian, T., Walsh, G., & Zenz, R. (2008). Word-of-Mouth im Web 2.0 am Beispiel von Kinofilmen. In T. Kilian (Ed.), *Web 2.0. Neue Perspektiven für Marketing und Medien* (pp. 321-338). Berlin: Springer.

Kolokythas, P. (2010). *Aktuelle Marktanteile von OS, Browser & Suchmaschinen.* PC-WELT.DE. Retrieved April 2010, from: http://www.pcwelt.de/start/software_os/windows/news/2341344/aktuelle-marktanteile-von-os-browser-suchmaschinen/

Levine, R. (2009). But how does it taste? In R. Levine, C. Locke, D. Searls, D. Weinberger (Eds.), *The cluetrain manifesto* (pp. 23-36). (10th anniversary edition). NY: Basic Books.

Liehr, K., Peters, P., & Zerfaß, A. (2009). *Reputationsmessung. Grundlagen und Verfahren.* DPRG; Universität Leipzig. Retrieved August 2010, from: http://www.communicationcontrolling.de /fileadmin/communicationcontrolling/pdf-dossiers/communication controllingde_Dossier1_Reputationsmessung_April2009_o.pdf

Regele, U. (2009). *DIHK-Saisonumfrage: Erwartungen an die Wintersaison 2009/10, Bilanz der Sommersaison 2009* (Survey). Berlin/Brüssel: Deutscher Industrie- und Handelskammertag e.V.

Sidali, K. L., Schulze, H., & Spiller, A. (2009). The impact of online reviews on the choice of holiday accommodations. *Paper presented at the ENTER 2009.* Amsterdam, The Netherlands.

Sonntag, U., & Aderhold, P. (2010). *ReiseAnalyse 2010: Erste Ergebnisse ITB 2010.* FUR Forschungsgemeinschaft Urlaub und Reisen e.V. Retrieved March 2010, from: http://www.fur.de/fileadmin/user_upload/RA_Zentrale_Ergebnisse/FU R_Reiseanalyse_RA2010_Erste_Ergebnisse.pdf

Spielberger, M., Schöpe, S., & Chehimi, N. (2009). Die besten Seiten für Hotel-Detektive. *Urlaubperfekt, 1,* 60-63.

Steinmann, C., & Ramseier, T. (2008). Community und Marke: Die Bedeutung von Communities im postmodernen Markenmanagement. In C. Steinmann (Ed.), *Community Marketing. Wie Unternehmen in sozialen Netzwerken Werte schaffen* (pp. 33-51). Stuttgart: Schäffer-Poeschel Verlag.

Stiftung Warentest (2010). Jeder ein Tester. *Test, 2,* 76-79.

The Nielsen Company (2009). *News release: Personal recommendations and consumer opinions posted online are the most trusted form of*

advertising globally. The Nielsen Company. Retrieved March 2010, from:
http://uk.acnielsen.com/site/documents/TheNielsenCompanyRevealsth
eMostTrustedFormsofAdvertisingAcrosstheWorld.pdf

Trivago (2009). *Hotelbuchungen 2009: Die Deutschen sind Schnäppchen-Jäger.* trivago.de. Retrieved March 2010, from:
http://imgpe.trivago.com/contentimages/press/texts/pm_hotelbuchung.
pdf

Westbrook, R. A. (1987). Product/consumption-based affective responses and postpurchase processes. *Journal of Marketing Research,* 24(3), 258-270.

World Tourism Organization (2010). *UNWTO World Tourism Barometer.* World Tourism Organization. Retrieved July 2010, from:
http://unwto.org/facts/eng/pdf/barometer/UNWTO_Barom10_2_en_ex
cerpt.pdf

Xiang, Z., & Gretzel, U. (2010). Role of social media in online travel information search. *Tourism Management,* 31(2), 179-188.

PART 5:

INNOVATION AND COMPETITIVENESS

Chapter Eleven

Innovation Orientation and Performance in Hotels in Spain

Sara Campo, Ana M. Díaz Martín and María J. Yagüe

Abstract

The current research has two main objectives. First, the study analyzes the effect of the innovation investment made by hotels in Spain on their performance. Second, it aims to explore the influence of perceived market technological turbulence and contextual variables on the innovation-performance relationship. The results obtained confirm that innovation has a positive effect on hotel performance. Perceived technological turbulence does not act as a moderator variable of this relationship, but it does have a direct and positive effect on hotel performance. The influence of the perception about the crisis and firm age on performance is negative and significant, whereas the effect of belonging to a chain is not significant.
Keywords: Innovation orientation, technological turbulence, performance, hotel innovation.

1. Introduction

Traditionally, tourist services and especially hotels have been seen as low innovative firms operating in a context characterized by low technological turbulence. However, with the development of ICTs (mainly the Internet and e-commerce), which has affected all business sectors and particularly hotels, the view that tourism-related services being technologically backward, with innovation playing only a marginal role on performance, has begun to change.

In this sense, hotel managers have realized that present day tourists have little in common with tourists of previous decade, especially regarding their knowledge and use of information and communication technologies. They play an active role when searching for information about tourist destinies on the Internet and they compare an ample number of alternatives before making a decision. Moreover, the information provided by hotels and their commercial policies are no longer the only data taken into account by tourists when choosing an accommodation. Before making up their minds, tourists can now consult new types of data generated by other tourists and seek their advice through blogs, discussion boards, forums, user groups and other social media platforms. In fact, customers place more trust in consumer-generated media than they do in traditional marketers and advertisers (Blackshaw & Nazzaro, 2006).

On the other hand, the world-wide economic crisis has seriously affected the competitiveness of Spain's hotel sector: it has sparked a reduction in average prices and has increased the pressure on cost control, including investments in innovation and technological improvements.

This work aims to understand how all these changes have occurred, from the hotel managers' viewpoint, and analyze whether this perception has a moderating effect on the relationship between innovation and business performance. Researching these issues is important for several reasons. First, innovation has clearly become a critical factor, not only for company survival, but also for growth and the fight against increasing competition and environmental uncertainty (Han *et al.,* 1998). Second, a large body of literature has already explored the link between innovation and performance, but empirical studies researching the innovation-performance relationship do not reach conclusive results (in some cases, they are even contradictory). Finally, there is little empirical evidence on this topic in the service sector (Cainelli *et al.,* 2004), since most existing studies have focused on manufacturing firms, and few works have analyzed the moderating effect of environmental variables.

This research seeks to extend previous findings by empirically analyzing the impact that innovation orientation has on performance in services and to what extent this relationship is moderated by the technological turbulence perceived by hotel managers.

In the next section, we review the literature on service innovation and performance to set out the main relationships of the present research work. Then, we present the methodology of the study carried out, a description of the data collection process and the techniques used in the empirical analysis. Finally, we discuss the results obtained, the study's implications, its limitations and future lines of research.

2. Literature Review

As already mentioned, empirical studies researching the relationship between innovation and company performance fails to reach conclusive results (for an extensive review, see Rosenbusch *et al.,* 2010). Results found in the literature are mixed and even contradictory.

On one hand, Birley & Westhead (1990), Jaworski & Kohli (1993) and Heunks, (1998) find no significant relationship between innovation and company performance. Other researchers report a negative impact of innovation on performance (McGee *et al.*, 1995; Vermeulen *et al.,* 2005). In service firms, the implementation of innovation and their impact on company performance is usually shorter than in other manufacturing sectors and this could be the reason for the non-significant and negative results found in the literature.

On the contrary, Han *et al.* (1998), Li & Atuahene-Gima, (2001, 2002), Matsuno *et al.* (2002), Gunday *et al.,* (2008) and Chen *et al.* (2009) conclude that the effect is positive. More precisely, Matsuno *et al.* (2002) state that the degree of innovation within a firm is an indicator of its entrepreneurial proclivity, and that this, in turn, has a direct and positive effect on company performance.

Additionally, Han *et al.* (1998) verified that the innovation-performance relationship was stronger in turbulent environments and the explanation given by these authors for the mixed results found in literature is based on the sector analyzed.

In the tourism industry, innovation research is a young phenomenon and there is very limited empirical knowledge about the effects of innovation action in tourism enterprises (Hjalager, 2010). Specifically, in the hotel sector Agarwall *et al.* (2003) show that innovation mediates the relationship between market orientation and company performance, as already demonstrated for other services (Han *et al.*, 1998; Sheelagh *et al.,* 2002). These authors found that hotel managers' perceptions about performance, as well as the objective data about chain performance, are positive and significantly influenced by innovation. Likewise, market orientation only has a positive effect on real performance in the presence of innovation activities. Victorino *et al.* (2005) also verified that innovative hotels gain a competitive edge and subsequent customer preference.

Based on the previous comments, and given that innovation is, for hotels, one of the principal means of gaining an advantage in a highly competitive and turbulent environment, we hypothesize that:

H1: Innovation has a positive and direct effect on hotel performance.

Moreover, according to Gunday *et al*. (2008), innovation directly affects economic and marketing performance (H1a), and these contribute to increased financial performance (H1b). In the short term, innovation allows the firm to improve customer satisfaction and perceived value, and achieve better economic performance (increased sales, market share, etc.). In the long term, innovation has an indirect effect on financial performance through economic and marketing performance.

2.1. Moderators of the innovation-performance relationship

The moderating role of the environment, and more specifically of variables such as competitive hostility or market turbulence, has already been taken into account in studies on the relationship between market orientation and business performance (Subramain & Gopalakrishna 2001). According to these, the omission of the various environment variables in this type of research can lead to non-significant results for studies carried out in different contexts. However, few studies have analyzed the moderating effect of the technological and competitive environment on the relationship between innovation orientation and organizational performance (Deshpandé *et al.,* 1993; Matsuno *et al.*, 2002) and their results are inconclusive.

According to Han *et al*. (1998), the positive relationship between innovation and performance is stronger for companies operating in more turbulent markets. The underlying argument is that innovation is crucial for companies facing a certain degree of uncertainty because of the market setting or market turbulence (Ettlie & Puentes, 1982; Han *et al.,* 1998).

Damanpour & Evan (1984) (cited by Han et al, 1998) propose that organizations are able to cope with market uncertainty through technical and administrative changes in their organizational structure, and thus improve the achievement of objectives and performance. Nevertheless, Han *et al.* (1998) contradict the conclusions reached by the seminal research by Jaworski & Kohli (1993) who failed to obtain a significant effect of technological turbulence, or those of Slater & Narver (1994) who found that technological turbulence negatively moderates the market orientation-performance relationship. Taking into account the aforementioned studies, the second hypothesis is:

H2: The technological turbulence of the environment moderates the relationship between innovation and performance.

Consequently, as we propose in the model depicted in Figure 1, the innovation-performance relationship is stronger when managers perceive environments as highly turbulent.

Figure 1. Proposed Model

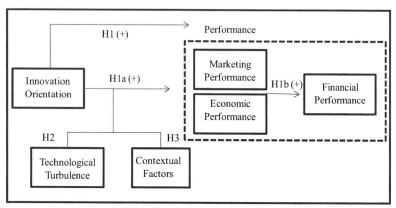

Previous studies also suggest that the innovation-performance relationship is moderated by contextual factors (Li & Atuahene-Gima, 2001) that act as control variables (H3). According to Rosenbusch *et al.* (2010), potential moderators include company and company-environment specific factors, such as company age and culture. They argue that new firms can be expected to be more flexible and agile than established firms, while older firms benefit from the specialization of their resources. However, specialization comes at the cost of more limited flexibility. Thus, they propose that new ventures benefit more from innovation than mature firms do. This leads us to posit that:

H3a: The positive impact of innovation on business performance is stronger in newer hotels that in older hotels.

Secondly, belonging to a hotel chain or not may also affect the innovative propensity of hotels and their performance, since it acts as a stimulus for investment and a protection against market volatility (Hjalager, 2010). In this sense, we expect that:

H3b: The positive impact of innovation on performance is stronger for chain hotels.

Finally, a specific company-environment factor that could also affect the relationship between innovation and performance in an unstable economic situation is the management confidence on the effects of the crisis. If managers are optimistic about the consequences of the crisis and its duration, their perceptions about the effect of innovation on performance will differ from those of managers with a pessimistic perception. To be more precise:

H3c: the effect of innovation orientation on performance will be higher in hotels where managers are optimistic about the crisis, than in hotels managed by people with a pessimistic perception.

3. Methodology

To test the relationships proposed in this study, data was collected through an on-line survey addressed to managers of 357 four-star hotels located in 52 cities throughout Spain. The hotel listing was extracted from the website Booking.com, which is currently the main site for hotel reservations in Spain. We obtained a total of 149 valid surveys (response rate of 42%). The field study was carried out between the months of March and May 2010.

The questionnaire contained information about company investment in innovation. In their research applied to tangible goods, Gunday *et al.* (2008) explain that there are four different types of innovation: product innovation, process innovation, marketing innovation and organizational innovation. Agarwal *et al.* (2003) applied the research to hotel services stating the importance of collecting both administration and technological innovation for the innovation variable. In this paper, we have followed these guidelines with the inclusion of three items on the questionnaire. First, in the process of service delivery, employees occupy a preferential place and as such, the questionnaire includes investment in human resources for the innovation of hotel services (I1), product innovation is included with investment in innovation to develop new services (I2), and marketing and organizational innovation through I3 with a question for management on the degree of process innovation (accounting, financial, and marketing).

To measure perceptions about technological turbulence of the environment, the research by Han *et al.* (1998) is used, which includes measuring service sector turbulence as well as market and technological environment turbulence. In this paper, we have expanded the Han et al.

(1998) scale to the hotel accommodation context and have used a 7-item scale including various aspects of technological and market turbulence.

To analyze business performance, two types of measures are used: the first is a direct measure of managers' perceptions about the level of performance achieved; perceptual judgments have a potential for self-reporting bias, but prior research has shown that perceived performance may be a reasonable substitute for objective measures and that managers prefer to avoid offering precise quantitative data (Taylor & Wright, 2003). In the second measure, performance is evaluated against the companies' main competitors (Jaworski & Kohli, 1993; Matsuno et al., 2002; Narver & Slater, 1990; Slater & Narver, 1994).

The results obtained in the exploratory analysis of the data showed that the direct measure is more reliable and valid and therefore this was the only measure finally used in the study. Three types of results are included: marketing performance (4 items), economic performance (3 items) and financial performance (3 items). To measure marketing and economic performance, we followed the research of Campo et al. (2010) and Agarwal et al. (2003). Regarding marketing performance, variables such as customer satisfaction (MK1), added customer value provided (MK2), quality of service offered (MK3) and hotel market image (MK4) are included. To measure economic performance, objective measures such as sales trends (E1), market share developments (E2) and employment rate developments (E3) are included. To measure financial performance, financial indicators commonly cited in previous studies are used, (Matear et al., 2002 and Snoj et al., 2007) such as gross profit (F1), return on investment (F2) and financial profitability, (F3).

Furthermore, the literature states that there are contextual moderators, which are expected to impact on the innovation-performance relationship. In this case study, we consider two types of contextual factors which may influence the innovation-performance relationship: firm specific factors (company age and chain affiliation) and company-environment specific factors (the opinion of management about the effects of the economic crisis on their business).

4. Results

To analyze the data obtained, a descriptive analysis of the variables is made first (see Table 1). The data reveals that the degree of hotel innovation perceived by the interviewees is relatively low (with an average of 4.93 on a 7-point Likert scale). The most important innovation made by the hotels is a process innovation for internal management, which has higher average values (5.16). This scale has a relatively high reliability (0.86), and the variance explained by these three items is greater than 70% (78.60).

Table 1 - Descriptive Analysis, Reliability and Variance Scores

Variables	Average*	DT	N	Reliability level (α)	Variance explained
Degree of innovation	**4.93**	1.17	137	0.86	78.60
I1	4.77	1.28			
I2	4.88	1.37			
I3	5.16	1.33			
Degree of turbulence	**5.91**	0.80	145	0.78	45.60
T1	5.65	1.36			
T2	5.63	1.28			
T3	6.03	1.07			
T4	6.57	.70			
T5	5.54	1.66			
T6	6.24	1.01			
T7	5.74	1.21			
Marketing performance	**5.73**	0.79	148	0.85	76.07
MK1	5.55	1.06			
MK2	5.86	0.90			
MK3	5.81	1.02			
MK4	5.70	.80			
Economic performance	**5.09**	1.14	147	0.93	88.05
E1	5.01	1.27			
E2	5.16	1.15			
E3	5.12	1.22			
Financial performance	**4.67**	1.19	135	0.94	89.14
F1	4.64	1.24			
F2	4.70	1.31			
F3	4.67	1.23			
Contextual variables					
AGE	17.32	18.65	151		
CRISIS	4.09*	1.32	148		
CHAIN					
Yes	86.8%		151		
No	13.2%				

* 7-point scale (minimum 1; maximum 7)

The perception of market turbulence in terms of technological change is high, on average 5.91, and fairly homogenous; the standard deviation is relatively small (0.80). Specifically, variables with higher averages are those concerning the opinion of management that new technologies: have opened new customer access routes (T4=6.57), have increased customers bargaining power (T6=6.24) and have presented significant business opportunities in the hospitality sector (T3=6.03). This scale presents a reliability greater than 0.7 (0.78), but the explained variance is greater than 50% (45.60).

The analysis of the various types of company performance supports the conclusion that managers perceive a substantial improvement in marketing results in recent years: improvement of customer satisfaction (5.55), added customer value provided (5.86), level of quality offered (5.81) and hotel market image improvement (5.70). The evaluation of economic performance is somewhat lower (average 5.09), perhaps due to a fall in the average prices of Spain's hotel accommodation due to the economic crisis. Consequently, financial performance is assessed to a lesser degree than the rest of the results (average 4.67). The different performance types obtain high values with regard to reliability, greater than 0.8 in all cases, and satisfactory results in terms of extracted variance, which is greater than 75%.

With respect to contextual variables, descriptive analysis results reveal that the average age of four-star, urban hotels in Spain is 17.32 years, but the high standard deviation obtained (18.65) suggests the coexistence in the market of hotels with varying degrees of seniority and experience. The managers' evaluation of the impact of the crisis on performance is 4.09, on average. In this case, the standard deviation is also relatively high (1.32), allowing for differences in evaluations among managers at each hotel. Finally, most of the hotels in the sample (86.8%) belong to hotel chains, a common characteristic of four- and five-star hotels in Spain.

To test the influence of innovation on the different types of performance, a step-by-step regression analysis is performed. The dependent variable is each type of outcome while the explanatory variables are innovation orientation (INNOV) and technological turbulence (TURB). The control variables of the hotel are hotel age, chain affiliation, and perception on the effect of the crisis. We analyze whether TURB influences performance as an explanatory variable or as a moderator. To verify the moderating effect, a new variable is created as a result of the product of INNOV * TURB.

Three types of performance are considered in this study: marketing performance (MK.P), economic performance (EC.P) and financial performance (FIN.P). The first two, MK.P and EC.P, are established as dependent variables in the regression equation, with the explanatory variables being the independent variables (INNOV and TURB), the moderator variable (INNOV*TURB), and the hotel contextual variables (AGE, CRISIS and CHAIN). Financial performance is a consequence of marketing and economic performance, thus creating a fourth equation in which the dependent variable is FIN.P and the explanatory variables are MK.P and EC.P.

$$Performance = f(MK.P, EC.P, FIN.P)_{EQ1}$$

$$MK.P = \alpha_1 + \chi_1 INNOV + \chi_2 TURB + \chi_3 INNOV * TURB + \chi_4 AGE + \chi_5 CRISIS + \chi_6 CADENA_{EQ2}$$

$$EC.P = \alpha_2 + \partial_1 INNOV + \partial_2 TURB + \partial_3 INNOV * TURB + \partial_4 AGE + \partial_5 CRISIS + \partial_6 CADENA_{EQ3}$$

$$FIN.P = \alpha_3 + \beta_1 MK.P + \beta_2 EC.P_{EQ4}$$

Table 2 presents the regression model outcomes. The results presented are those that provide the best fit in the R^2. In equation 4 ($EQ4$), the TURB variable does not enter as an explanatory variable when performing regression estimation by stages.

The results obtained confirm the direct effect of innovation and the degree of market turbulence on performance (H1 not rejected), but the effect as a moderator variable is not significant (H2 rejected). Investment in innovation has a direct and significant effect on marketing performance (χ_1 =0.34), but its effect on economic performance is weak and insignificant (∂_1 =0.09) (H1a partially rejected). On the other hand, technological turbulence has a direct, positive and significant effect on marketing (χ_2=0.34) and economic (∂_2=0.23) performance.

With respect to the contextual variables, belonging or not to a hotel chain has no significant effect on performance, although it should be noted that the four-star hotel sample in Spain is biased towards hotel chain affiliations; therefore, these results need to be considered with caution.

The hotel's age (number of years operating) has a negative and significant effect on marketing (χ_4 = -0.19) and economic (∂_4= -0.14) performance; thus, managers of the newest hotels perceive greater improvement in business performance in recent years.

As expected, manager perception on the effects of the economic crisis on their businesses negatively and significantly affects both economic (∂_5= -0.31) and marketing (χ_5= -0.29) performance. Manager perception of marketing and economic performance achieved is also lower depending on the extent to which managers perceive that the economic crisis has had a significant effect on their business. The effect is stronger in the latter, as they are more easily measured in the short term. These results support H3 about the moderating effect the contextual variables have on the innovation-results relationship, except for the chain variable (CHAIN) which exercises no significant effect.

Table 2 - Regression Analysis

Dependent variables	MK. P ($_{EQ2}$)	EC.P ($_{EQ3}$)	FIN.P ($_{EQ4}$)
Explanatory variables			
INNOV	0.34***	0.09 (ns)	
TURB	0.21**	0.23**	
Moderator variable			
INNOV*TURB	0.10 (ns)	0.13 (ns)	
Contextualized variables			
AGE	-0.19**	-0.14*	
CRISIS	-0.29***	-0.31***	
CHAIN	-0.12 (ns)	-0.03 (ns)	
MK.P			0.17**
EC.P			0.55***
R^2 adjusted	0.242	0.15	0.44
F	8.121***	4.8***	51.8***

*** $p<0.001$; ** $p<0.01$; * $p<0.05$; (ns = not significant)

Equation 4 ($_{EQ4}$) analyzes the effect of marketing and economic performance on financial performance. The effect of both performance types on financial performance is positive and significant, and the percentage of variance in the relationship, measured by R^2, is high (44%). An improvement in marketing performance can improve the company's financial performance ($\beta_1=0.17$), but the effect of economic performance on financial performance is much stronger ($\beta_2=0.55$) (H1b not rejected). This result is consistent, to the extent that an increase in sales, occupancy rate or in market share (EC.P) has an immediate effect on gross profit, in ROI, and in financial performance (FIN.P).

5. Conclusion

This chapter analyzes the impact of innovation orientation on the hotel sector in Spain for a number of business performance types, namely economic, marketing and financial, and the effect of perceived market turbulence and company's contextual variables on this relationship. The results of the exploratory analysis are useful for managers and academics as they provide reliable and valid scales applied to the hospitality industry to measure and quantify the innovative propensity of firms, perceived technological turbulence, and the different types of results applied. These scales may be useful for future research applied in other contexts within the hospitality industry.

The results obtained in the dependency analysis show that hotel innovation does not directly contribute to economic performance, hotel occupancy rates, or sales in the short term. However, they show the importance of investing in innovation to improve the hotel services in the medium and long term. These results confirm those obtained by previous research about the direct and positive influence of innovation on marketing performance. That is, on customer satisfaction concerning service quality, value offered, and the hotel's market image, which are key variables to obtain sustainable competitive advantages and corporate profits in the long term.

The effect of perceived technological turbulence on performance is direct and does not act like a moderator variable as previous studies suggested. The impact of this variable on performance is positive and significant. The explanation may go in line with the argument of Greenley (1995) and Han et al. (1998) who defend that the effect of market turbulence on the innovation-performance relationship depends on the sector being analyzed, and also on the time needed for the innovation to start contributing to company performance within that particular sector. Additionally, they claim that for service firms, the period of time between the application of the innovations and its impact on performance is usually shorter than the time needed in the manufacturing sector. New technologies, especially the Internet, have had a major impact on the tourist industry in general, and more particularly, on the hotel industry. Direct access to tourist information for hotel services from home as well as the possibility of making on-line reservations has led to increased hotels bargaining power against tourist service suppliers in addition to an increased level of hotel industry competition. In this sense, we can say that the Internet opened up new avenues for communication and customer access and provided significant opportunities for the hotel industry, which is reflected in an increase in economic and marketing advantages.

Outcomes of this study also reveal that some hotel features, such as age or management perception on the effect of the crisis on their business, significantly and negatively influence economic and marketing performance. Hotels which have been operating for fewer years may have a more modern infrastructure, a more flexible corporate structure, and a greater innovative propensity to allow greater adaptation to changing environments and, consequently, improved economic and marketing performance. On the other hand, perceptions of economic and marketing profits achieved are lower depending to what extent managers are pessimistic about the effect of economic crisis on their businesses. Finally, financial performance is a consequence of economic and marketing performance, which exerts a strong and positive effect on the former.

Belonging to a hotel chain affiliation has no significant effect on performance, but this may be because most of the hotels in the sample belong to a hotel chain. The limited sample of independent hotels can explain these insignificant results and should be resolved in subsequent research.

There are a number of limitations in the work that need to be kept in mind. First, this was an exploratory cross-sectional study. Therefore, it is impossible to be certain that the relationships identified will not vary or even lose meaning over time. Second, the constructs are measured based on the subjective perceptions of a single informant per firm. This procedure may possibly be a source of bias. Using objective performance measures could contribute to explain the phenomenon analyzed with greater clarity. Thirdly, it would be interesting to test the model proposed in other tourist services.

References

Agarwal, S., Erramilli, M.K., & Dev, C.S. (2003). Market orientation and performance in service firms: role of innovation. *Journal of Services Marketing*, 17(1), 68 – 82.

Birley, S., & Westhead, P. (1990). Growth and performance contrasts between 'types' of small firms. *Strategic Management Journal*, 11(7), 535–557.

Blackshaw, P., & Nazzaro, M. (2006). Consumer-Generated Media (CGM) 101. Word-of-Mouth in the Age of the Web-Fortified Consumer. A Nielsen BuzzMetrics White Paper. Retrieved January 2012 from http://www.nielsen-nline.com/downloads/us/buzz/nbzm_wp_CGM101.pdf

Cainelli, G., Evangelista, R., & Savona, M. (2004). The impact of innovation on economic performance in services. *The Service Industries Journal*, 24(1), 116-130.

Campo, S., Rubio, N., & Yagüe, M.J. (2010). Information technology use and firm's perceived performance in supply chain management. *Journal Business to Business Marketing*, 17 (4), 336-364.

Damanpour, F., & Evan, W.M. (1984). Organizational innovation and performance: The problem of "organizational lag". *Administrative Science Quarterly*, 29(September), 392-409.

Ettlie, J., & Bridges, W.P. (1982). Environment uncertainly and organizational technology policy. *IEEE Transactions on Engineering Management*, 29(February), 2-10.

Greenley, G.E. (1995). Market orientation and company performance: Empirical Evidence from UK Companies. *British Journal of Management*, 6(March), 1-13.

Gunday, G., Ulusoy, G., Kilic, K., & Alpkan, L. (2008). Modeling innovation: Determinants of innovativeness and the impact of innovation on firm performance. *4th IEEE International Conference on Management of Innovation and Technology*, Bangkok.

Han, J.K., Kim, N., & Srivastava, R.K. (1998). Market orientation and organizational performance: Is innovation a missing link? *Journal of Marketing*, 62(4), 30-45.

Hjalager, A.M. (2010). A review of innovation research in tourism. *Tourism Management*, 31(1), 1–12.

Heunks, F.J. (1998). Innovation, creativity and success. *Small Business Economics*, 10(3), 263–272.

Jaworski, B.J., & Kohli, A.K. (1993). Market orientation: Antecedents and consequences. *Journal of Marketing*, 57(July), 53-70.

Li, H., & Atuahene-Gima, K. (2002). The adoption of agency business activity, product innovation, and performance in Chinese technology ventures. *Strategic Management Journal*, 23(6), 469–490.

—. (2001). Product innovation strategy and the performance of new technology ventures in China. *Academy of Management Journal*, 44(6), 1123–1134.

Matear, S., Osborne, P., Garret, T., & Gray, B.J. (2002). How does market orientation contribute to service firm performance? An examination of alternative mechanism. *European Journal of Marketing*, 36(9/10), 1058-1075.

Matsuno, K., Mentzer, J.T., & Özsomer, A. (2002). The effects of entrepreneurial proclivity and market orientation on business performance. *Journal of Marketing*, 66(July), 18-32.

McGee, J.E., Dowling, M.J., & Megginson, W.L. (1995). Cooperative strategy and new venture performance: The role of business strategy and management experience. *Strategic Management Journal*, 16(7), 565–580.

Narver, J.C., & Slater, S.F. (1990). The effect of a market orientation on business profitability. *Journal of Marketing*, 54(October), 20-35.

Rosenbusch, N., Brinckmann, J., & Bausch, A. (2010). Is innovation always beneficial? A meta-analysis of the relationship between innovation and performance in SMEs. *Journal of Business Venturing*, in press.

Matear, S., Osborne, P., Garrett, T., & Gray, B.J. (2002). How does market orientation contribute to service firm performance?: An examination of alternative mechanisms. *European Journal of Marketing,* 36(9/10), 1058-1075.

Slater, S.F., & Narver, J.C. (1994). Does competitive environment moderate the market orientation-performance relationship? *Journal of Marketing*, 58(January), 46-55.

Snoj, B., Milfelner, B., & Gabrijan, V. (2007). An examination of the relationships among market orientation, innovation resources, reputational resources and company performance in the transitional economy of Slovenia. *Canadian Journal or Administrative Sciences*, 24, 151-164.

Subramanian, R., & Gopalakrishna, P. (2001). The market orientation-performance relationship in the context of a developing economy: An empirical analysis. *Journal of Business Research*, 53, 1-13.

Subramanian, R., Kumar, K., & Yauger, C. (1994). The scanning of task environments in hospitals: An empirical study. *Journal of Applied Business Research*, 10(4), 104-115.

Vermeulen, P.A.M., De Jong, J.P.J., & O'Shaughnessy, K.C. (2005). Identifying key determinants for new product introductions and firm performance in small service firms. *Service Industries Journal*, 25(5), 625–640.

Victorino, L., Verma, R., Plaschka, G., & Dev, C. (2005). Service innovation and customer choices in the hospitality industry, *Managing Service Quality*, 15(6), 555-576.

Yeh-Yun Lin, C. & Yi-Ching Chen, M. (2007). Does innovation lead to performance? An empirical study of SMEs in Taiwan, *Management Research News*, 30(2), 115-132.

CHAPTER TWELVE

INNOVATION: A PRIMARY COMPETITIVE TOOL FOR THE SUCCESS OF TOURISM DESTINATIONS

MARICA MAZUREK

Abstract

The implementation of tools of competitiveness becomes one of the major preconditions for successful performance. Successful tourist destinations are those that use their comparative advantage more effectively than other places. Especially during economic crises, successful tourist destinations benefit from the positive influence of image, the high quality of the destination's services, and innovative approaches to management: one such country is Austria. This chapter seeks to define and compare the applied concepts of competitive advantage and innovation in management, with specific reference to the financing of tourism at the national, regional and municipal levels in two neighboring countries in Europe—Slovakia and Austria. **Keywords:** destination competitiveness, innovation, competitive advantage, knowledge diffusion, institutional innovation.

1. Introduction

Competition, competitiveness and innovation all work towards one identical goal—success. Competitiveness in tourism destinations has been discussed by researchers and academics (Bordas, 1994; Buhalis, 2000; Crouch & Ritchie, 2003; Dwyer & Kim, 2003; Hassan, 2000; Heath & Wall, 1992; Kozak & Rimmington, 1999), and it tends to be very closely related to innovation. Thus, competitiveness is a goal, and innovation is one of the tools for enhancing the comparative advantages of tourist destinations. In Baumol's words (2000), "innovation [is] a primary competitive weapon." The principles of innovation have been discussed in general terms by various authors (Breukel & Go, 2009; Hjalager, 1996; Johannesson, Olsen, & Lumpkin, 2001; Kanter, 1983; Novelli *et al.,* 2006), however, with specific reference to tourism, the latest publication by Hall and Williams (2008) has clearly highlighted the major drivers of tourism innovation as being "competition, economic performance, demand-led innovation, technology, and firm-level strategy and resources." Innovation offers "first mover advantage" (Hall & Williams, 2008, p. 33); however, some disadvantages stemming from innovation could be risk in the forms of vulnerability, cost increases, new technology, or unanticipated employees' attitudes to changes. The comparison of approaches to competitiveness and innovation reveals different approaches in specific countries. Their innovative marketing and management strategies are decisive points of success.

2. Innovation and Innovative Techniques in Tourism

Innovation in tourism should be perceived as a response to social, economic, political and environmental changes. The changes in tourism in the last twenty years have forced tourism destinations to start to think "out of the box" if they want to become successful, which means being focused more strategically in their managerial or marketing practice. These changes are especially concerned with new forms of tourism and tourism products, new technologies, managerial and marketing strategies, and information processes.

Kanter (1983, p. 20) defined innovation as "the process of bringing any new, problem solving idea into use … the generation, acceptance and implementation of new ideas, processes, products or services." Hjalager (1996, p. 202) defined innovation "as new modes of social and economic action either derived from the invention of a physical product or process, or from the redefinitions of interrelationships between actors." Hall and Williams (2008, p. 18) described "competition, economic performance, demand-led innovation, technology, and firm-level strategy and resources" as drivers of tourism innovation. A symbiotic, mutual and mostly positive relationship between competition and innovation is based on the pressure on tourism businesses to be more effective, efficient and productive. Comparative advantage can be utilized differently through innovation, and innovation offers the possibility of gaining strategic advantage. Strategic approaches and innovative thinking influence differentiation and positioning of tourism destinations, and Porter (2000a, p. 19) has pointed out the importance of strategic thinking and innovation in connection with success and competitiveness.

The theory of innovations is based on Schumpeter's theory of economic development, developed in 1911, but the notion of innovation originates from Smith and Ricardo in the eighteenth and nineteenth centuries. The concept of innovation was transferred from biology through Schumpeter's notion of economic development. Sundbo (2001, p. 22) explains that "the idea of evolution comes from biology, primarily from Darwinian theories … as the 'survival of the fittest,'" which means that innovation is required for continuous economic development and success, and competitiveness depends on innovation and knowledge implementation. A competitive or changing environment forces entrepreneurs or a society to develop and apply new ways of thinking and doing things, a process which requires the acquisition and diffusion of knowledge.

Innovation and competitiveness are influenced by knowledge and the knowledge economy. Competitiveness and innovation are interrelated, where innovation is at the core of destination competitiveness. An increase in competitive forces and in demand for innovation is emerging in today's global economy. Knowledge is an important competitive tool for innovation in the new, post-capitalist society, which is based on a knowledge economy. Drucker (1993, p. 38) states that "knowledge is the only meaningful resource today"; however, this might be a little misleading because what is key is not only the possession of knowledge, but also the diffusion and use of knowledge. Diffusion and transformation of knowledge is crucial. In tourism, transformation of knowledge through innovative processes is dependent on new tourism policies, marketing concepts, infrastructure, or technological changes. The continual change from the Fordist to the post-Fordist society—which transformed the production patterns of the economy through stronger managerial, marketing and service patterns with a more innovative character—required continual innovations in products, processes, markets and institutions.

Modern innovation theory is based on industrial and technical innovation, as has been discussed by Sundbo (1998). Authors associated with this theory (e.g., Dosi *et al.,* 1988; Hjalager, 1997; Johanesson, Olsen, & Lumpkin, 1991) have disputed the character of innovations, especially as regards whether they are more focused on products or processes. Both types of innovations are common in tourism. Hjalager (2002) for example, discusses the importance of product innovation (new products and services), process innovation (the new role of customers in service delivery processes), market innovation (new modes of communicating with customers), logistics innovations (new constellations of services and the organization of flows) and institutional innovation (the emergence of new organizations and new ways of providing, financing, marketing, producing and collaborating).

One new strategy emerging in the tourism industry, which is making a significant contribution to the development of tourism businesses and their competitiveness, is consumer-centric tourism marketing (CCM). CCM is based on the creation of a relationship (kinship) between a customer and a tourist destination. It is a relatively innovative approach to marketing and branding. This type of relational marketing is highly focused on evoking a strong loyalty relationship between a tourist destination and customers.

The process of tailoring tourism services and offers to the demands of customers requires a sophisticated marketing and management approach, and the presence of skilled labor in the tourism industry. Some countries, such as Switzerland and Austria, have based their tourism business and strategy on the provision of highly sophisticated and strictly consumer-demand-tailored tourism services. For this reason, Switzerland and Austria are the most highly ranked countries in terms of tourism competitiveness. Consumer-centric marketing requires centralization of information systems, allowing the collection of information on customers. In order to develop or expand the use of CCM or CRM in tourism services, diffusion of new technologies or even business modeling is required in a destination. Just as product innovation is important for improving and innovating marketing strategies, institutional innovations (the emergence of new organizations and new ways of providing, financing, marketing, production and collaboration) lead to the continuous improvement of methods of financing by applying more strategic and advanced techniques in management, marketing, and branding. Additionally, good practice from countries with successful tourism industries can be applied in other countries in order to improve their competitiveness.

Branding as a tool of competitive advantage is based on the principles of value-added effect for customers (demand side) and equity creation (tourism destinations, demand side). Pike (2005) mentions that "the future of marketing [is] a battle of brands." Branding simplifies the visitors' decisions; it simplifies the process of segmentation and positioning. Tourism destination branding could be understood as a process of "bringing together two or more adjoining communities of similar natural and cultural compositions and attractions" (Cai 2002, 734). Tourism destinations are becoming among the largest brands, and their complexity represents a challenge for marketers and planners. Buhalis (2000, p. 3) notes that "tourists perceive the destination as a brand comprising a collection of suppliers and services … and consume it as a comprehensive experience during the visit." A separation of experience from the physical components and attributes is not recommended for successful branding and marketing of a destination. The idea of a strong brand umbrella (destination brand family tree) and the co-ordination of activities at the destination under the same brand concept (logo, slogan, brand identity, mission, vision, values, etc.) are crucial in brand extension and in the concept of co-operative branding. Co-branding and the creation of partnerships within tourist destinations have been recommended by academics (Cai, 2002; Prideaux & Cooper, 2002; Telfer, 2001) because, with a common vision and synchronization of branding and marketing processes, the implementation of branding will be easier and more effective.

The process of branding tourism destinations is influenced by primary (natural) resources and secondary resources (infrastructure, superstructure, culture, history), but also by external conditions of the macro-environment (economic, political, social factors). The existence of the private and public sectors, and of different managerial approaches, also complicates the process of branding. The influence of the macro-environment might be crucial for marketing and management strategies, and the examples of successful countries such as Switzerland or Austria attest to the importance of a supportive economic, political and legal environment for the implementation of strategic marketing and management. Morgan and Pritchard (1999, p. 215) mention that destination managers and tourism planners might have to cope with significant obstacles during the implementation of marketing and branding strategies in destinations, especially three unique challenges: "a lack of control over the total marketing mix, their relatively limited budgets, and often, over-arching political considerations."

Co-operation and strategic marketing (creation of strategic alliances), strengthening the role of DMOs in a destination, and branding are important for the competitiveness and success of tourist destinations. Recent authors have explained that destinations need to bring together all parties to collaborate rather than to compete, and to pool resources toward developing an integrated management and delivery system (Fyall & Garrod, 2005; Prideaux & Cooper, 2002; Telfer, 2001). Experience and relationships in branding have a strong impact on the success of destinations, which can later be converted into repeated visits or the creation of positive image. Cohesiveness and co-ordination (for example, in building and maintaining a consistent positioning strategy) is not easy to pursue, but without a common vision and synchronization among stakeholders, success cannot be achieved. This goal could be more easily achieved once all parties begin to "recogniz[e] that collaboration is likely … the *sine qua non* for successful destination marketing" (Fyall *et al.*, 2006, p. 83). The creation of partnerships in destinations improves competitiveness and the relationship of visitors to destinations, and consequently enables the implementation of effective marketing and branding tools. Partnerships cannot be understood as being a result of branding because branding concepts have a specific role in marketing, but partnerships can still improve the implementation of branding principles and create better relationships between visitors and destinations.

DMOs play an important role in the establishment of contact with visitors and in implementation of specific visitor programs, which might improve brand loyalty and increase repeat visits. The creation of partnerships in a destination can also support the funding process and simplify the availability of finances for marketing and promotion. It is important, however, to note that "successful brand campaign[s] leading to increased yields for local businesses do not translate into increased revenue of DMOs" (Pike, 2005, p. 181). Good practices of DMOs in countries with successful tourism outcomes as well as a sophisticated managerial and financial system at the national, regional and municipal levels might be helpful for other countries seeking more innovative and competitive approaches. Similarly, branding as an innovative approach to tourism destination management could be used as an example of a tool for success in other countries. One method which can be applied in order to compare similarities and discrepancies in service provision is benchmarking, particularly destination benchmarking, and tourism is predominantly a service-based industry.

Benchmarking at the micro-level (in enterprises) or macro-level (in a society or in destinations) is a method that can improve performance and competition. Kozak (2004, p. 41) mentions that the macro-level implication or Tourism Destination Benchmarking was overlooked during the last period. He defines destination benchmarking as

> the continuous measurement of the performance of tourism destinations (strengths and weaknesses) not only against themselves or other destinations in the same or in a different country, but also against national/international quality grading systems by assessing both primary and secondary data for the purpose of establishing priorities, setting targets and gaining improvements in order to gain competitive advantage. (Kozak 2004, p. 41)

In other words, competitive advantage can be achieved through the implementation of destination benchmarking techniques and practices. Hall and Williams (2008) discuss the impact of benchmarking on innovation and competitiveness and especially the possibility of looking at other organizations and their successes in order to pool the best ideas and so be more competitive. For this reason, Austria, as a country ranking second in tourism competitiveness, is a good example of the innovative approach to tourism development and a model of success for other countries—for instance for Slovakia, as a neighboring country which is still in great need of more innovative and sophisticated approaches to tourism development.

3. Methodology

Case studies from both countries—Austria and Slovakia—have been used in the present research. In Slovakia, primary and secondary data were collected via an exploratory approach from the bodies governing tourism at the national level (the Slovak Tourism Agency and the Ministry of Economy), and from the regional and municipal levels of government (interviews with tourism representatives and experts).

The primary research was conducted in the form of questionnaires given to fifteen experts in tourism in Slovakia selected from staff at the Tourism Department of the Ministry of Economy (at that time the governing body of tourism development in Slovakia); staff at the Slovak Agency of Tourism (SACR), academics teaching tourism at universities in Slovakia (Faculty of Economics at the University of Matej Bel, Department of Tourism and Economy at the University of Bratislava), representatives of selected autonomous bodies involved in tourism policy, staff at Departments of Tourism in Slovakia (Zilina), representatives and mayors of selected municipalities in Slovakia (Poprad and Kremnica), and other experts in tourism. The questionnaire contained fifteen semi-structured questions dealing with opinions concerning the innovative approach to marketing and management in tourism and financial strategies in Slovakian tourism policy. The questionnaire used the five-point Likert scale from 1 = strongly agree to 5 = strongly disagree. The content of the questions concerned the innovative approach to the financing of tourism in Slovakia from public sources and satisfaction with the contemporary system of financing, marketing and management of tourism in Slovakia.

Table 1 - Financing, Management and Marketing in Slovakia

Types of questions in the questionnaire	Mean
The financing of tourism in Slovakia is suitable for tourism development.	4.0
Government should play an important role in managing and financing tourism.	2.1
A complex managerial and financial approach is required for governance of tourism at governmental level.	1.3
The reason for the involvement of government in financing and innovations is the character of the tourism "product" (public goods).	2.5
Promotion and marketing is the main goal of government participation in tourism financing and support.	4.1
The development of tourism at regional level is supported effectively by government.	4.2
Fiscal changes and support for tourism from the regional budget could be helpful for the improvement of tourism strategy, management, innovation and financing.	2.3
Reinvestment of financial gains from tourism could improve tourism management, marketing and innovations.	1.8
Mutual financing from different financial sources could improve tourism performance.	1.6
A regional strategic approach could be helpful in the improvement of tourism development in regions.	2.2
Tourism development at municipal level does not experience lack of financial, organizational or legislative support.	4.4
Fiscal changes could improve tourism financing at the municipal level generally and in terms of the implementation of innovations in tourism.	2.5
Reinvestment of financial gains from tourism at the municipal level could help tourism development.	1.9
Tax from accommodation should be used for tourism development in municipalities.	1.4
A new taxation system in municipalities in Slovakia could be helpful in supporting tourism development, managerial improvements in tourism, and the implementation of innovations in tourism.	3.0

The secondary research in Slovakia consisted of studying, reviewing, and analyzing the relevant governmental and regional documents, and marketing strategies focused on tourism development at national, regional and municipal levels available on the Internet, or from governmental, regional and municipal agencies (the Ministry of Economy, the Slovak Agency of Tourism, the regional government, the Department of Tourism, Zilina, the municipal governments of Poprad and Kremnica).

The results were compared with the secondary data and examples of best practice from Austria; however, primary research similar to that conducted in Slovakia with tourism experts, using the same type of questionnaire, was missing. This could be considered a weakness of the research. This type of research might be undertaken in the second phase of research at a future date. In Austria, the secondary research was focused on information about innovative approaches to tourism marketing; management or financing by the Bundes Ministry for Economy and Employment (BMWA) and the Austrian National Tourism Organization (ANTO); and on documents and Internet materials and information concerning innovations at regional and municipal levels. We focused especially on the region of Lower Austria. One of the important sources of information was also the Research Institute of Tourism and Leisure in Vienna, Austria, where we conducted personal interviews with academics. A particular priority was to learn about innovative techniques and methods, which could be transferred from Austria to Slovakia. The Slovakian content of the research is stronger due to the relevance of materials and primary research; however, the results from Austria evidently offer a stronger innovative content.

4. Results

Slovakia, a country with favorable conditions for tourism development (especially due to the mountains, spas, and historical places such as castles), has a strong comparative advantage. Despite this, the deployment of resources into tourism and into managerial and marketing practices is still underdeveloped, especially in terms of financing tourism and implementing branding strategies and other innovative managerial and marketing strategies. A precondition for effective managerial and marketing processes is a proper legislative and organizational environment with strong financial support, which Slovakia still lacks. As a result of innovative destination management initiatives, clusters have been created in some regions in Slovakia. The most successful tourism clusters in Slovakia are in Liptov, Turiec and Orava in the Zilina region, which enabled this region to gain competitive advantage. Clustering and innovative approaches in destination management of tourism regions have also been applied successfully in Austria. The marketing strategy of this region is based on Porter's strategy of innovation. Zilina region has formed clusters around three major regional centers (Liptov, Orava and Turiec) and has created partnerships between the public and private sectors. Zilina region is the second most successful region in terms of tourism development; the most successful in Slovakia is the Bratislava region. Besides marketing research in regional centers, the concept of tourism development in the Zilina region has included implementation of e-marketing, creation of a logo, branding, formation of the identity and image of the territory, customer-centered marketing (CCM), and a successful customer relational marketing (CRM) strategy. For these activities, the regional government decided to spend public funds. Whereas other regions are currently suffering economic difficulties, Zilina region is benefiting from the presence of the South Korean automobile producer, Kia, and the region has enormous potential for tourism. The most crucial factor is, however, the innovative approach of local government to tourism development and the willingness to invest and improve marketing strategies in tourism and to co-operate with private sector, forming partnerships between the public sector and tourism entrepreneurs.

Adopting a similar approach to that taken at the municipal level in Zilina, we explored which innovative practices in tourism management and financing were applied in two municipalities, Kremnica and Poprad in Central Slovakia. Kremnica is located in the Region of Banska Bystrica and Poprad is located in the Region of Presov (NUTS III). Both municipalities have enormous potential for tourism development. Kremnica is a famous old gold mining town, one of the richest towns in the Austro-Hungarian Empire, and is surrounded by mountains, offers good ski facilities, and boasts a number of historical monuments. Poprad is the gateway to the High Tatras mountain range and national park. In light of these facts, we were curious to find out whether the Slovakian national government and the regional governments have recognized the tourism potential of these areas and whether an innovative approach to tourism has been implemented in these municipalities, as it has been in the Zilina region. Our main focus was the municipal budgets of Kremnica (see Table 2).

A rapid decrease of revenues in 2009 was caused by economic recession. We investigated if tourism development in a municipality was influenced by an increase or decrease of revenues in the municipal budget of Kremnica, and if there is any correlation between the growth of revenues generally and the expenditures on tourism. On the contrary, however, the graph below (Figure 1) shows that the revenues from tourism (accommodation tax) had a significant influence on tourism financing in each municipality, as was the case in Austria. In Slovakian municipalities, finance from municipal budgets is used primarily for expenditures such as social services, infrastructure and police, while tourism is not considered a

Table 2 - Expenditures and Revenues in Kremnica (2005–2009)

Year	2005	2006	2007	2008	2009
Revenue	76 396	257 319	236 950	139 034	6 476 917
	80 327	156 863	223 599	139 652	4 384 510
	105.20%	60.96%	94.36%	100.44%	67.69%
Expenditure	93 318	210 478	191 073	127 545	4 854 819
	94 982	104 849	180 643	90 267	2 545 403
	101.78%	51.19%	94.54%	70.77%	52.43%

Source: Kremnica municipality representatives, 2009–2010.
Note: In thousands of Sk; year 2009 in thousands of EUR.

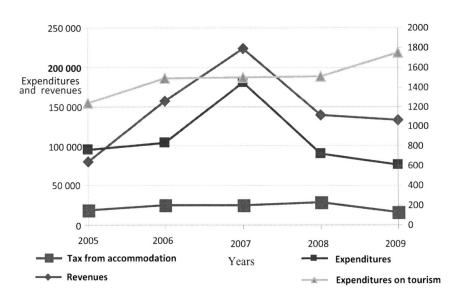

Figure 1: Revenues and expenditures for the municipality of Kremnica (2005–2009)

priority; this is very different from the Austrian approach. In Kremnica, the tax from accommodation did not significantly influence tourism development because the amount is not sufficient to finance tourism without any additional financial resources from the municipal budget or government. This means that the system of financing and supporting tourism development uniquely from public sources is not sufficient and needs to be changed.

Similar results were found in Poprad (regarding the budget of the municipality during the period 2005–2009). The intention of this part of the study was to explore whether innovative management strategies and techniques for supporting competitiveness might be influential in tourism development in this municipality. Table 3 shows revenues and expenditures in Poprad during the period studied, while figure 2 (below) presents data concerning the revenues and expenditures of Poprad generally and the relationship between general revenue and expenditure on tourism development.

Table 3 - Expenditures and revenues in Poprad (2005–2009)

Year	2005	2006	2007	2008	2009
Revenue	864 809	1 067 968	868 918	1 078 225	36 523 020
	956 976	1 113 231	880 218	1 183 036	37 773 269
	110.7%	104.2%	101.3%	109.7%	103.42%
Expenditure	864 809	1 067 968	868 918	1 078 225	36 523 020
	827 023	1 113 231	714 272	1 066 129	36 032 625
	95.6%	98.00%	82.20%	98.90%	98.66%

Source: Municipality of Poprad, 2005–2009.
Note: In thousands of Sk; year 2009 in thousands of EUR.

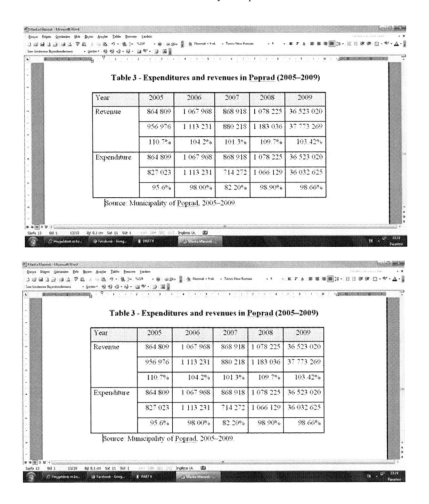

Table 3 - Expenditures and revenues in Poprad (2005–2009)

Year	2005	2006	2007	2008	2009
Revenue	864 809	1 067 968	868 918	1 078 225	36 523 020
	956 976	1 113 231	880 218	1 183 036	37 773 269
	110.7%	104.2%	101.3%	109.7%	103.42%
Expenditure	864 809	1 067 968	868 918	1 078 225	36 523 020
	827 023	1 113 231	714 272	1 066 129	36 032 625
	95.6%	98.00%	82.20%	98.90%	98.66%

Source: Municipality of Poprad, 2005–2009

Figure 2: Revenues and expenditures: Poprad (2005–2009)

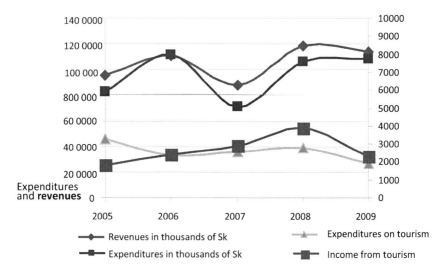

In some states (for example, Austria, Switzerland, the state of California in the United States), tax from accommodation serves as an important source of tourism development, since in these places there is a functioning system of tourism financing (either in the form of public financing or through partnerships). In Slovakia, this sort of system does not yet exist.

The graph indicates results similar to those found in Kremnica. It would seem, however, that in 2008, Poprad gained more income from tourism than did Kremnica, but that this income was not spent adequately on tourism development. This indicates that emergent expenses such as social services, health care and infrastructure were prioritized above tourism development in the municipality of Poprad. Even where there is potential for competitive tourism development, local government decisions and priorities can influence tourism development in a region. This case fully supports Crouch and Ritchie's (2003, p. 80) concept of the "onion skin taxonomy," which describes how political, economic and other macroeconomic or microeconomic decisions can significantly influence competitiveness in tourism.

Austria has a more systematic approach to tourism development, and especially to financing of regional and municipal policy, in comparison to Slovakia; for example, there is a rule in Austria that if a region offers more than 150,000 overnight stays per year, the regional government must set up a tourism association to finance tourism development. This amount has been calculated as a specific percentage of the annual revenue. The members of this association are not only tourism entrepreneurs but also entrepreneurs and businesses benefiting indirectly from tourism. Entrepreneurs contribute 40% of the fund income—the so-called "tourism tax"—which is a tax-deductible item. Activities undertaken by the association generate 10% to 15% of the fund income, and 5% to 10% is transferred from the state budget. The rest of the funding comes from fundraising activities. So-called "special funds" for financing tourism are created from various sources including the state budget, cities, municipalities, enterprises, banks and citizens (financing from mutual sources). The Tyrolean law on tourism has been in force since 1991 and deals with questions of membership in tourism partnerships and the collection of finances (obligatory flows from the state budget and the grants from government). This law is one example of functional legislative support for tourism, which allows implementation of innovative decisions and supports tourism development financially, managerially and organizationally.

Tourism creates approximately 16.3% of GDP in Austria, which ranks first in tourism receipts per capita in the world and second (after Switzerland) in terms of competitiveness in tourism, as measured by the Tourism Competitiveness Index. Vienna is one of the most successful tourist destinations in the world, generating 15% of the total income from tourism in Austria. The main goal of Austrian tourism is to highlight "quality rather than quantity." Innovative tourism destination strategies and customer-oriented marketing strategies have been identified as among the most important approaches in Austrian tourism development strategies. State funding is primarily focused on developing high standards of quality in tourism, especially in the service sector. Co-operative marketing and the creation of partnerships have played important roles in the implementation of tourism policy and marketing strategies.

Our attention was focused on the Lower Austria region (Niederösterreich Region). Despite the unfavorable economic climate in the world and in Austria over the last two to three years, this region achieved positive results in tourism development. A special company, Niederösterreich Bergbahnen, was established in Lower Austria to organize the sale of shares in the mountain destinations of this region. Tourism support, financing and the creation of partnerships are important goals, which require common marketing and branding in a region. According to the research findings, Niederösterreich Bergbahnen has shares in different municipalities—for example in Annaberg, St. Coronna, Mönichkirchen-Mariansee—and the rest of the municipalities are set to negotiate further development (Semmering, Hochkar, Ötscher, Mitterbach). In this region there is one more interesting initiative which has enabled the creation of more innovative marketing strategies, and this approach is based on cross-border co-operation and partnerships.

Recently, a partnership was initiated between Austria and Bratislava region in Slovakia, oriented around wine tourism. A common initiative for co-operation between the regions has been included into the "Program of cross-border co-operation in the tourism destination management of Lower Austria–Bratislava region." This program is focused on financing common marketing activities, promoting wine routes in the Bratislava and Lower Austria regions, and transferring good practices (the benchmarking approach). Wine production in the Lower Austria Region dates back to the Roman Empire, and the most recognized variety of wine from this region is called Weinviertel. In a model similar to this initiative in the Bratislava region, the Lower Austria region cooperated with Zilina region in a common initiative with Zilina university, Zilina Municipality, and also with partners from Södermanland (Sweden).

Another example of cross-border cooperation is the Regional Cooperation Management linking of Lower Austria with the Czech Republic, Slovakia and Hungary (RECOM), which is part of the European Territorial Cooperation program, 2007–2013. Each program established a joint technical secretariat in Austria (Vienna), Hungary (Budapest), and the Czech Republic (Brno), but no Slovakian office was opened for this program. The main focus of this co-operation is the funding of tourism projects. During the research, Slovakian partners commented that the lack of financial and managerial support from the Slovakian government was an obstacle to effective co-operation. In Austria, obstacles to co-operation that were reported included a low level of involvement and willingness to co-operate among public, private and other representatives from the border area. Other obstacles include national and regional legislation; different power structures (top-down or bottom-up approaches); lack of coordination or homogeneity between different tourism funding systems in countries interested in co-operating in tourism; language barriers; and different approaches to management and decision-making processes.

5. Conclusion

The research reported in this paper was focused on the notion of innovation in tourist destinations in Austria and Slovakia, on differences in tourism policy in each country, on innovative approaches to marketing and management strategies, and on benchmarking analysis of measures at the NTA level. The research in Slovakia and Austria sought to answer questions as to whether similar success stories in tourism management, marketing and policy could be useful for other countries, and whether the concept of the innovative approach to tourism, which has been used in the tourism strategies of the most successful countries in tourism such as Austria, might be one of the decisive factors in tourism success. The originality and value of this research is the attempt to compare two neighboring countries with different trajectories of tourism development in the past—due to political and economic considerations—and to find out whether Slovakia could learn from innovative practice in Austria, the world's second most successful country in terms of tourism competitiveness, and improve its competitive advantage.

Our focus was especially on institutional innovation, based on Hjalager's (2002) classification and the application of comparison of different approaches to marketing and management in Slovakia and Austria. One tool for improving quality and implementing innovative techniques, which is based on comparison of approaches and learning from best practice, is benchmarking. Benchmarking has been studied by various academics (for example, Dorsch & Yasin, 1998; Kozak, 2004; Lennon *et al.,* 2006) and, in the innovation classification, benchmarking stems from market needs and is strategically easier to implement than other approaches. For this reason, the process of continual change and novel implementation, which has been applied in benchmarking, forms part of an incremental innovative approach.

In Slovakia, some regions implemented innovative approaches to marketing and management strategies, based on Porter's theory of competitiveness. These approaches have been implemented in Austria for a longer period of time. In Slovakia, most regions are not familiar with innovative destination management and marketing principles and branding. This chapter has compared and discussed two case studies from these countries. The innovative tourism marketing strategy of Zilina region in Slovakia was compared with the innovative techniques and approaches to marketing and management in Austria.

The benchmarking method, which is based on the transfer of best practice from different countries, could help to provide solutions for the problem of tourism competitiveness everywhere. Austria's successful tourism policy and innovative approach has enabled it to gain approximately 20% of its annual export earnings from tourism, and to earn the third highest income from foreign currency per capita in Europe.

Austria is definitely a success story, lending strong support to the idea of "quality rather than quantity."

References

Baumol, W. (2002). *The Free Market Innovation Machine: Analyzing the Growth Miracle of Capitalism*. Princeton, NJ: Princeton University Press.

Bordas, E. (1994). Competitiveness of tourism destinations in long distance markets. *Revenue de Tourisme,* 3(3), 3–9.

Breukel, A., & Go, F.M. (2009). Knowledge-based network participation in destination and event marketing: A hospitality scenario analysis perspective. *Tourism Management,* 30, 184–193.

Buhalis, D. (2000). Marketing the competitive destination of the future. *Tourism Management,* 21, 97–116.

Cai, L.A. (2002). Cooperative branding for rural places. *Annals of Tourism Research,* 29(3), 720–742.

Crouch, G. I., & Ritchie, J.R.B. (2003). *The Competitive Destinations: A Sustainable Tourism Perspective.* Cambridge: CABI.

Dorsch, J. J., & Yasin, M.M. (1998). A framework for the benchmarking in public sector. *International Journal of Public Sector Management,* 11(23), 91–115.

Dosi, G. et al. (1988). *Technical Change and Economic Theory.* London: Pinter.

Drucker, P.F. (1993). *Post-Capitalist Society.* Oxford: Butterworth-Heinemann.

Johanesson, J.A., Olsen, B., & Lumpkin, G.T. (2011). Innovation as newness: What is new, how is new, and new to whom? *European Journal of Innovation Management,* 4(1), 20–31.

Dwyer, L., & Kim, C. (2003). Destination competitiveness: Determinants and indicators. *Current issues in Tourism,* 6(5), 369–414.

Fyall, A., & Garrod, B. (2006). *Tourism Marketing: A Collaborative Approach.* Clevendon: Channel View Publications.

Hall, C.M., & Williams, A.M. (2008). *Tourism Innovation.* NY: Routledge.

Hassan, S. (2000). Determinants of market competitiveness in and environmentally sustainable tourism industry. *Journal of Travel Research,* 38(3), 239–245.

Heath, E., & Wall, G. (1992). Marketing tourism destinations: A strategic planning approach. In *Relevance of Power in the Collaborative Process of Destination Branding*, ed. G. Marzano. 11th annual conference on graduate education and graduate student research in hospitality and tourism, 5–7 January, 2006, Seattle.

Hjalager, A.M. (1996). Tourism and the environment: The innovation connection. *Journal of Sustainable Tourism,* 4(4), 201–217.

—. (1997). Innovation patterns in sustainable tourism: An analytical typology. *Tourism Management,* 18(1), 35–41.

—. (2002). Repairing innovation defectiveness in tourism. *Tourism Management,* 23(5), 465–474.

Johannesson, J.A., Olsen, B. & Lumpkin, G.T. (2001). Innovation as newness: What is new, how is new, and new to whom? *European Journal of Innovation Management,* 4(1), 20–31.

Kanter, R.M. (1983). *The Change Masters.* NY: Simon & Schuster.

Kozak, M. (2004). *Destination Benchmarking: Concepts, Practices and Operations.* Wallingford: CABI.

Kozak, M., & Rimmington, M. (1999). Measuring tourist destination competitiveness: Conceptual considerations and empirical findings. *Hospitality Management,* 18, 273–283.

Lennon, J.J., Smith, H., Cockerell, N., & Trew, J. (2006). *Benchmarking National Tourism Organisations and Agencies – Understanding best practice.* Amsterdam: Elsevier.

Morgan, N.L., Pritchard, R., & Pride, R. (1999). *Destination Branding: Creating the Unique Destination Position.* Oxford: Butterworth-Heinemann.

Novelli, M. et al. (2006). Networks, clusters and innovation in tourism: A UK experience. *Tourism Management,* 27(6), 1141–1152.

Pike, S. (2005). Tourism destination branding complexity. *Journal of Product Brand Management,* 14(4), 258–259.

Prideaux, B. & Cooper, C. (2002). Marketing and destinations growth: A symbiotic relationship or simple coincidence? *Journal of Vacation Marketing,* 6(1), 35–48.

Poon, A. (1993). *Tourism, Technology and Competitive Strategies.* Wallingford: CABI.

Sundbo, J. (2001). *The Strategic Management of Innovation.* Cheltenham: Elgar.

Sundbo, J., ed. (1998). *The Theory of Innovation: Entrepreneurs, Technology and Strategy.* Cheltenham: Edward Elgar.

Telfer, D. (2001). Strategic alliances along the Niagara wine route. *Tourism Management,* 22(1), 21–30.

CHAPTER THIRTEEN

NEW PRODUCT DEVELOPMENT IN ALPINE DESTINATIONS

RUGGERO SAINAGHI

Abstract

The traditional fragmented structure of the European market has spurred the development of meta-management firms defined as destination management organisations (DMOs). The present chapter explores some critical conditions that DMOs must manage in order to become a focal organisation for local firms. The analysis is based on a case study represented by an Alpine destination (Livigno, Italy). The local DMO (APT Livigno) has created a performing new product able to significantly increase the number of clients for the lodging and skiing sector during the beginning and the end of the season. The chapter identifies some critical factors and above all shows some synthetic drivers which a DMO has to manage in order to stimulate the development of a tourism destination.
Keywords: DMOs, product development, destination management, destination competitiveness.

1. Introduction

Tourism is a leading sector for modern economies. Over the past six decades, tourism has experienced continued expansion and diversification to become one of the largest and fastest growing economic sectors in the world. Many new destinations have emerged alongside the traditional ones in Europe and North America. In spite of occasional shocks, international tourist arrivals have shown virtually uninterrupted growth – from 25 million in 1950, to 277 million in 1980, 438 million in 1990, and 681 million in 2000, and the current 880 million (WTO, 2011).

In the tourism market, it is destinations that compete, not individual firms. Growing competition, both national and international, is making this more and more apparent. In fact, every destination has to position its products in such a way as to give them character and personality (Go & Govers, 2000).

European snow tourism, after a long development stage (Cockerell, 1988, 1994; Sainaghi, 2008; Spring, 1998), is subject to increasing competition. It is, indeed, a market characterised by low growth rates (Fredman & Heberlein, 2003) and has been faced with continuing expansion of supply driven both by the creation of new destinations and the growth in available resources in those already in existence (Flagestad & Hope, 2001; Hudson, 2000). In this context, many destination operators (businesses, associations, DMOs) are undecided as to the strategy to adopt in order to maintain or increase their own market share and, above all, how to create a sustainable competitive advantage (Porter, 1985, 1991).

The increasing competition characterising modern territorial systems has shifted the competitive rules from firms to destinations (Claver *et al.*, 2007; Go & Govers, 2000; Sainaghi & Canali, 2011). Some authors have defined tourism destinations as "competitive subjects" (Bieger, 1997; Sainaghi, 2004). The first level of competition is between different territories and if, and only if, one destination is chosen by a client or a target, then the second level of competition starts, i.e. between local firms.

The relevance of destination strategy suggests the existence of a strong link between the competitive positioning of the system and local firm performance. The "meta-management" strategy (Sainaghi, 2006) tends to significantly influence the development of the destination (Ingram and Inman, 1996) and, more generally, the structural characteristics of local firms (Baum & Mezias, 1992; Sainaghi & Canali, 2011).

The chapter identifies some critical drivers that public territorial governance must manage in order to become a leading company in the field of tourism destinations. The reflection is supported by an empirical case, represented by the Livigno destination (Italy) and by the "Skipassfree product". Using analytical operative data from firms involved in this product (hotels and ski companies), the analysis shows that, in the presence of rigid cost structures and high demand elasticity, it is possible to profoundly modify the competitive results, by working on collaborative strategies. The performance of the companies involved confirms that the development of a new product could create "win, win" situations, where many actors can increase their value.

The chapter reports details about the governance structure of the Skipassfree product, showing some major, original choices that can be important for the literature on the theme of public territorial governance.

2. Destination Management of Tourism Places

The literature has, over time, defined the concept of "destination" as both a system of attractions and the geographic area that encompasses them (Sainaghi, 2004, 2006). In the European context, winter destinations operate principally in the Alpine region, serving a target customer group interested in sports, skiing being of particular importance. For this reason Bieger (1997) refers specifically to "winter *sports* destination" (italics added). Snow tourism can be seen as a special form of the more general "mountaineering" phenomenon (Beedie & Hudson, 2003; Mitchell, 1983; Pomfret, 2006).

The Alpine destinations display the characteristics typical of the community model (Bodega *et al.,* 2004). It is a model with a fragmented supply side, centred on independent small and medium enterprises operating in a decentralised way, where no single unit has any dominant administrative power or dominant ownership within the destination (Flagestad & Hope, 2001). This fragmentation is reflected in the structural complexity of the strategic positioning sought by local businesses, by potentially conflicting views of the course the destination should take in its future development (Buhalis, 2000; Needham & Rollins, 2005; Williams *et al.,* 2004). On the other hand, one often finds a sense of shared values at these destinations, an indispensable point of departure for any dialogue between operators. Precisely such characteristics have led a number of authors to describe "community based" destinations as "social networks" (Godde *et al.,* 2000; Price *et al.,* 1997), "complex systems" (Baggio, 2008; Baggio & Sainaghi, 2011; Scott & Laws, 2005; Zahra & Ryan, 2007) or "tourist districts" (Dredge, 1999; 2006; Sainaghi, 2004, 2006).

The supply fragmentation, on the one hand, and the unitary perception of the destination by the clients, on the other, have encouraged the development of some local agencies in charge of the development of the destination. These organisations are usually called "destination management organisations" (DMOs) and are typically non-profit making firms (Flagestad & Hope, 2001; Sainaghi, 2006). The financial mechanisms can range from (d'Angella *et al.,* 2010):

- "cooperative models", where local tourism companies themselves finance the DMO;

- "public structures", where a local public organisation (usually the municipality) contributes to financing the tourism agencies;
- "normative structures", where a law obliges some actors (usually tourism actors) to finance the DMOs. The normative model requires a fraction of the lodging price to finance the DMO and requires a deep involvement mainly with hotel firms;
- "market models", where the DMO receives its grant by selling some services and products to tourism clients.

In reality there are many "mixed models", in which these polar archetypes are linked and overlapping, creating specific empirical models (Sainaghi, 2004). DMOs are asked to manage some primary processes able to influence the endowment of infrastructures, the development of new products and the communication and marketing activities (Sainaghi, 2006). On the other hand, DMOs should also manage support processes, able to create a consensus and a strong involvement with local actors. Support processes primarily include internal marketing, training and research. The present paper focuses on new product development and shows how a DMO could contribute to influencing collaborative strategies.

3. Methodology

The research methodology is centred on a single case study (Yin, 1994), represented by the Livigno destination, and in particular by the Skipassfree product. The fieldwork made it possible to collect different sources of evidences (interviews, documentation, measures of performance) based both on qualitative and quantitative data (Jick, 1979).

Interviews were carried out with the operative and managerial employees responsible for the event and communication management by the local DMO, called "Azienda di Promozione Turistica Livigno" (hereafter APT Livigno). The interviews also involved some managers of hotel firms, the owner of an important local ski company and some managers of commercial shops. A total of twelve open interviews were made, with the aim to understand: i) the functioning of the Skipassfree product, ii) the collaborative mechanisms, iii) the results, iv) the future perspectives.

Documentation includes a set of written pieces represented by some power point presentations and internal documents describing the functioning and the results achieved by the Skipassfree product. The field analysis also made it possible to collect the presentation of the project in the social financial statements. Furthermore, APT Livigno top management presented the project at some public events. The researchers have received all the documents used on these occasions.

Finally, the articles use some *archival records*, represented by daily data of the hotel sector and operative data of ski corporations.

Concerning the lodging data, the local DMO is responsible for collecting daily information relating to the number of clients (arrivals and overnights), segmented by the country of origin (domestic or international). Domestic clients are segmented by regions and provinces, and international customers by countries. Usually these data are available in all Italian destinations but with a monthly detail. APT Livigno has developed sophisticated software able to collect data in a daily format. This fact made it possible to develop the evolution of tourism movement over the years with and without the Skipassfree product. Operative indicators focus on customers, showing the number of arrivals, overnights and occupancy.

Concerning the ski company, the analysis used daily data of "first entries". A first entry measures the real number of ski days. In fact, when a customer uses his or her ticket for the first time in a day, this generates a first entry. In the case of multi-day tickets, the customer usually generates many first entries. This operative measure is very useful to perceive the movement generated by a new product. The analysis also collected the number of daily passages. This indicator counts the number of mountain railways used in a day by a client.

The Skipassfree product was launched in the winter season '07-'08. For this reason the time series cover four years: two seasons without the event ('05-'06 and '06-'07) and two with the Skipassfree ('07-08 and '08-'09). The season '09-'10 has been excluded because the data were not available when the field analysis was conducted.

4. The Skipassfree Product: Object and Structure

The goal of Skipassfree is to increase the number of tourism flows at the beginning and at the end of the winter season, offering a package inclusive of lodging and ski service. The promotion starts from the beginning of the season (from the end of November until Christmas) and lasts until its end (after Easter to May 1). Both periods are characterised by low occupancy (lodging sector) and by a limited number of skiers (first entries). Occupancy, in fact, is below 20% before Christmas, while it shows a high variability at the end of the season, according to the position of the Easter holidays.

The average length of stays, during the winter season, roughly amounts to 6 days. The target attracted is customers interested in a "white week" skiing holiday. This strategic positioning was also examined by the Skipassfree project. In fact, this product requires a minimum length of stay of 4 days in the case of hotels and 7 days for customers using an apartment.

The product is anchored around four main actors: i) the client, ii) the lodging sector, iii) the ski companies, and iv) the local DMO (APT Livigno).

Focusing on the *customer*, promotion is very easy: on buying a bed in a hotel or in an apartment taking part in the Skipassfree scheme, the client receives the ski pass without any additional cost. The affiliated lodging structures are shown in all the communication products used by the DMO – price list, web page for the DMO and for Skipassfree, leaflets distributed in workshops and trade fairs.

Focusing on the *lodging sector*, owners and managers taking part in the Skipassfree project pay 50% of each ski ticket offered free to their own clients. The nature of this additional cost is therefore a variable one and its absolute value is related to the actual number of attracted customers. The economic advantage for the lodging sector is primarily related to an increase in occupancy and to a possible increase in the average room revenue. In fact, owners and managers are free to price their service during both promotional periods, according to their strategic positioning and to the level of demand. The prices are communicated to potential customers through different channels, such as: the web page of the lodging firm and of the DMO, the paper material of the APT, the web pages of tourism intermediaries (tour operators and agencies).

Analysing the Skipassfree project from the point of view of a hotel, it involves bearing an additional cost (50% of the ski ticket), but this product can increase the average room price and occupancy.

From the point of view of *ski companies*, Skipassfree requires granting a 50% discount to affiliated lodging structures. The increase in profitability is also in this case researched by an increase in sold volumes (number of tickets or skiers).

The whole architecture is quite simple: expressing the ski ticket price in base 100, the latter will be offered free to the customer and the cost is shared equally by the affiliated lodging firms and the ski companies. For the hotel sector, taking part in the Skipassfree project does not involve bearing fixed costs; the success of this product is strongly linked to the additional volume generated. It is well known that the sensitivity of operating profit to the operating leverage (variation in volume, which means number of customers) is much higher when the fixed costs are also higher (Koller et al., 2005; Sainaghi, 2010a, 2010b, 2011). Both the firms involved (lodging and ski companies) have a cost structure largely dominated by fixed costs, determined by the presence of high investments (attributed to the income statement in terms of amortisation or in terms of rentals) and high personnel costs.

Focusing on the *DMO*, APT Livigno is the Skipassfree orchestrator. Local firms in fact asked this organisation to design the communication campaign, in order to present Skipassfree to potential targets. The promoting budget was supported by the Livigno Skipass Association – an organisation that includes all the local ski companies –, which made available an annual contribution of approximately 150,000 Euros. The DMO was made responsible for designing the marketing plan in terms of channels, markets and targets. The sole fixed component (marketing cost) was borne by the ski companies. *Ex post*, the involvement of the DMO was strategic for mainly two reasons.

First, APT Livigno has a consolidated know-how in the field of marketing and communication and therefore it was not necessary to create an *ad hoc* team, reducing the developing cost and complexity. Second, the local DMO manages many other promotional activities. It was therefore possible to generate some positive synergies with other processes, further reducing the costs. Finally, the local DMO is highly involved in the local network and has a good reputation and trust.

5. Critical Points and the Marketing Plan

The Skipassfree development revealed some critical points from the beginning, especially:

- the risk of attracting components of excessively price-sensitive demand, with possible consequent image damage for Livigno;
- the natural resistance of many lodging firms to giving free of charge a service usually bought by its clients (ski ticket) and to bearing an important part of this cost (50%);
- the risk of significantly reducing the economic margin generated by loyal customers that usually choose Livigno as their holiday destination during the Skipassfree periods.

At destination level, some actors were worried about generating an "avalanche effect" produced by this promoting strategy in the competitive games against other rival mountain resorts. In fact, if the Skipassfree strategy were to be widely implemented by other destinations, the result would be to risk offering the actual product to potential clients with a considerable discount.

All these elements were assessed more as critical points to be managed, rather than as impedimental variables for the whole project. In fact, the usage of a price lever in order to make the beginning and the end seasonal periods more attractive is widely adopted by many destinations (not only Alpine ones) and many firms, and this strategy necessarily attracts more price-sensitive demand components. In any case, the entrepreneurial challenge of the Skipassfree project is definitely seen in an increase in volumes (number of customers for both the lodging and ski sectors). These two sectors in fact have high fixed costs and low occupancy; in these conditions it may be advantageous to offer a lower unitary margin and increase occupancy.

Concerning the reluctance on the part of some hotels to giving free ski tickets, this problem was solved simply by also making participation in this promoting product free of charge. Consequently, all owners and managers not sharing the Skipassfree goals and principles did not take part. During the last three years the number of affiliated firms significantly increased and even some entrepreneurs who were initially firmly opposed to the project, subsequently joined.

The risk of reducing the economic margin generated by loyal customers was immediately defined as a theoretical problem. In fact, as outlined in the following paragraphs and in particular in Tables 3 and 5, the attracted target during the beginning and the end of the season consists of Italian customers, coming from the neighbouring provinces, with a shorter length of stays. It is a different target from those attracted by the Skipassfree, centered on a long length of stays. Consequently loyal Italian customers and their economic margins will not be impaired by the Skipassfree product.

Having explained some operating doubts, we will now examine in detail the marketing plan and communication activity. APT Livigno was responsible for designing and implementing the marketing plan.

To communicate the first edition of Skipassfree, a structured client segmentation was outlined. APT Livigno was in charge of collecting all statistical data from the lodging sector. This organisation developed software able to maintain the daily structure of recorded data. Consequently, the marketing plan developed an in-depth analysis of the main segments, choosing Livigno at the beginning and at the end of the winter season. Some target markets were identified at national and international level. Concerning the domestic market, the targets already attracted come primarily from neighbouring provinces, interested in short breaks, especially during the holiday periods and at weekends. For this reason, new segments were identified in the marketing plan, staking mainly on distant regions (centre and south of Italy), with the aim to increase the length of stays. The most important communication channel was identified in attending trade fairs and the distribution of written materials.

Focusing on foreign countries, much attention was placed on the Western European nations already acquainted with Livigno, such as Germany, Belgium, Switzerland, the UK, Ireland and Denmark. Little energy was invested in Eastern European countries – Poland and the Czech Republic – and South Africa was the only non-European country involved in the Skipassfree project. The marketing plan for foreign countries involved some intermediaries, together with targeted communication activities.

6. Achieved Results: The Beginning of Winter

The results can be appreciated by simply comparing the number of overnights and first entries during the two years without and with the Skipassfree. Due to the profound diversity of the variations obtained at the beginning and at the end of winter, the present paragraph focuses only on December, while the following one presents the performance achieved in April and May.

The early season values (see Table 1) show an important increase affecting both the lodging and the ski sector. In particular, the data measure a dramatic growth for both sectors (more than 100%) comparing the last two seasons (with the Skipassfree) with the first two (without the event). It is interesting to see the significant increase marked between the first and the second winter with Skipassfree. In fact, the average number of daily overnights develops a growth from 1,834 (2005) to over 4,000 (2008), with a progress of 126%. The number of first entries shows a similar progression and collects an increase of 118%, moving from 2,387 to over 5,000 (penultimate column of Table 1).

Table 1. Evolution of tourism data at the beginning of winter season.

Winter season	Periods		# of days	Average daily overnights	Total overnights	Length of stays	Average daily # of skiers	Tot. # of skiers
	Seasonalities			Hotels			Ski companies	
	From	To						
'05-'06	01/12/05	23/12/05	22	1,834	40,342	3.4	2,387	52,521
'06-'07	01/12/06	23/12/06	22	1,852	40,742	2.7	2,511	55,245
'07-'08	30/11/07	22/12/07	22	2,555	56,199	3.0	3,614	79,499
'08-'09	29/11/08	23/12/08	24	4,144	99,454	4.6	5,201	124,820
	% Var. ('08 over '05)		9%	126%	147%	34%	118%	138%
	% Var. ('08 over '06)		9%	124%	144%	70%	107%	126%
	% Var. ('08 over '07)		9%	62%	77%	53%	44%	57%

Furthermore, the average length of stays also shows an important progression, primarily during the year 2008 when it collects a value of just under 5 days (4.8), compared with a lower amount during the year '05 (3.4 days) and '06 (2.7).

Based on these results, we can conclude that the Skipassfree has achieved the main targeted results in terms of volume, increasing the number of clients for both the two main sectors (lodging and ski) involved in the project.

At this point, it is interesting to compare the markets with most growth with those on which the greatest promotional efforts were focused, in order to evaluate the effectiveness of the marketing strategy. Table 2 segments the lodging data, distinguishing between national and international markets. The analysis focuses only on the hotel sector because in the case of ski flows there is no available information on nationality. In fact, when clients purchase a ski card, their nationality is not recorded.

Table 2. Evolution of hotel flows segmented per nationalities - beginning of season.

Seasonalities			Hotel sector							
			Domestic market				International market			
Periods From	To	# of days	Arrivals	Overnights	%	Length of stays	Arrivals	Overnights	%	Length of stays
01/12/05	23/12/05	22	8,340	23,434	58%	2.81	3551	16,908	42%	4.76
01/12/06	23/12/06	22	10,068	23,060	57%	2.29	5087	17,682	43%	3.48
30/11/07	22/12/07	22	11,054	23,564	42%	2.13	7791	32,635	58%	4.19
29/11/08	23/12/08	24	9,392	27,988	28%	2.98	12419	71,466	72%	5.75
% Var. '08 over '05		9%	13%	19%	-52%	6%	250%	323%	71%	21%
% Var. '08 over '06		9%	-7%	21%	-50%	30%	144%	304%	66%	66%
% Var. '08 over '07		9%	-15%	19%	-33%	40%	59%	119%	24%	37%

A first observation suggests a very different participation in the Skipassfree product between national and international clients. The domestic market, in fact, generally speaking shows a smaller increase: the number of overnights rises from 23,434 ('05-'06) to 27,998 ('08-'09), registering an increase of 19%. On the contrary, foreign countries show an increase of 323%, moving from 16,908 overnights ('05) to over 70,000 ('08). This variation is reflected in the commercial mix (the squared percentages in Table 2): in 2005 58% of total clients are domestic, in 2008 the number of foreigners peak at 72%; Italians accounted for only 28%.

Furthermore, analysing the length of stays, it is possible to record a second important gap. The domestic tourist continues to show a low value, less than 3 days, suggesting an interest only in weekends and short breaks. On the contrary, foreign guests significantly increase their length of stays, reaching 6 days during the last year (2008), with an average increase of 21% (2008 in comparison with 2005). In fact, the initial value was 4.76 days.

A second observation considers the details of foreign countries, showing the first five international markets (Table 3) and the five most important Italian provinces. The values are depicted in descending order.

Table 3. Evolution of hotel flows of top five foreign countries and top five domestic provinces – beginning of season.

	2005	2006	2007	2008	% Var. '08 over '05	% Var. '08 over '06	% Var. '08 over '07
Top five international markets							
Poland	3,445	3,622	13,732	35,060	918%	868%	155%
Czech Republic	3,369	2,290	5,743	11,794	250%	415%	105%
Germany	2,517	2,665	4,549	6,585	162%	147%	45%
Belgium	375	708	1,188	2,790	644%	294%	135%
UK	1,187	1,351	2,147	2,583	118%	91%	20%
Other markets	6,015	7,046	5,276	12,654	110%	80%	140%
Foreigners	**16,908**	**17,682**	**32,635**	**71,466**	**323%**	**304%**	**119%**
Top five Italian provinces							
Milan	6,346	6,067	5,276	4,944	-22%	-19%	-6%
Bergamo	1,443	1,830	1,923	1,712	19%	-6%	-11%
Brescia	657	974	1,145	1,056	61%	8%	-8%
Rome	539	288	627	989	83%	243%	58%
Como	609	747	957	868	43%	16%	-9%
Other provinces	13,840	13,154	13,636	18,419	33%	40%	35%
Italy	**23,434**	**23,060**	**23,564**	**27,988**	**19%**	**21%**	**19%**

Focusing attention on the domestic market, it is interesting to note that, apart from the significant presence of tourists from Rome, the primary provinces in numerical terms are Livigno's neighbouring territories. The flow evolution shows a decrease for the Lombardy region (Livigno is located in this Region) and a parallel increase for the Rome province. Concerning international countries, all nations show an increase measured numerically, with the sole exception of the UK. Poland is the country showing the most significant increase, moving from 3,445 overnights ('05) to over 35,000 in 2008.

The results achieved are interesting because they show an asymmetric evolution of the attracted market and marketing efforts. The marketing plan invested primarily in the domestic country, secondly in consolidated western European nations, and marginally in Eastern European markets. On the contrary, the success of Skipassfree is based on the latter nations.

8. Results: The End of Winter

To interpret end-of-season performance it is important to consider some elements of calendar variability able to influence the number of days covered by Skipassfree. In fact, in some years Easter falls at the end of March or at the beginning of April, and therefore the promoting period is longer, as in 2008 (28 days); in other years the promotional period is quite short, as in 2009 (15 days). A similar situation characterises the previous two years (not covered by the Skipassfree). For this reason it is more effective to use the average daily number of tourists rather than the absolute value of clients.

A second useful observation to interpret the results concerns the position of the two holiday periods of 25 April (Liberation Day, a national holiday) and May 1 (Labour Day). In some years these two holidays create a "bridge" or long weekend, favouring a last period of skiing; in other years they fall mid-week and do not generate a particular increase in the tourism movement.

Added to these calendar factors, we must also consider some aspects of climate. Temperatures do not always guarantee optimal snow conditions at the end of the season. However, generally speaking, the four years analysed show good or very good snow conditions even at the end of the season and so it is possible to compare the achieved results.

With this methodological premise, it is possible to interpret the quantitative results. Table 4 depicts a substantial stability of overnights, comparing the last year to the initial values, and a significant increase (+149%) assuming 2007 as base year. The variation in the last two years ('07-'08) is positive (7%). Focusing attention on average daily values, we may say that in the last two years the data are very close to the initial ones ('06). This is a positive result, especially if we focus attention on 2009, when the calendar structure made the end of the season particularly short (15 days).

The comparison between 2007 and 2009 (two years with a short end season) shows the significant results achieved by the Skipassfree project. In fact, in 2007 the average daily number of overnights amounted to 865; in 2009 this number grew, peaking at 2,149. A similar trend, but marked by a stronger increase, is shown by the ski companies: in 2009 the number of daily first entries stood at 2,890, while a value of 488 in 2007 (short end of season, 19 days) and a figure of 2,516 was seen in 2006 (longer end of season, 28 days).

Table 4. Evolution of tourism data at the end of winter season.

Seasonalities		Hotels			Ski companies	
Periods	# of days	Average daily overnights	Total overnights	Length of stays	Average daily # of skiers	Tot. # of skiers
From To						
05/04/06 03/05/06	28	2,156	60,357	4.8	2,516	70,445
14/04/07 03/05/07	19	865	16,427	2.8	488	9,276
05/04/08 03/05/08	28	2,007	56,206	4.0	2,587	72,426
18/04/09 03/05/09	15	2,149	32,232	3.9	2,890	43,353
% Var. '09 over '06	-46%	0%	-47%	-19%	15%	-38%
% Var. '09 over '07	-21%	149%	96%	36%	492%	367%
% Var. '09 over '08	-46%	7%	-43%	-3%	12%	-40%

The detail of lodging tourism flows segmented by nationality (see Table 5) does not show particular breakdowns comparing the two years without and with the event. In fact, the domestic and international mix remains substantially stable (especially excluding 2007) and shows a number of foreign clients slightly greater (56%-58%) than Italian tourists (42%-44%). The latter account for a short length of stays, moving from 2.5 and to 3 days, while international guests peak at a value higher than 6 (excluding 2007). The evolution on daily Italian overnights shows a significant increase in the last two years (+32% and +3%), while international customers stabilise around 1,200 daily average overnights, both in the presence of a long (2008, 28 days) or a short end of season (2009, 15 days).

Table 5. Evolution of hotel flows segmented per nationalities - end of season.

Seasonalities			Hotel sector							
			Domestic market				International market			
Periods From	To	# of days	Arrivals	Overnights	%	Length of stays	Arrivals	Overnights	%	Length of stays
05/04/06	03/05/06	28	8,567	26,428	44%	3.08	4116	33,929	56%	8.24
14/04/07	03/05/07	19	5,190	13,121	80%	2.53	576	3,306	20%	5.74
05/04/08	03/05/08	28	9,033	24,816	44%	2.75	4971	31,390	56%	6.31
18/04/09	03/05/09	15	5,366	13,649	42%	2.54	2945	18,583	58%	6.31
% Var. '09 over '06		-46%	-37%	-48%	-3%	-18%	-28%	-45%	3%	-23%
% Var. '09 over '07		-21%	3%	4%	-47%	1%	411%	462%	186%	10%
% Var. '09 over '08		-46%	-41%	-45%	-4%	-7%	-41%	-41%	3%	0%

Lastly, the analysis of generating markets shows a strong positioning between end of the season and Eastern Europe, with the exception of Germany, in the case of international clients. The domestic market remains dominated by neighbouring provinces.

Generally speaking, variations are very large if measured using percentages. This result is strong compared with the initial low values. The evolution of both markets (national and international) shows a recovery after the considerable drop depicted in 2007, primarily generated by the calendar structure (short end of season). More recently, the average values are slightly higher than the initial ones (2006). We may conclude that end of season does not register a discontinuity (like that depicted in December), but in any case the Skipassfree project has made it possible to level up the average daily values of both the lodging and skiing sectors, especially during years when the end of season is fairly short (as in 2008); and make more stable the average number of international clients 56%-58%, last two years). This is an important result because these clients show a longer length of stays, on the one hand, and because they reduce the dependence on national (and neighbouring) provinces.

9. Conclusion

The case study suggests some conclusions whose implications go far beyond the Skipassfree project. A first remark concerns the nature of cost structure. It is easier to develop a new territorial governance when local firms have a rigid structure, dominated by fixed costs and low occupancy. This scenario makes firms extremely sensitive to volume increases, creating a good premise for collaboration. Furthermore, the high fragmentation of the tourism destination reduces the role played and playable by single firms. It is very difficult for one single, small company to develop a complex new product requiring new investments, involving many actors, and generating positive externalities to free riders.

A second interesting point is related to the ability of the territorial governance structure (APT Livigno in the Skipassfree project) to sustain fixed cost investment and to design financial mechanisms in order to involve local firms. The decision to centralise investment was very important, in that it made it possible to design financial mechanisms involving local hotels (usually small) built around variable costs. The risk of participation, for a single firm, is thus very small. If the new product is a flop, firms do not increase volumes, but also do not pay additional costs.

Another observation concerns the commercial mix. During the beginning and the end of season, single firms are able to attract neighbouring clients, interested in short breaks and presumably coming during weekends or non-working days. Given this market positioning, a critical value added factor for a local agency, is the ability to attract new, possibly completely new targets. This situation creates a clear perception by local firms of the "commercial power" held by the territorial governance structure. On the contrary, if the local agency creates events or products that focus on the same targets and markets, local firms have an impaired perception of the DMO's commercial ability, reducing trust.

Finally, a critical value for a territorial governance structure is to possess the critical skills and core competencies in order to collect local resources and to "increase" the value of money. Without APT (in the case of Skipassfree) local firms with a limited marketing budget would probably not have been able to design the project, to involve companies, or to attract so many international customers.

References

Baggio, R. (2008). Symptoms of complexity in a tourism system. *Tourism Analysis,* 13(1), 1-20.

Baggio, R., & Sainaghi, R. (2011). Complex and chaotic tourism systems: towards a quantitative approach. *International Journal of Contemporary Hospitality Management,* 23(6), 840-861.

Baum, J., Mezias S.J., & S.J. (1992). Localized competition and organizational failure in the Manhattan hotel industry, 1898-1990. *Administrative Science Quarterly,* 37(4), 580-604.

Beedie, P., & Hudson, S. (2003). Emergence of mountain-based adventure tourism. *Annals of Tourism Research,* 30(3), 625-643.

Bieger, T. (1997). *Management von Destinationen und Tourismus- organisationen* (Dritte Auflage ed.). München/Wien: Oldenburg.

Bodega, D., Cioccarelli, G., & Denicolai, S. (2004). New inter- organizational forms: evolution of relationship structures in mountain tourism. *Tourism Review,* 59(3), 13-19.

Buhalis, D. (2000). Marketing the competitive destination of the future. *Tourism Management,* 21(SI), 97-116.

Claver-Cortés, E., Molina-Azorìn, J.F., Pereira-Moliner, J., & Lopez- Gamero, M. D. (2007). Environmental strategies and their impact on hotel performance. *ClJournal of Sustainable Tourism,* 15(6), 663-679.

Cockerell, N. (1988). Skiing in Europe – potential and problems. *EIU Travel and Tourism Analyst,* 5, 66-81.

—. (1994). Market segments: the international ski market in Europe. *EIU Travel and Tourism Analyst,* 3, 34-55.

d'Angella, F., De Carlo, M., & Sainaghi, R. (2010). Archetypes of destination governance: A comparison of international destinations. *Tourism Review,* 65(4), 61-73.

Dredge, D. (1999). Destination place planning and design. *Annals of Tourism Research,* 26(4), 772-791.

—. (2006). Policy networks and the local organization of tourism. *Tourism Management,* 27(2), 269-280.

Flagestad, A., & Hope, C.A. (2001). Strategic Success in Winter Sports Destinations: A Sustainable Value Creation Perspective. *Tourism Management,* 22(5), 445-461.

Fredman, P., & Heberlein, T.A. (2003). Changes in skiing and snowmobiling in Swedish mountains. *Annals of Tourism Research,* 30(2), 485-488.

Go, F.M., & Govers, R. (2000). Integrated quality management for tourist destinations: A European perspective on achieving competitiveness. *Tourism Management,* 21(SI), 79-88.

Godde, P.M., Price, M.F., & Zimmermann, F.M. (2000). Tourism and Development in Mountain Regions: Moving Forward into the New Millennium. In P.M. Godde, M.F. Price, & F.M. Zimmermann, *Tourism and Development in Mountain Regions* (p. 1-25). NY: CABI.

Hudson, S. (2000). *Snow Business. A Study of the International Ski Industry.* London: Cassell.

Ingram, P., & Inman, C. (1996). Institutions, intergroup competition, and the evolution of hotel populations around Niagara Falls. *Administrative Science Quarterly,* 41(4), 629-658.

Jick, T.D. (1979). Mixing qualitative and quantitative methods: Triangulation in action. *Administrative Science Quarterly,* 24(4), 602-611.

Koller, T., Goedhart, M., & Wessels, D. (2005). *Valuation. Measuring and managing the value of companies* (4th Ed.). NJ: John Wiley.

Mitchell, R.G. (1983). *Mountain experience: The psychology and sociology of adventure.* Chicago: The University of Chicago Press.

Needham, M.D., & Rollins, R.B. (2005). Interest group standards for recreation and tourism impact at ski areas in the summer. *Tourism Management,* 26(1), 1-13.

Pomfret, G. (2006). Mountaineering adventure tourists: A conceptual framework for research. *Tourism Management,* 27(1), 113-123.

Porter, M.E. (1985). *Competitive Advantage.* NY: The Free Press.

—. (1991). Towards a dynamic theory of strategy. *Strategic Management Journal,* 12(SI), 95-117.

Price, M.F., Moss, L.A., & Williams, P.W. (1997). Tourism and amenity migration. In B. Messerli, & J.D. Ives, *Mountains of the World: A Global Priority* (p. 249-280). London and NY: Parthenon Press.

Sainaghi, R. (2004). *La gestione delle destinazioni turistiche.* Milano: Egea.

—. (2006). From contents to processes: versus a dynamic destination management model (DDMM). *Tourism Management,* 27(5), 1053-1063.

—. (2008). Strategic positioning and performance of winter destinations. *Tourism Review,* 63(4), 40-57.

—. (2010a). A meta-analysis of hotel performance, continental or worldwide style? *Tourism Review,* 65(3), 46-69.

—. (2010b). Hotel performance: state of the art. *International Journal of Contemporary Hospitality Management,* 22(7), 920-952.

—. (2011). RevPAR determinants of individual hotels: evidences from Milan. *International Journal of Contemporary Hospitality Management,* 23(3), 297-311.

Sainaghi, R., & Canali, S. (2011). Exploring the effects of destination's positioning on hotels' performance: The Milan case. *Tourismos: An International Multidisciplinary Journal of Tourism,* 6(2), 121-138.

Scott, N., & Laws, E. (2005). Tourism Crises and Disasters: Enhancing Understanding of System Effects. *Journal of Travel & Tourism Marketing,* 19(2/3), 149-158.

Spring, J. (1998). Subtle but important shifts in customers. *Ski Area Management,* 37(5), 57-58.

Williams, P.W., Gill, A.M., & Chura, N. (2004). Branding mountain
    destinations: the battle for "placefulness". *Tourism Review,* 59(1), 6-
    15.

WTO. (2011). *Tourism highlights.* Retrieved from http://www.world-
    tourism.org/facts/menu.html

Yin, R. (1994). *Case Study Research* (2nd Ed.). California: Sage.

Zahra, A., & Ryan, C. (2007). From chaos to cohesion - Complexity in
    tourism structures: An analysis of New Zealand's regional tourism
    organizations. *Tourism Management,* 28(3), 854-862.

CHAPTER FOURTEEN

CREATIVITY AND INNOVATION IN TOURISM: THE ROLE OF EVENTS

TONINO PENCARELLI, MIRELLA MIGLIACCIO, SIMONE SPLENDIANI AND FRANCESA RIVETTI

Abstract

For a local tourist system, the ability to innovate its offers becomes a crucial strategic factor in global competition with other destinations. The study first discussed the conceptual links among creativity, innovation, and tourist areas, following two basic perspectives: territorial or destination level and individual company or organization level. The goal is to clarify the relationships between creativity, innovation and territory through knowledge transmission and sharing within the geographically located and interconnected system of actors. On the empirical level, the aim is to analyze cases of Italian events, highlighting underlying creative and innovative processes. The chapter has important managerial implications. At meta-level management it highlights the role of the learning destination, while at the organizational level it stresses the key role of the project team in making events effective. **Keywords:** experience economy, creativity, innovation, event management, destination management, learning destinations.

1. Introduction

In the "post-modern economy", where the consumer has become more and more fickle and is looking for new and authentic experiences, the tourist enterprises and tourist destination offers need to be original and continually innovative. In an information and knowledge economy, innovative tourism products and experiences are developed by processes of knowledge generation, knowledge sharing, and knowledge combination, generated by the creative capabilities possessed by tourist enterprises and tourist destinations. This chapter focuses on tourist events as emblematic cases of innovative products offered by the tourism industry. This topic is examined by describing the relationships between knowledge, creativity, and innovation. The link between creativity and innovation is considered to be the linchpin of knowledge theory.

Scholars have examined knowledge from different perspectives. Initially they considered it a resource acquired by an organization (e.g. Drucker, 1985). Nonaka (1994) changed this perspective, by defining knowledge a "justified true belief" created by the organization. Wenger and Snyder (2000) emphasize the crucial role of community consensus in improving the effectiveness of the process of knowledge creation (Migliaccio, Addeo, & Rivetti, 2010). Boisot (1998) suggests that it is "a capability based on information", depending on organizational structure and data sharing. Nootebom (2009) refers to knowledge in a broad sense, going beyond rational inference, know-what, and know-how, to include perception, interpretation, value judgements, morality, emotions, and feelings.

Regarding innovation, Nelson and Winter (1982) consider it to be a structurally unpredictable "mutation" of routines. Nonaka (1994) points out that innovation can be regarded as a process by which the organization creates and defines problems, which require the development of new knowledge to be resolved. Rogers (1998) stresses both the creation of new knowledge and the dissemination of existing knowledge in the innovation process. However, according to Dodgson, Gann, and Salter (2002), innovation is the productive use of knowledge manifested in the successful development and introduction of new products, processes, and/or services.

Amabile (1996) points out that the concept of creativity is the production of new and appropriate ideas in every field of human activity. Other scholars believe that it is the ability to generate new and useful ideas (Schilling, 2004; Sternberg & Lubart, 1999). Binning (1991) suggests that it should be defined as the attitude of a system to evolve. With reference to the level of analysis, initially scholars have focused on the construction of individual creativity (e.g. Amabile, 1996), subsequently shifting to organizational creativity (Woodman, Sawyer, & Griffin, 1993; West, 2002). The last construction represents a turning point in management studies, because it also highlights the need to streamline the path to innovation in the generation of ideas, drawing attention to the "collective dimension" of knowledge (Weick, 1995). Creativity is the organizational ability to generate new and useful ideas at different stages of the innovation process by making use of available knowledge that then feeds into new discoveries. The transformation of new ideas through innovation requires social or scientific validation (Csikszentmihalyi, 1999). This is a non-sequential dynamic circle (see Figure 1), with particular characteristics depending on both the context and the types of innovation.

Figure 1 – From ideas to innovation

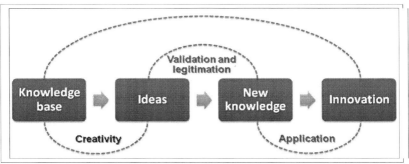

Source: our data

In sum, knowledge, creativity and innovation are closely linked and feed each other in a potentially infinite process. The relationship between creativity, knowledge and innovation should be analyzed in a tourist destination from two basic perspectives:

- *Territorial or destination level* – (paragraph 2)
- *Individual company or organization level* (paragraph 3).

Events are an example of social and cultural innovation. They allow consumers to act as "consumer-actors," as co-designers and co-producers, living the various dimensions of experience, describing it, enhancing it, and sharing it among all participants. The active role of local communities suggests that these events can be qualified as "social innovations" (Norman, 1992), over and above the organizational and managerial skills involved, becoming i.e. "innovations that create new types of social behaviour, using human and social energy more efficiently and connected to each other - in new ways – and to social contexts".

2. Events as Creative and Innovative Tourism Products

Networking relationships among enterprises - more or less intense for individual destinations – facilitate processes of knowledge transfer, learning, and coordination of actors' activities, in line with the strategic network theory (Shaw & Williams, 2009), based on a 'continuous interactive learning' process (Heunks, 1998).

For the successful implementation of a creative idea, and thus the innovation process an organization's ability to draw external capital (in terms of human resources, information, and knowledge) is as crucial as the ability to effectively transfer knowledge among actors - promoting learning processes (Golinelli, 2002; Pencarelli & Forlani, 2002; Sacco, 2006; Sundbo *et al.*, 2007; Weidenfeld *et al.*, 2010). This implies a variety of information flows within firms, among firms, producers and consumers, and between the public and private sectors. All this requires a "weakening" of the traditional boundaries of the enterprise (Weidenfeld *et al.*, 2010), which requires the ability to manage knowledge and its applications, to identify the knowledge resources needed and evaluate those possessed, and to acquire and re-distribute knowledge within the organization (Nonaka & Takeuchi, 1995).

This approach can be effectively reflected in local tourist contexts through the "Learning Tourist Destination Model", or LTD (Pencarelli & Splendiani, 2010; Schianetz, Kavanagh, & Lockington, 2007), which is borrowed from the concept of the "learning organization." Following Napier and Nilsson (2006), we can state that collective creative processes of destinations are effective if they are based on the capacity of the actors to interact and to absorb input from the context. They depend on relational resources (such as reputation and trust) and intellectual resources (such as knowledge) held by firms and embedded within the destination (local social capital). In this conceptual framework, innovation can be seen as the result of the creative ability of businesses and the tourist destination, which in turn depends on their stock of knowledge, people, and local actors, and the ability to combine and link people, actors, and knowledge (Vicari, Cillo, & Verona, 2005). Output of these processes can be different, have a different degree of intensity, and involve a number of areas.

For the purpose of our study, maintaining the dialectical relationship between business and destination, we can place the output of innovative processes in the following categories:

- *strategic innovation*, linked to new combinations of customers served, needs met, and technologies that define new market segments and new competitive business models (Abell, 1986);
- *innovation of products / services*, related to something relatively new to the supply system, both in absolute terms - something never seen before - and in relative terms - that is, referring to that

particular business or destination (Hjalager, 2010). In service management literature, the concept of innovation is generally linked to purely behavioural or process changes, even before technological process changes (Normann, 1992; Sudbo *et al.,* 2007).

- *process / technological innovations.* These innovations are related to production and delivery processes - even of a technological nature - aimed at increasing efficiency and productivity without affecting the quality of supply.
- *meta-managerial and managerial innovations.* This type of innovation acts both at the enterprise level and destination level, including new ways of organizing relations within the company or the network operators to drive people within the network. These innovations have a strong influence on the ability of the company to encourage organizational creativity, through the preservation of knowledge and the definition of learning models.

In this context, the role of events should be analyzed as examples of "knowledge-intensive" and highly creative tourist products. Events are potentially innovative because they are based on individual and organizational creativity, and are customizable for communities, enterprises, and tourist destinations. From the conceptual point of view, tourist products are packages of goods and services which tourists enjoy during their stay and which correspond to their motivation for travel (Pencarelli & Forlani, 2002). In other words, tourist products allow tourists to live tourist experiences, understood as personal and engaging events that involve a shift in spatial and temporal duration and include an overnight stay (Rispoli, 2001). Following this approach (Fortezza & Pencarelli, 2010), experiences can create value for people when they:

- gratify and enhance the senses;
- create opportunities for socializing (Cova, 2003);
- affirm their identities, or offer new temporary ones, as part of a theatrical performance;
- create opportunities for self-realization.

Events, in this sense, are experience-products par excellence, that is the archetypal form on which experience is built, following the progression of the economic value model developed by Pine and Gilmore (2000). For this reason, to be appreciated, experiences must be unique and must fully involve the consumer and host communities at the emotional, physical and cognitive levels. Therefore they must be innovative, offering new solutions and original formats in terms of content, time, or location. Events can be the result of initiatives undertaken by permanent or temporary organizations and/or collaboration between them, by collaboration with an underlying network of professionals (artists, experts, etc..) coordinated as hierarchical models, or through network approaches, through the activation of "chains of cooperation" (Sedita, 2009). In this respect, it is important to understand the connections between event management and organization, the governance of tourist destination and the destination management approach followed by the key players.

Events are the results of creative capabilities (shared, but also not shared and unconscious) of the various players in the destination - or coming from other areas. Creative capital qualifies the attractiveness of places and expresses development potential. Events also provide an opportunity to actively involve tourists, who are driven by the emotional aspects in the decision making process, as protagonists and co-producers of their own experiences. The consumer can identify new classes of needs and provide useful information for designing the event. This involvement also affects the atmosphere within which the event is experienced, enhancing the perception of authenticity on the part of other users. The viewer of the event can contribute to its innovation by making available their own creativity or by facilitating access to creativity through related social networks.

3.1. Creativity, knowledge and innovation in project teams

As previously highlighted, on the demand side, the role of consumer is highlighted. Alternatively, on the supply side, the management of the event becomes crucial. The following paragraphs are focused on the relationships between creativity, knowledge, and innovation at the organizational and firm levels, particularly considering teams. Originally studies on creativity were focused on the individual. Creativity was conceived as a mental or cognitive capacity acting within social contexts, and the collective process of generating ideas remained opaque.

Starting from the 1990s, scholars have developed multilevel models with reference to social entities. These models were often not defined in detail, and sometimes used interchangeable terms (i.e. groups and teams). In this view, groups and teams play a key role in organizational creativity. This is more evident considering how interactions work in organizational and environmental contexts. However, the emphasis remained on structural and managerial practices designed to stimulate individual creativity, and to their impact on the group and organizational levels.

Woodman *et al.* (1993) carried out one of the first attempts to discover how to develop organizational creativity according to a multilevel perspective (individual-group-organization). However, even in this case, the focus is on the individual. In fact, the group is defined as "the social context in which creative behaviour occurs" (p. 303). In this view creativity is the complex product of a person's behaviour in a specific situation, and it is influenced by contextual and social factors.

Studies on group creativity have advanced due to West (2002), who examines how creativity and innovation are implemented in work groups in an integrated way. Unlike previous scholars, he emphasizes the influence of the external environment; moreover, he highlights the crucial role of "group integrated processes", through which specific tasks and individual knowledge can function as mediators "for creativity and innovation." However, in order for groups to be effective agents in this process, they must be characterized by both strong integration processes and a high level of safety (supportive), and the context must be demanding (challenging) (West & Sacramento, 2006, pp. 39-40).

From these studies, a growing awareness emerges concerning the role of the group as an agent for organizational creativity. Through this new perspective, one can examine how knowledge is combined and recombined within the organization and, consequently, how the creative process should be managed. It does not seem enough to "build" the team properly, because its structure does not exhaust its potential for creativity. Similarly, it is no longer sufficient to define managerial routines as acting only on the individual level. It is our contention that this phenomenon has particular features in the context of cultural events.

3.2. Cultural events and project teams

Cultural events are developed by "project" organizations, which differ in terms of time, nature, and level of formalization. Regarding the time, there are both temporary and permanent units; moreover, in temporary units there is often a stable "core", flanked by *pro-tempore* figures. The nature of the organization (public, private or mixed) has a strong political impact on all managerial and operational decisions, resource allocation and role assignment in particular. Concerning the level of formalization, we must emphasize the role of "latent organizations", which are located in networks of professionals linked by reputational and experiential factors (Sedita, 2009, p. 41).

Project teams constitute the basic units of these organizations. Within cultural events, they follow a product-driven logic. The event is the result of a collective effort of creation and sharing of meaning, mediated by social legitimation. In this context, aesthetic attributes and symbolic knowledge must be managed in an appropriate way. Therefore, cultural events must be managed through adhocratic logics (Mintzberg, 1983), in contrast to projects in science-based and technology-based industries.

The structure of the team changes during the life cycle of the event, depending on the specific activities to be implemented. The subunits which design the event generally last for a long period, although they can be characterized by temporary components. The temporary components encourage creativity, but only through a stable core is it possible to create knowledge. In addition, during the implementation of the event, other individual or collective actors can be linked to the team. At this stage the role of stimulating creativity falls mainly to the leader. He/she acts as a creative entrepreneur (Napier & Nilsson, 2006), a "promoter" of the team's creative capacity, while the team and its components are the primary agents of creativity. During the implementation, the leader becomes an "orchestrator" of individual and collective units, which contribute to the generation of new useful ideas. With regard to the nature of the event's financial support, both public and private sponsors are often extremely important.

Considering the level of formalization, the "hard" component of the organization managing the event is generally limited. In fact, the organizational structure largely corresponds to the team, which includes professionals involved for the specific edition and, in many cases, volunteers. This structure encourages creativity by reducing hierarchy and favoring logics of mutual adaptation. In our opinion, it is possible to identify critical factors that stimulate creativity within teams that organize and manage cultural events:

- enhancing the absorptive capacity (Cohen & Levinthal, 1990)
- removing all cognitive and emotional barriers to creativity
- enhancing relational skills.

With reference to the first factor, teams should find information, recognize its value, and apply it. This depends not only on the team's knowledge base, which comes from the stable core and the individuals, but also on all relations with the external environment and between the sub-groups. Thus, communication between the team members and the sub-groups, and with the external environment, is extremely important. In this situation, both an "open" culture and the presence of mediators are crucial to overcome obstacles to creativity. In sum, for an event to reach its creative and innovative potential, project teams should:

- use communication techniques and tools which enable systematic listening and dialogue, encouraging interaction through shared language;
- set appropriate selection and recruitment mechanisms, in order to build a conflicting, and so potentially innovative, environment, heterogeneous in terms of professional skills and knowledge (Paulus, 2000); therefore, adhocratic coordination mechanisms are also necessary;
- use motivation techniques and incentive systems; many people should hold multiple and temporary roles;
- be managed by a charismatic team-leader, initially as a creative entrepreneur and then as an "orchestrator", who aligns different approaches without jeopardizing innovation, and who encourages and manages diversities, through trust and reciprocity mechanisms;
- provide the presence of innovative leaders at the territorial level, capable of ensuring coordination and cooperation between actors, and exchange of information and knowledge, in order to develop a stimulating environment for shared creativity as a requirement for innovative processes;
- have cognitive inter-mediation and relational connection figures, promoting inter-group and external relations.

These aspects will align with the specific event to be organized and implemented. In the following paragraphs two cases from Italy: the Sannio FilmFest, which takes place in Sant'Agata De' Goti, and the Summer Jamboree held in Senigallia are examined.

4. Case Study Analysis

The case study is exploratory in nature and is designed to develop hypotheses and propositions to be verified in further investigations. We have chosen to implement a multiple qualitative case study (Yin, 1994), which allows us to focus on the interaction with the subjects investigated (Corbetta, 1999), not simply as a matter of rigour (Eisenhardt, 1989), but also in order to point out in each case the analysis of specific facets of the phenomenon investigated. Events analysis is aimed at understanding the degree of innovation, the link with the creativity of the area and possible management choices stimulating the creativity of those involved.

Consistent with the type of survey chosen, use of primary and secondary data was made, collected through participant observation, semi-structured interviews with organizers, and documents. The main topics discussed during the interviews are related to the following research questions:

- Which characteristics do project teams need to have in order to stimulate creativity and innovation? What is the role of the team leader?
- Which approach to regional governance is more effective in stimulating creativity and innovation at the destination level?

The table below describes the case studies. It is divided into two main areas:

- The first describes the events and their sub-activities, through information, including type, number of visitors, promoting body, etc.
- The second analyzes the team, clarifying its organizational structure and internal relations.

Table 1 – Case Studies

EVENT PROFILE		
	Sannio FilmFest	Summer Jamboree
First Year	1997	2000
Time of performance	First ten days of July	First ten days of August
Location	Sant'Agata De' Goti (BN) – Campania Region – Italy	Senigallia (AN) – Marche Region - Italy
Event type	International Film Festival dedicated to costume movies.	International festival of music and culture of America in the '40s and '50s
Promoting body-organizer	Cultural association "Sotto il segno dei Goti"	Association "Summer Jamboree"
Number of visitors (last edition)	35.000 in the 10-day event	150.000 in the 9-day event
Offering	Costume movies are the central theme. Screenings, exhibitions, meetings with filmmakers, seminars, training courses and award ceremonies.	Music is the central theme. In addition to numerous live concerts - with world-renowned artists as well as young talent - the whole city gets moving and the whole environment is "themed".

THE ROLE OF TEAMS: CONFIGURATION, INTERNAL AND EXTERNAL RELATIONS, LEADERSHIP		
	Sannio FilmFest	Summer Jamboree
Configuration	50 people split into two temporary teams and one permanent team. Permanent team: the festival's Artistic Director (the leader), head of economic planning, head of film office, head of general planning. First temporary team (six months a year): administration, hospitality, media relations, ceremonial. Second temporary team (one month a year): assistants, service personnel, drivers and technicians.	The team has a pyramidal structure. At the top there are three individuals, namely: 1) the festival's Artistic Director, 2) Head of Communications, Media, Sponsor Relations, Relations with public authorities; 3) Logistics Manager. The three subjects - who represent the "hidden network" referred to in paragraph 3 - are joined by a number of middle managers for ancillary activities (stands and structures, ticket office, hostess / reception, artists reception, food and beverages, merchandising.
Internal relations	Permanent team: periodic meetings and informal contact. First temporary team: formal and informal contact. Second temporary team: mainly formal interaction.	The team works all year to organize the event, due to the existence of events connected to the main one, dispersed at different times of the year.
External relations (with public and private entities)	External communication is formal and largely involves the leader and other members of the permanent component. Relations with public organizations and sponsors are collaborative.	The most important relationship with the public is with the town of Senigallia, in which the team shares the objectives and every matter. Also with private sponsors there is a highly collaborative relationship, especially with the main two.

The role of team leader	Charismatic profile. Great experience in the film industry. Dense network of relations, used for the benefit of the event. Transfer of knowledge and skills to other team members. Support from other members of the permanent team in defining the program, economic planning and coordination.	The role of team leader is covered by the three managers. They supervise the event and the treatment of external relations. They are also responsible for selecting employees.
The role of viewers and local people	Two main occasions of interaction with visitors and residents: the campus of scenography and costume and the initiatives called "Borgo in Fest", which take place in the Old Town Square.	The entire city gets moving and everything is "thematic" This includes not only objects from the street, but also a strong involvement of traders and local crafts.

Analysis of these cases shows how different team-organizational models may lead to high levels of innovation and creativity. Both teams tend to favor heterogeneity as a factor potentially facilitating the generation of new ideas, but also guaranteeing the presence of a common language - in one case concerning the film industry and in the other, the music and style of America in the 40s and 50s. The "common language" is appropriately assessed in the recruitment of new members of both teams, since it facilitates interaction and communication among people, both through formal channels and through informal ones. The coordination of activities is made easier by the common language, as well as by the established relationships that bind most of the permanent team members. These aspects are reflected in the characteristics of leaders.

In both cases the assignment of roles and responsibilities is characterized by a growing degree of flexibility up the pyramid, which supports creativity at higher hierarchical levels. In particular, this structure creates opportunities for people to engage in problem-solving activities, which not only leads them to go beyond their areas of responsibility, but above all makes creativity a type of "response" as defined by Unsworth (2001). This "Responsive Creativity" is the ability to find a solution to a specific problem that has a definite solution.

Through examining these two contexts, two main differences between the teams' organizational models can be identified. The first is about the nature of the leader. At the Sannio FilmFest, leadership is exercised by a single subject - involving other members of the permanent component in the assessment of crucial management aspects: planning, organization, implementation, and ex-post activities. Trust is the critical factor for success through the creation of long-term relationships at all levels. In the case of the Summer Jamboree, however, leadership is exercised by a collegial body composed of three American music fans who first created the event and subsequently have been able to maintain high enthusiasm and stimulus to continuous innovation. The second difference regards the active role of visitors and residents. During the Sannio Film Festival, spectators have two kinds of experiences:

- An "entertainment" experience, i.e. passive participation by the viewer with only "intellectual" involvement (Pine & Gilmore, 2000).
- A "learning" experience, through the "campus" of scenography and costume.

In the case of the Summer Jamboree, however, the experience of the viewer can be defined as one "of evasion", that is - the result of active participation. Spectators wear period clothing and are physically involved in the festival through parties and events. In both cases we find a supportive environment for the teams organizing the events, due to the contribution of territorial leaders and local community - especially through organizational support, information and knowledge dissemination, and so on. This helps the system's ability to generate creativity and thus innovation. The local communities welcome both events enthusiastically, helping with ideas, participating actively, and spreading positive word of mouth and viral communication (through photos and messages on Facebook or other social networks). Also tourist entrepreneurs have contributed in a positive way, extending the opening hours of local activities and providing logistical support.

5. Conclusion

The creative and innovative potential of the destination is one of the distinctive characteristics that can be critical in the competition among territories to attract tourists. In highlighting the innovative output of tourist destinations (paragraph 2), we have chosen to focus on events as products of creativity and - at the same time – as a potential source of additional innovative steps. Starting from this assumption, the study first discussed the conceptual links among creativity, innovation, and tourist areas, following two basic perspectives:

- *Territorial or destination level* (paragraph 2), with particular reference to the role of the local community as a context of people and organizations capable of generating social innovations (Normann, 1992);
- *Individual company or organization level* (paragraph 3). First of all, it emerges that cognitive dynamics have a circular and non-sequential course, as cause and effect of creativity and innovation (par.1). This is characterized differently, depending on the context in which it occurs and on the forms of innovation.

At the territorial/destination level, the importance of social networks in promoting innovative dynamics emerges. They leverage creative intelligence and collective knowledge, based on organizational cohesion factors, typical of local systems (e.g. trust, reciprocal listening among network participants, shared and co-identified mission views, opening up of involved cognitive systems). In other words, in tourist destinations the focus shifts from the stock of knowledge to the flow of knowledge, particularly with reference to the ability to generate, transfer, and share knowledge between the actors. This emphasizes not only the role of network relationships (clusters, districts), but also the need to loosen current business boundaries (Weidenfeld *et al.,* 2009). Creativity and knowledge are "disseminated" in this context, within the destinations as well as within the organizations and among the local actors, individuals who play a critical role (Figure 2).

This chapter has important managerial implications. Meta-level management (destination manager) and team or business leaders play the most important role in increasing and enhancing creativity and knowledge. It highlights the role of the learning destination (Pencarelli & Splendiani, 2010) that invokes the system's ability to make available to local actors (local agencies, businesses, non-profit organizations, local people, tourists, etc.) information and knowledge within a collaborative environment, as well as inspire trust. At organizational level we stress the key role of the project team in making events effective, since the project team favors organizational creativity, thus allowing continuous innovation (par 3). The role played by local community and tourists is also very important, as "prosumers" (Normann, 1992) of innovation, in that they help socialization, creative combination, and conversion of knowledge (Nonaka, 1994).

These events constitute innovations (Fig.2), as the output of creative processes made by individuals or "hidden networks". In addition, events are tourism products, that is, packages of goods and services that tourists consume to satisfy their experiential needs. As such, they represent the connection between supply and demand in tourism (Pencarelli & Splendiani, 2010).

Fig. 2 – Creativity, Knowledge and Innovation in Tourist Destination

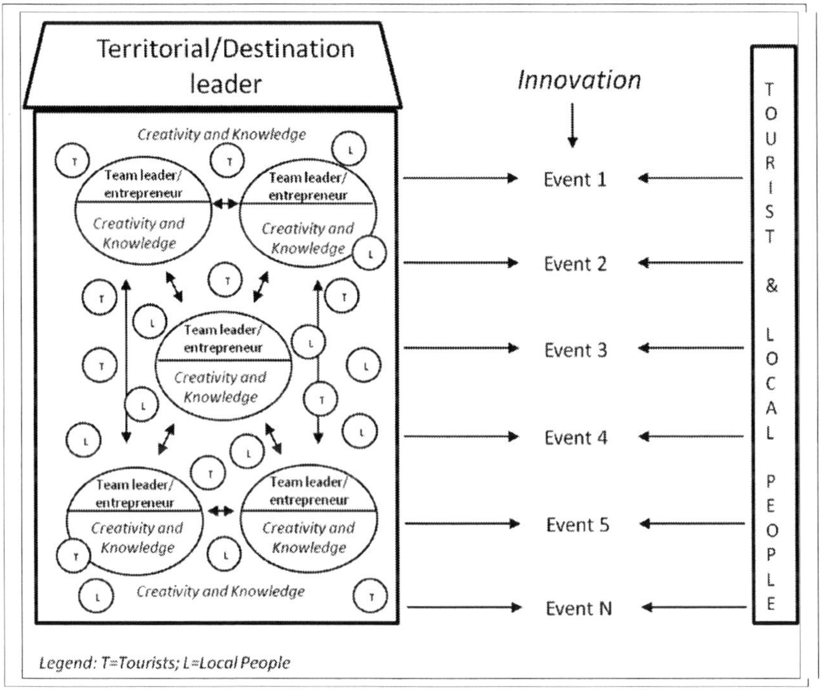

Although limited to two exemplary experiences that do not allow generalizations, this case analysis highlights and strengthens some assumptions in the literature, such as:

- the circular interdependence between knowledge, creativity, and innovation in organizations and tourist destinations in setting up unique tourism products

- the importance of a common language to promote collective learning and transfer of knowledge and skills to enterprises as well as to the territorial level
- the vital role of the charismatic leader, or the governing body of the "event system", in combining unsettled knowledge and new knowledge and sharing creative processes and innovative solutions with regional and institutional stakeholders.

Moreover, in a world where the economy of experience is driving the new trend of consumptions (Pine & Gilmore, 2000), the cases analyse suggest that events are highly-experiential tourism products. Therefore, the ability to use and connect knowledge through creative processes, both within and outside the boundaries of tourist destinations, is crucial. This requires the selection of the right "experience activators," which Schmitt (1999) defines "strategic experiential modules": *sense* activates experiences of a sensory nature; *feel* activates affective experiences; *think* activates learning experiences; *act* activates experiences of a physical nature; *relate* activates experiences of a social nature.

Each event is like a stage play, a special product: unique, difficult to standardize and containing different degrees of innovativeness. Its innovativeness depends on variations in its theme, composition and the attitude of the "players" in their setting, the role of spectators (tourists), who are sometimes passive spectators of the show, but sometimes become actors themselves and generators of new forms of innovation.

As with all experience-products, however, in a world of fickle consumers, the risk is to trivialize and make the experience unattractive to the public who must choose it as a way of spending their free time. For this reason, processes of knowledge management and creative processes must be continuously stimulated at the regional, organizational, and personal levels, in order to guarantee continuous innovation, to remain competitive, and to differentiate it from other competing products. In this perspective, one needs to stimulate the growth of "learning organizations" and "learning destinations".

Continuous innovation, however, must avoid excessive proliferation of events, especially events in the same period. This is to prevent giving tourists too many choices or to "destination"overload. The risk, in this sense, is that the events will become "unsustainable," which will compromise the quality of enjoyment and satisfaction of tourists and residents. It is necessary for the governing leader of the destinations to serve the functions of direction and coordination, identifying the main events for those in tourism development planning, also in order to avoid forms of product cannibalization. However, this activity is very complex due to the fact that in the innovative processes that take place within events, leadership is "shared" and "spread" across multiple levels, involving destination government, event organizing companies, tourist entrepreneurs, leaders of non-profit organizations, leaders of local community groups and so on. In other words, innovation springs from "disseminated" processes and has to be shared among the various levels of leadership, as the case studies show.

Despite the limitation from the small number of cases studies, this research points out the links between knowledge, creativity, and innovation in tourism, highlighting the importance of the charismatic leader at both the enterprise and destination levels; the results of the study also open the way for new paths and research questions, such as: What role can innovation play in the product portfolios of the destinations? How do we build experiences while avoiding the risk of their massification and trivialization? What experiences are necessary for creating sustainable tourism destinations? How can a leader improve the knowledge, creativity and innovation processes in tourism organizations and tourism destinations, conceived as learning subjects?

References

Abell, D.F. (1986). *Business e scelte aziendali*. Milano: Ipsoa.

Amabile, T.M. (1996). *Creativity in context: Update to "the social psychology of creativity"*. Boulder, CO: Westview Press.

Bilton, C. (2007). *Management and creativity: From creative industries to creative management*. Oxford: Blackwell.

Binning, G. (1991). *Dal nulla. Sulla creatività dell'uomo e della natura*. Milan: Garzanti.

Boisot, M.H. (1998). *Knowledge assets: Securing competitive advantage in the information economy*. Oxford: Oxford University Press.

Cohen, W.M., & Levinthal, D.A. (1990). Absorptive capacity: A new perspective on learning and innovation. *Administrative Science Quarterly,* 35(1), 128-152.

Corbetta, P. (1999). *Metodologia e tecniche della ricerca sociale*. Bologna: Il Mulino.

Cova, B. (2003). *Il marketing tribale*. Milano: Il Sole 24 Ore Libri.

Csikszentmihalyi, M. (1999). Implications of a systems perspective for the study of creativity. In R. Sternberg (Ed.), *Handbook of Creativity* (pp. 313-335). Cambridge: Cambridge University Press.

Dogson, M., Gann, D.M., & Salter, A.J. (2002). The intensification of innovation. *International Journal of Innovation Management*, 6(1), 53-84

Drucker, P.F. (1985). *Innovation and entrepreneurship. Practice and principles*. NY: Harper & Row.

Eisenhardt, K.M. (1989). Building theories from case study research. *Academy of Management Review*, 14(4), 532-550.

Fortezza, F. & Pencarelli, T. (2010). *Il marketing delle esperienze fra specificità e tendenze evolutive: il caso Wish Days*. Paper presented at International Congress "Marketing Trends", Venice, 21-23 January.

Golinelli, C.M. (2002). *Il territorio sistema vitale*. Turin: Giappichelli.

Grönroos, C. (2002). *Management e Marketing dei Servizi. Un approccio al management dei rapporti con la clientela*. Torino: ISEDI.

Heunks, F.J. (1998). Innovation, creativity and success. *Small Business Economics*, 10(3), 263-272.

Hjalager, A. (2010). A review of innovation research in tourism. *Tourism Management,* 31(1), 1-12.

Lubart, T. (1994). Creativity. In R.J. Sternberg (Ed.) *Thinking and problem solving*. NY: Academic Press.

Migliaccio, M., Addeo, F., & Rivetti, F. (2010). Market knowledge exploration and Web 2.0: Initial empirical evidence on hotel chains. In J.C. Spender, & G. Schiuma (Eds.), *Intellectual capital in a complex business landscape*, IFKAD proceedings, Matera, Italy, June 24-26.

Mintzberg, H. (1983). *Structure in fives. Designing effective organizations*, Englewood Cliffs, NJ: Prentice Hall.

Napier, N., & Nilsson, M. (2006). The development of creative capabilities in and out of creative organizations: Three case studies. *Creativity and Innovation Management*, 15(3), 268-278.

Nelson, R.R., & Winter, S.G. (1982). *An evolutionary theory of economic change*. Cambridge MA: Harvard University Press.

Nonaka, I. (1994). A dynamic theory of organizational knowledge creation. *Organization Science*, 5(1), 14-37.

Nonaka, I., & Takeuchi, H. (1995).*The knowledge-creating company: How Japanese companies create the dynamics of innovation*. NY: Oxford University Press.

Normann, R. (1992). *La gestione strategica dei servizi*. Milan: Etas Libri.

Paulus, P.B. (2000). Groups, teams and creativity: The creative potential of idea-generating groups. *Applied Psychology: An International Review*, 49(2), 237-262.

Pencarelli, T., & Forlani, F. (2002). Il marketing dei distretti turistici-sistemi vitali. *Sinergie*, 58, 231-277.

Pencarelli, T., & Splendiani, S. (2010). *Il governo delle destinazioni turistiche in una prospettiva di sostenibilità. Profili concettuali ed evidenze empiriche.* Paper presented at 9th International Marketing Trends Conference. Venice, January 21-23.

Pine, B.J., & Gilmore, J.H. (2000). *L'economia delle esperienze.* Milan: Etas Libri.

Rispoli, M. (Ed.) (2001). *Prodotti turistici evoluti. Casi ed esperienze in Italia.* Turin: Giappichelli.

Rogers, M. (1998). The definition and measurement of innovation. *Melbourne Institute Working Paper*, n.10.

Sacco, P. (2006). Il distretto culturale evoluto: competere per l'innovazione, la crescita e l'occupazione in *Nuove dinamiche di sviluppo territoriale: i distretti culturali evoluti*, Forlì: AICCON.

Sedita, S.R. (2009). Le organizzazioni project-based. In S.R. Sedita, M. Paiola (Ed.), *Il management della creatività. Reti, comunità e territori.* Rome: Carocci.

Schianetz, K., Kavanagh, L., & Lockington, D. (2007). The learning tourism destination: the potential of a learning organization approach for improving the sustainability of tourism destinations, *Tourism Management,* 28(6), 1485-1496.

Schilling, M. (2004). *Strategic management of technological innovation.* NY: McGraw-Hill.

Schmitt, B.H. (1999). *Experiential marketing.* NY: The Free Press.

Shaw, G., & Williams, A. (2009). Knowledge transfer and management in tourism organisations: An emerging research agenda. *Tourism Management,* 30(3): 325-335.

Sternberg, R.J. & Lubart, T.I. (1999). The concept of creativity: Prospects and paradigms. In R.J. Sternberg (Ed.), *Handbook of Creativity.* Cambridge: Cambridge University Press.

Sundbo, J., Orfila-Sintes, F., & Sorensen, F. (2007). The innovative behaviour of tourism firms - Comparative studies of Denmark and Spain. *Research Policy*, 36(1), 88-106.

Taggar, S. (2002). Individual creativity and group ability to utilize individual creative resources: A multilevel model, *Academy of Management Journal*, 45(2), 315-330.

Unsworth, K. (2001). Unpacking creativity. *The Academy of Management Review,* 26(2), 289-297.

Vicari, S., Cillo, P., & Verona, G. (2005). Capacità creativa e innovazione. Un modello interpretativo resource-based. *Sinergie*, 67, 123-147.

Weick, K.E. (1995). *Sensemaking in organizations.* London: Sage Publications.

Weidenfeld, A., Williams, A.M., & Butler, R.W. (2010). Knowledge transfer and innovation among attractions. *Annals of Tourism Research*, 37(3), 604-626.

Wenger, E.C., & Snyder, W.M. (2000). Communities of practice: The organizational frontier. *Harvard Business Review*, 78(1), 139-145.

West, M.A. (2002). Sparkling fountains or stagnant ponds: An integrative model of creativity and innovation implementation in work groups. *Applied Psychology: An International Review*, 51(3), 355-387.

West, M.A. & Sacramento, C.A. (2006). Flourishing in teams: Developing creativity and innovation. In J. Henry (Ed.), *Creative management and development* (3th Ed). London: Sage.

Woodman, R.W., Sawyer, J.E., & Griffin, R.W. (1993). Toward a theory of organizational creativity. *Academy of Management Review*, 18(2), 293–321.

Yin, R.K. (1994). *Case study research: Design and methods*. Thousand Oaks: Sage.

Yoeman, I., Robertson, M., Ali-Knight, J., Drummond, S., & McMahon-Beattie, U. (2003). *Festival and events management: An international arts and culture perspective*. Oxford: Butterworth-Heinemann.

Chapter Fifteen

How Hotels Can Learn from Failures: An Integrated Service Recovery System

Ana M. Díaz Martín, María Leticia Santos Vijande, Leticia Suárez Álvarez and Ana B. del Río Lanza

Abstract

Appropriate management of service failures involves a complex organizational response that enables tourism firms to learn from their current mistakes and transform such information into process improvements, in order to prevent future problems and introduce innovations into the service. Empirical evidence on this issue is limited. The current research seeks to identify, from the provider's perspective, the potential dimensions of an Integrated Service Recovery System (ISRS). The psychometric and performance-related properties of the proposed scale were tested against the data from a sample of 240 hotels in Spain. The results obtained confirm the existence of three key dimensions for service recovery in hotels: failure detection, failure analysis and response to failure.
Keywords: service failure, recovery, scale development.

1. Introduction

Service recovery has traditionally been seen as a set of specific actions in response to an unsatisfied consumer, or as an operational mechanism of damage control (East *et al.*, 2007; Grewal *et al.*, 2009; Reynolds & Harrys, 2009; Vaerenbergh *et al.*, 2009). However, over the last two decades, a new stream of contributions to the literature has begun to challenge this old view stressing the need to pay more attention to the information on service failures. Nowadays, it is crucial for organizations to learn from mistakes, transform such information into process improvements, and increase the understanding of how recovery affects the firm's overall performance in the long term and/or its future relationships with clients (Hart *et al.*, 1990; Johnston, 2005; Johnston & Michel, 2008; La & Kandampully, 2004; Lovelock *et al.*, 2009; Michel e*t al.*, 2009; Reichhel, 1996; Schıbrowsky & Lapidus, 1994; Slater, 2008; Smith *et al.*, 2009; Spreng *et al.*, 1995; Tax & Brown, 1998).

Under this renewed approach, failure management achieves a strategic consideration since it involves a deep revision of firms operations and the commitment of all the employees to proactively prevent failures and efficiently recover from mistakes. Talking about tourism firms specifically, adopting this new perspective implies that learning from mistakes and transforming such information into process improvements is for them as critical as recovering after a failure has occurred. Empirical evidence on this topic is scarce and the present study seeks to extend the existing literature by determining the dimensions that constitute an Integrated Service Recovery System (ISRS) in the hotel industry.

The identification of these management dimensions implies analyzing service recovery and gathering information from the viewpoint of the supply side, not from that of the demand side, which has been by far the more studied. Recently, Smith *et al.* (2009) proposed and validated seven possible dimensions related with service recovery management, but without considering the issue of learning from mistakes.

The paper is organized as follows. First, in order to identify the dimensions that constitute the ISRS scale developed in the present study, we review the literature on service recovery and its managerial implications. The following section presents the methodology of the study carried out, including a description of the process of development of the scale, data collection, and the techniques used in the empirical analysis. Finally, we discuss the results obtained and future research lines.

2. Literature Review

The ideal situation is one in which service firms have warning systems available to prevent impending failures or detect them immediately. From this perspective, proactive service recovery strategies involve detailed evaluation and monitoring of service provision so as to identify all the relevant information needed to anticipate and/or rectify any failures as they occur, even before the client is aware that there has been a problem, and, in any event, before the client actually formulates any a complaints or claims (Smith *et al.*, 1999; Smith & Bolton, 1998).

The ISRS should therefore offer the possibility of carrying out proactive and reactive responses as efficiently as possible. The literature presents various alternative logical sequences of the phases a firm should go through when implementing service recovery practices. Thus, Hart *et al.* (1990) describe four key stages: anticipating the requirements of recovery, acting rapidly, training employees, and keeping clients informed about the changes or improvements made to the service as a result of having identified and corrected the problem. Schibrowsky and Lapidus (1994) suggest that the customer service department has to develop two fundamental tasks: first, to handle individual complaints in order to resolve problems and satisfy the clients, and second, to analyze the information obtained from each complaint to uncover its cause and make the necessary improvements to the process to minimize the likelihood of a repeat of the failure.

In the same vein, Tax and Brown (1998) identify a sequence of four stages to help managers achieve effective recovery: identifying the failures, resolving the clients' problems, communicating and classifying the failures, and integrating the information available to improve the overall service. According to La and Kandampully (2004), service recovery that leads to value enhancement takes the firm through three phases of service orientation: operational, or the act of recovery in itself; strategic, or learning derived from an analysis of the failures; and service vision, or transforming the information or knowledge about the failures into changes and improvements in the organization.

Johnston and Michel (2008) opted for distinguishing three outcomes of recovery which they denominated customer recovery (satisfied clients), process recovery (improved processes), and employee recovery (satisfied staff). The three outcomes together constitute what the authors call service recovery. Consumer and process recovery are linked to damage control measures and improving the provision of service to avoid future failures. These thus coincide with practices also identified in the previous works. The third outcome is the most novel, since the authors include the need to support the employees in their task of dealing with client complaints and claims, what is called internal service recovery.

Recently, Michel *et al.* (2009) have explained how tensions among customer recovery, process recovery and employee recovery cause service recovery to fail and they suggest that effective recovery management requires an integrated approach. In the same vein, Smith *et al.* (2009) suggest the need to look at service recovery as an integrated system and they propose seven "structural dimensions" of effective service recovery systems. Among these dimensions three are clearly related to supporting employees when dealing with service failures and recoveries -"formality", "decentralization" and "human intensity"-, two other dimensions are linked to failure analysis -"comprehensiveness" and "system intensity"-, another factor named "accessibility" refers to failure identification and the last one, "influence", is linked to customer involvement in the recovery process.

In the present work, drawing on the contributions described above, we propose the existence of three main dimensions or factors underlying the construct we denominate Integrated Service Recovery System. These are: failure detection, failure analysis, and response to failure. The response dimension, as shown in Figure 1, comprises four different initiatives: rapid response, fair outcome, employee empowerment, and learning–innovation.

Figure 1 - Dimensions of an Integrated Service Recovery System

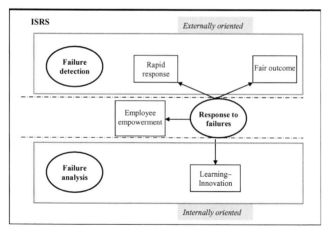

It is proposed that taking into account all these dimensions the organization can implement the strategic, relational and proactive focus described as desirable in service recovery management as well as to meet both the external and internal service recovery requirements (with clients and employees). Similarly, this system involves adopting a wide perspective of the failure-recovery process that allows understanding both its external and internal implications for the firms. In the following, we shall proceed to explain the content of each of these dimensions.

2.1. Failure detection

The percentage of formal complaints made by dissatisfied clients is very low, compared with the total number of services rendered deficiently (Harari, 1992; Singh, 1990; Tax & Brown, 1998). In these cases firms do not have the option of recovering from the failure, facing uncontrollable consequences for their image, long-term relationships, and/or market share. Most users who have a problem either change their provider quietly, or, worse, change their provider and trigger a negative word-of-mouth communication by speaking badly of the organization to others. Thus, obtaining information from clients by designing simple and accessible communication channels for them to make their views known is the first essential step in any recovery system (Colgate & Norris, 2001; Johnston & Michel, 2008; La & Kandampully, 2004; Michel *et al.,* 2009; Tax & Brown, 1998).

However, the firm needs to know immediately both whether there have been specific shortcomings in service provision, and whether there are potential problems or failures that either the clients or the employees can anticipate. It will have to develop specific procedures to obtain this information from both customers and employees. The user of the service must perceive that it is not going to be complicated to participate in these tasks; otherwise there will be a greater likelihood of losing the client's immediate feedback. Also, management must have timely availability to the data generated as an aid in taking the opportune decisions. We believe that such practices, with a clear external focus, allow the recovery process to be anticipated even before or at least immediately after the failure occurs, as well as to promptly ascertain the client's recovery needs, once failure occurs, and facilitate their instant fulfillment. Smith *et al.* (2009) named failure identification as "accessibility", although these authors limit this dimension to capturing the voice of customers when the failure occurs.

2.2. Failure analysis

Failure detection presupposes the existence of an organizational culture centered on creating customer value understood as a dynamic concept (Parasuraman, 1997), which in turn requires a continuous effort of adaptation and improvement by the organization (Slater,1997; Woodruff, 1997). Accordingly, given the potential complexity of the organizational response necessary to achieve service recovery and value creation, it is essential to share and analyze information on service problems and failures at all levels so as to foster the joint interpretation of its implications, reach a consensus on service improvement priorities (Johnston & Clark, 2008), and achieve long-term improvements in performance (Tax & Brown, 1998). Johnston and Michel (2008) include the analysis and interpretation of information on failures within the so-called "process recovery", and Smith *et al.* (2009) use the "system intensity" and "comprehensiveness" dimensions as a measure of the magnitude of the resources devoted to monitoring and controlling failures and gathering information about all potential recovery activities. We therefore believe that the ISRS should include the analysis and collective assessment of information available on the failure in order to establish proactively the necessary measures for improvement and to respond as efficiently as possible when failures do occur.

Efficient practices of analysis can also reinforce the identification of problems by overcoming two main obstacles to failure detection:

Total quality management fosters a "zero defects" culture. These extended practices can generate a certain aversion among both management and workers against recognizing that mistakes still occur (Homburg & Fürst, 2007), and the customer service department may find itself becoming more and more isolated within the organization the more negative feedback it provides. Sometimes it is the employees themselves who have little interest in listening to clients' problems with the service, and they end up treating complaints as occasional incidents which do not require a detailed report to the firm's management (Tax & Brown, 1998, p. 83). This type of behavior has been called "see no evil, hear no evil, speak no evil" (Homburg & Fürst, 2005). In this way, employees, by suppressing information about failures, neutralize their perceived potential threats to their self-esteem, reputation, autonomy, resources, and job security. In both cases, the lack of cooperation of managers and/or employees restricts the opportunity for customer and process recovery.

The above situation will be further exacerbated if, in addition, employees feel trapped between what they see as clients' reasonable complaints and management and/or organizational policies and procedures which leave no room for change, all of which generates a high level of stress in their work. Management therefore needs to provide effective support (internal service recovery) to avoid the employees developing feelings of impotence and helplessness that can induce them to display passive, maladaptive behavior to the customer. This employee alienation will be compounded when management is felt to make no effort to recover them from this situation, for example, by improving the processes of service provision to avoid the employees having to deal with constantly recurring failures (Michel *et al.,* 2009).

If the organization's usual practice includes a critical review of service operations, conducted at all levels in a spirit of improvement, we believe that it will contribute primarily to creating a climate in which employees do not feel threatened when they identify and report service failures, allowing internal service recovery. In addition, a willingness of workers and managers to admit mistakes and discuss their implications will also foster the possibility of both proactively and reactively improving the external service recovery.

2.3. Response to failures

In the present work response to failures has a twofold orientation. One is external, targeted at the consumer, and primarily related to front-office corrective actions that seek to maintain or even increase client satisfaction and avoid damaging the intention to repurchase (Kau & Loh, 2006). The other is internal, and corresponds to back-office operations that seek to transform the knowledge generated within the firm into service improvements, innovation and allow employees' recovery (La & Kandampully, 2004).

With respect to front-office corrective actions, among the recovery practices most studied in the literature are the speed of the response, the suitability of the final outcome of the service, and the interactive process involved in resolving the problem (McCollough *et al.,* 2000; Tax & Brown, 1998). In light of this evidence, we propose breaking the consumer-oriented response down into three factors: rapid response, fair outcome, and employee empowerment. Figure 1 shows this last factor as lying between the external and internal orientation. The reason is that this dimension contributes to both customer recovery and employee recovery, with the latter having a positive effect on the capacity to generate knowledge from failures. These three dimensions are closely related to the concept of perceived justice (rapid response is related to process justice, fair outcome to distributive justice, and employee support to interactive justice). In the present work, however, we do not deal with the measurement of consumer perceived justice, for which there already exist validated scales, but with evaluating whether or not the firm provides the means with which to give a fair overall response.

2.4. Rapid response

Previous research reports a decline in clients' satisfaction and loyalty when the response to their complaints is perceived as too slow (Spreng *et al.,*

1995; Wirtz & Bateson, 2002), as well as that service users are very frustrated when recovery procedures involve long and cumbersome processes (Tax & Brown, 1998). In this sense, La & Kandampully (2004) reinforce that recovery primarily demands an immediate solution, and that the proximity in time between the problem and its recovery can be crucial to the service experience. The study of Gross *et al.* (2007), on 4000 clients of nearly 600 service firms, also confirms that most of the respondents still believe that service firms are slow to respond and fix recurring problems. Similarly, Río *et al.* (2009) find that, in the cell-phone sector, users invariably want the recovery to focus on restoring service as soon as possible.

The ISRS must therefore consider the speed with which the solution is offered to the consumer as a key activity in its management of failures. As noted by Hart *et al.* (1990) twenty years ago, rapid identification of a problem, even before the client is aware of it, will only be fruitful if the firm also responds rapidly; if possible by the first person who is contacted (Boshoff, 1997).

2.5. Fair outcome

According to Tax *et al.* (1988), as well as speed in the recovery process, consumers expect compensation for the damages the failure may have caused them and/or the costs they incurred to obtain a solution. In this sense, La and Kandampully (2004) propose that the second crucial recovery action is to compensate the clients and thank them for their understanding.

Such compensation may be both tangible and psychological (Webster & Sundaram, 1998). On the one hand, firms assign tangible resources to correct problems and restore the interchange with the client by returning the money, replacing the service, or offering discounts on a future purchase. And on the other, psychological efforts seek to minimize the problem by showing concern for the client's needs, desires, and concerns. Two approaches are recommended for psychological compensation: empathy and apology (Miller *et al.,* 2000). Normally, the client will respond more favorably to tangible efforts or to a combination of psychological and tangible efforts (Webster & Sundaram, 1998). In this sense, we believe that the ISRS should include explicit recognition of the failures committed, the design of solutions tailored to user expectations, and the fulfillment of the acquired rectification commitments.

According to Johnston and Michel (2008), rapid response and fair outcome are related to "customer recovery". The fair and rapid response dimensions, which are not considered Smith's *et al.* (2009) research, represent the management practices that strongly support the firm's ability to effectively react to failures. The recovery system designed by Smith *et al.* (2009) is more internally focused and the only aspect related to the external response included is the "influence dimension", defined as the ability of the system to adapt to different customers' recovery needs. Smith and Karwan (2010) consider recovery speed and fairness as an outcome of their recovery system, although we believe that the practices leading to these types of results should be inherent to an integral recovery system.

2.6. Employee support

A basic principle of quality management is that quality is the responsibility of all members of the organization. Employees therefore need to have minimum levels of responsibility and authority to detect and resolve any quality-related problem. This premise is especially applicable to front-line employees. It is essential to empower them to prevent failures and fix them rapidly if they should occur (Dewitt & Brady, 2003). The positive effects of the allocation of service recovery responsibilities to the employees have been demonstrated in several studies (de Jong & de Ruyter, 2004; Miller *et al.*, 2000). Responsibility has to be backed up with appropriate training in how to recover the service (Tax & Brown, 1998), which encourages employees in their work and gives them confidence to use the discretion they have received appropriately.

For some authors, however, empowering employees to fix problems in real time may lead to different service recovery solutions for any given case depending on which person is dealing with it, hence diminishing recovery justice (Michel *et al.,* 2009). From this standpoint, it would be advisable to set out clearly formalized service recovery policies and procedures, even if this is to the detriment of the employee's decision-making capacity (Smith *et al.,* 2009). Formalized procedures will also avoid managers' neglecting to give the employees the support and attention they need in practice to take effective responsibility for customer service recovery (Schneider & Bowen, 1995).

This aspect is less of a problem, however, in professional services. Since the employees are highly qualified, and usually experienced professionals, they naturally have the autonomy and authority to decide how to solve client problems. In other words, given a failure in the provision of the service, the judgment of the professional may be the only valid criterion to determine how to resolve conflicts in rendering the service. For this reason, in this type of firm it is common to find sector-wide ethical codes of behavior to prevent opportunism in the necessary autonomy of professional practice (Lowendahl, 2005).

The ISRS should therefore include a factor referring to the necessary combination of employee empowerment and training to develop successful recovery strategies. This dimension should contribute to employee satisfaction after the failure since it is the employee who can make decisions to rectify the process and to compensate the client immediately if necessary, and thus alleviate the tensions that arise from dealing with service recovery. In turn, all this can strengthen the employees' collaboration in the processes of detection and analysis of failures.

2.7. Learning and innovation

While correcting mistakes and ensuring the loyalty of the service user by means of rapid and fair compensation and appropriate treatment are important, one must not overlook the potential creation of knowledge from classifying and analyzing the failures that occur, and disseminating this information with the aim of implementing changes in the service. These will be transformations designed to allow the organization to prevent future failures, to minimize the risk of problems, and to reduce the costs of any lack of quality.

As observed by Nonaka (1991), successful firms are those that consistently create new knowledge, disseminate it throughout the organization, and embody it rapidly in new technologies and products. This knowledge can come from the field of technology or from the market (Slater, 2008). In the latter case, the reasons for client dissatisfaction are at least as valuable as their reasons for satisfaction. Both are experiences of the firm from which it can learn (Reichheld, 1996). Service failures in particular need to be seen as opportunities for learning (Nevis *et al.*, 1995). A firm's ability to learn from failures, and thereby offer improved or completely new services, can have an influence on its long-term results (La & Kandampully, 2004; Lovelock *et al.,* 2009; Slater, 2008; Vos *et al.,* 2008).

When service organizations achieve effective feedback from their clients' service failure perceptions and collectively distribute and interpret this information, the result is that they learn and thus attain a better position from which to improve their services and/or processes and to develop new innovative services based on the active incorporation of relevant information into the design process (Alam, 2006).

Smith *et al.* (2009, p. 169) state that the intensity of the recovery system -the ways in which data are gathered, maintained, and utilized-closes the loop to enable learning and system improvement, but their service recovery system does not explicitly take into account the learning and innovation arising from the management of failures. However, Smith and Karwan (2010) consider again learning as an outcome of their proposal of a recovery system.

3. Methodology

Potential constructs and their items are built based on the literature, as well as on experts and practitioners suggestions. Using the SABI database (June 2009 update) we randomly selected a stratified population of 1.481 hotel companies with three, four and five stars and at least 10 workers. Only one hotel in each hotel chain was included in the target population as we understand that companies in the same group share the same management strategy.

After speaking to the hotels chosen by telephone, to check the accuracy of available data and request their participation in the study, the final population consisted of 1.238 hotels. Information was gathered through personal interviews, using hotel managers as key informants as they are deemed to have the knowledge required to answer questions about all the variables analyzed (Thorpe & Morgan, 2007). The sample finally obtained comprised 240 firms (response rate of 19.4%). Of these, 57,5% were three stars hotels, 37,9% belonged to the four stars category and 4,6% were five stars hotels. The average number of employees per hotel was thirty three.

In line with the usual recommendations (Churchill, 1979; Deng & Dart, 1994; Menor & Roth, 2007), the ISRS measurement scale was developed in two main stages. Initially, we prepared a list of 47 items based on a literature review and also on in-depth interviews with a panel of nine academic and professional experts in the field of quality management, service failure and complaints management. Although the development of the scale was based on previous research, specific attributes were proposed for this research -the first attempt to empirically asses the integrative nature of service recovery was published during the accomplishment of our data collection (Smith *et al.,* 2009).

After checking for and removing duplicates, we were left with a set of 36 items that were assigned, according to the researchers' criterion, to the different dimensions of the ISRS proposed in the present study. The researchers pre-tested the resulting measurement instrument to verify: (1) the suitability of the ISRS concept and its different dimensions to the reality of the sector under study, (2) the correspondence of the items with the proposed dimensions of the ISRS, and (3) their readability and correct understanding. As a result, several items were re-drafted to facilitate their interpretation, to avoid confusion and thus prevent research bias and 11 of them, considered confusing and/or redundant were eliminated. The development of the items reinforced by an extensive literature review and the detailed evaluations by academics and practitioners try to ensure that the ISRS scale addresses all issues relevant to the content domain under study and that, therefore, the ISRS constructs have content validity. Following Ahire and O'Shaughnessy (1998), a seven-point Likert scale was used for all items to ensure higher statistical variability among survey responses. Thus, for each ISRS criterion, respondents evaluated how well the different statements described their companies practices on a scale from 1 ("strongly disagree") to 7 ("strongly agree").

4. Results

First, the attributes comprising the different measurement scales conforming to the ISRS construct were subjected to an exploratory factor analysis. However, given the exploratory nature of that analysis, we subsequently performed several confirmatory factor analyses, using the program EQS version 6.1 for Windows, and the maximum likelihood estimation method, to examine the psychometric properties of the ISRS scale.

In the first confirmatory analysis, we studied the correlation of the six dimensions that constitute the ISRS in order to determine their convergent and discriminant validities. These results confirmed the convergent validity of the different dimensions since the standardized lambda parameters relating each observed variable with the latent variable ranged between 0.62 and 0.93, and were significant in all cases at a 95% confidence level (BBNNFI= 0.87; CFI=0.89; GFI= 0.82; RMSEA=0.047). Construct reliability was again evaluated using estimated model parameters. In addition, the discriminant validity was confirmed since for any pair of factors the correlation was less than the square root of the respective AVE (Fornell & Larcker, 1981).

Then, in view of the theoretical existence of a concept underlying the first-order factors rapid response, fair outcome, employee empowerment, and learning–innovation, we performed a second-order confirmatory factorial analysis to determine whether these dimensions indeed converge onto a single latent factor denominated response. The results confirmed the theoretical indication: the standardized lambda values were between 0.60 and 0.89, and were significant in all cases at a 95% confidence level, and the goodness-of-fit indices were satisfactory (BBNNFI= 0.86; CFI=0.88; GFI= 0.83; RMSEA=0.050). The composite reliability index and the AVE of this construct are also above the recommended threshold values.

The next phase of validating the ISRS scale was to determine the existence of an underlying factor for the three major concepts considered in the ISRS: failure detection, failure analysis, and response. As a prior step we checked the existence of convergent and discriminant validity among the aforementioned three contructs. To do so we used the means of the response dimensions, in order to avoid violating the ratio of sample size to number of parameters (Jöreskog & Sörbom, 1995). As it can be seen in Figure 2, the scale proposed in the present study is reliable and valid, and a latent factor under lays the three ISRS dimensions.

Figure 2. Causal Model

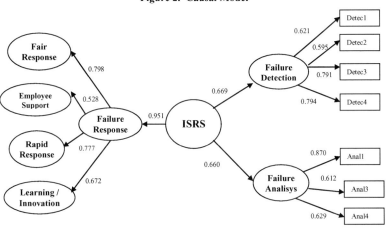

χ^2 S-B (38) = 108.3642 (p< 0.000) BBNNFI= 0.807 CFI= 0.866 GFI= 0.898 RMSEA= 0.088

5. Conclusion

In the last 20 years, several authors have theoretically suggested the need to assess the integrative nature of effective service recovery systems. The present work reinforces the advisability of considering service recovery as a comprehensive management system which provides the firm not only with procedures to recover from failures, but also with an invaluable way of learning. Such a system helps to improve the quality of the services provided by hotels as well as employee satisfaction and performance. Long-term competitiveness requires a service company to manage failure and recovery procedures in a proactive, relational, and ultimately strategic manner. The results of this research suggest that a service recovery system meeting this features can be developed around three basic constructs: failure detection, failure analysis and failure response.

The strategic approach means accepting that failure management is a continuing process, based on the systematic detection and analysis of all the failure-related information which provides a valuable source of learning to improve the future provision of services. All this processes are reinforced when implementing the ISRS.

The proactive approach is also supported within the ISRS by the collection and analysis of all the data related to potential failures. A fair service recovery (fair response), offered in the shortest time possible (rapid response), is also fundamental to the quality of the long-term relationship with the client. These aspects are further strengthened when the hotel's employees are trained and empowered to proactively prevent failures and, if they do occur, to respond to them as correctly as possible.

The dimensions here identified are in line with those proposed by Smith *et al.* (2009), although their research is based in the operations management literature and is more internally focused than ours. Our study, also takes into account the works on service recovery that have been reported in the Marketing literature and it contributes to a balanced internal and external orientation in service firms. The ISRS's failure detection procedures have a clear external orientation since the firm tries to know and/or anticipate any shortcomings related o service provision. The failure analysis dimension positively affects the recovery of internal clients or employees, since service shortcomings are recognized collectively, and the willingness to work to avoid them becomes tangible. And the response dimension includes measures for the organization's improvement both externally and internally.

There are a number of limitations in the work that need to be kept in mind. First, this was a cross-sectional study. Second, the constructs are measured based on the subjective perceptions of a single informant per firm. This procedure may possibly be a source of bias. And third, the ISRS scale was developed and validated in a specific context: hotels. It is clearly necessary to study its validity and composition in other tourism services.

Future research lines will be targeted at determining what type of management culture is the most likely to be effective for the development of the ISRS, and what will be the effects of such a system on the firm's image or brand value. Also, in the future, it will be interesting to verify if a well developed ISRS increases service companies' competitiveness by improving the results obtained from clients and analyze the differences among hotel segments. We have compared the scores given by each hotel to the 25 items included in the scale and the scores corresponding to the five stars hotels were slightly above the rest of the sample scores, but the difference was not statistically significant.

References

Ahire, S.L., & O'Shaughnessy, K.C. (1998). The role of top management commitment in quality management: An empirical analysis of the auto parts industry. *International Journal of Quality Science*, 3(19), 5-37.

Alam, I. (2006). Removing the fuzziness from the fuzzy front-end of service innovations through customer interactions. *Industrial Marketing Management*, 35(4), 468-480.

Bateson, J. (2002). Consumer performance and quality in services. *Managing Service Quality*, 12(4), 206-209.

Boshoff, C. (1997). An experimental study of service recovery options. *International Journal of Service Industry Management*, 8(2), 110-130.

Churchill, G. (1979). A paradigm for developing better measures of marketing constructs. *Journal of Marketing Research*, 16(February), 64-73.

Colgate, M., & Norris, M. (2001). Developing a comprehensive picture of service failure. *International Journal of Service Industry Management*, 12(3), 215-233.

De Jong, A., & De Ruyter, K. (2004). Adaptive versus proactive behavior in service recovery: The role of self-managing teams. *Decision Sciences*, 35(3), 457-491.

Deng, S., & Dart, J. (1994). Measuring market orientation: A multi-factor, multi-item approach. *Journal of Marketing Management*, 10(8), 725-742.

DeWitt, T., & Brady, M.K. (2003). Rethinking service recovery strategies: The effect of rapport on consumer responses to service failure. *Journal of Service Research*, 6(2), 193-207.

East, R., Hammond, K., & Wright, M. (2007). The relative incidence of positive and negative word of mouth: A multi-category study. *International Journal of Research in Marketing*, 24(2), 175-184.

Fornell, C., & Larcker, D.F. (1981). Evaluating structural equation models with unobservable variables and measurement errors. *Journal of Marketing Research*, 18(February), 39-50.

Grewal, D., Levy, M., & Kumar, V. (2009). Customer experience management in retailing: An organizing framework. *Journal of Retailing*, 85(1), 1-14.

Grönroos, C. (1995). Relationship marketing: The strategy continuum. *Journal of the Academy of Marketing Science*, 23(4), 252-254.

Harari, O. (1992). Thank heaven for complainers. *Management Review*, 81(1), 59-60.

Hart, C., Heskett, J., & Sasser, W.E. (1990). The profitable art of service recovery. *Harvard Business Review*, 68(July-August), 148-56.

Homburg, C.H., & Fürst, A. (2005). How organizational complaint handling drives customer loyalty: An analysis of the mechanistic and the organic approach. *Journal of Marketing*, 69(3), 95-114.

—. (2007). See no evil, hear no evil, speak no evil: a study of defensive organizational behavior towards customer complaints. *Journal of the Academy of Marketing Science*, 35(4), 523-36.

Johnston, R. (2005). Service operations management: from the roots up. *International Journal of Operations & Production Management*, 25(12), 1298-1308.

Johnston, R. & Clark, G. (2008). *Service operations management* (3rd ed.). Essex: Pearson.

Johnston, R., & Michel, S. (2008). Three outcomes of service recovery. Customer recovery, process recovery and employee recovery. *International Journal of Operations and Production Management*, 28(1), 79-99.

Jöreskog, K.G., & Sörbom, D. (1995). LISREL 8: *User's Reference Guide*. Chicago: Scientific Software International.

Kau, A.K., & Loh, E.W.Y. (2006). The effects of service recovery on consumer satisfaction: A comparison between complainants and non-complainants. *Journal of Services Marketing*, 20(2), 101-111.

La, K.V., & Kandampully, J. (2004). Market oriented learning and customer value enhancement through service recovery management. *Managing Service Quality*, 14(5), 390-401.

Lovelock, C.H., Wirtz, J., & Chew, P. (2009). *Essentials of Services Marketing*. Singapore: Prentice Hall.

Løwendahl, B.R. (2005). *Strategic management of professional service firms*. Copenhagen: Copenhagen Business School Press.

McCollough, M.A., Berry, L.L., & Yadav, M.S. (2000). An empirical investigation of customer satisfaction after service failure and recovery. *Journal of Service Research*, 3(2), 121-137.

Menor, L.J., & Roth, A.V. (2007). New service development competence in retail banking: Construct development and measurement validation. *Journal of Operations Management*, 25(4), 825-846.

Michel, S. (2001). Analyzing service failures and recoveries: A process approach. *International Journal of Service Industry Management*, 12(1), 20-33.

Michel, S., Bowen, D., & Johnston, R. (2009). Why service recovery fails: Tensions among customer, employee, and process perspectives. *Journal of Service Management*, 20(3), 253-273.

Miller, J.L., Craighead, C.W., & Karwan, K.R. (2000). Service recovery: A framework and empirical investigation. *Journal of Operations Management*, 18(4), 387-400.

Nevis, E., DiBella, A., & Gould, J. (1995). Understanding organizations as learning systems. *Sloan Management Review*, 36(2), 73-85.

Nonaka, I. (1991). The knowledge-creating company. *Harvard Business Review*, 69(November-December), 96-104.

Parasuraman, A. (1997). Reflections on gaining competitive advantage through customer value. *Journal of the Academy of Marketing Science*, 25 (2), 154-161.

Reichheld, F.F. (1996). Learning from customer defections. *Harvard Business Review*, 74(March-April), 56-69.

Reynolds, K.L., & Harris, L.C. (2009). Dysfunctional customer behavior severity: An empirical examination. *Journal of Retailing*, 85(3), 321-335.

Río-Lanza, A.B., Vázquez-Casielles, R., & Díaz-Martín A.M. (2009). Satisfaction with service recovery: perceived justice and emotional responses. *Journal of Business Research*, 62(8), 775-781.

Santos, M.L., Sanzo, M.J., Alvarez, L.I., & Vazquez, R. (2005). Organizational learning and market orientation: Interface and effects on performance. *Industrial Marketing Management*, 34(3), 187-202.

Schibrowsky, J.A., & Lapidus, R.S. (1994). Gaining a competitive advantage by analyzing aggregate complaints. *Journal of Consumer Marketing*, 11(1), 15-26.

Schneider, B., & Bowen, D.E. (1995). *Winning the service game*. Boston, MA: Harvard Business School.

Singh, J. (1990). Voice, exit and negative word-of-mouth behaviours: An investigation across three service categories. *Journal of the Academy of Marketing Science*, 18(1), 1-15.

Slater, S. (1997). Developing a customer value-based theory of the firm. *Journal of the Academy of Marketing Science*, 25(2), 162-167.

—. (2008). Learning how to be innovative. *Business Strategy Review*, 19(4), 46-51.

Smith, J.S., & Karwan, K.R. (2010). Empirical profiles of service recovery systems: The maturity perspective. *Journal of Service Research*, 13(1), 111-125.

Smith, J.S., Karwan, K.R., & Markland R.E. (2009). An empirical examination of the structural dimensions of the service recovery system. *Decision Sciences*, 40(1), 165-185.

Spreng, R.A., Harrell, G.D., & Mackoy, R.D. (1995). Service recovery: Impact on satisfaction and intentions. *Journal of Services Marketing*, 9(1), 15-23.

Tax, S.S., & Brown, S.W. (1998). Recovering and learning from service failure. *Sloan Management Review*, 40(1), 75-88.

Tax, S.S., Brown, S.W., & Chandrashekaran, M. (1988). Customer evaluations of service complaint experiences: Implications for relationship marketing. *Journal of Marketing*, 62(2), 60-76.

Thorpe, E.R., & Morgan, R.E. (2007). In pursuit of the ideal approach to successful marketing strategy implementation. *European Journal of Marketing*, 41(5/6), 659-677.

Vaerenbergh, Y.V., Larivière, B., & Vermeir, I. (2009). Assessing the additional impact of process recovery communications on customer outcomes: A comprehensive service recovery approach. *Working Paper* 2009/583, Faculteit Economie En Bedrijfskunde, Universiteit Gent. Retrieved from: http://157.193.52.32/nl/Ondz/WP/Papers/wp_09_583.pdf

Vos, J.F.J., Huitema, G.B., & de Lange-Ros, E. (2008). How organisations can learn from complaints. *TQM Journal*, 20(1), 8-17.

Webster, C., & Sundaram, D.S. (1998). Service consumption critically in failure recovery. *Journal of Business Research*, 41(2), 153-159.

Wirtz, J., & Bateson, J.E.G. (1999). Consumer satisfaction with services: Integrating the environment perspective in services marketing into the traditional disconfirmation paradigm. *Journal of Business Research*, 44(1), 55-66.

Wirtz, J., & Mattila, A.S. (2004). Consumer responses to compensation, speed of recovery and apology after a service failure. *International Journal of Service Industry Management*, 15(2), 150-166.

Woodruff, R. (1997). Customer value: The next source for competitive advantage. *Journal of the Academy of Marketing Science*, 25(2), 139-153.

SUBJECT INDEX

Adverse selection 160
Advertising effectiveness 21
Agent-based modeling 161, 163, 167, 168
Alternative tourism 7
Australia 148-151
Austria 203, 206, 207, 209, 211, 216-220

B2B 145
Belgium 230, 233
Benchmarking 208, 218, 219
Blogs 143, 146, 148, 189
Brand awareness 24
Brand equity 22, 23, 72
Brand identity 24, 25
Brand image 20, 23, 25-27
Brand logos 23, 24
Brand loyalty 31
Brand names 24, 25
Brand personality 15, 23, 25
Brand positioning 31
Brand recognition 24
Brand slogans 24
Branding 22, 23, 206, 208, 212, 217
    attributes 20
    nations 23
    regions 23
    states 23
    strategies 21, 26
Britain 23
Business tourism 21

Carbon offsetting schemes 115-117, 119-125, 127-131
City branding 21, 24
Climate change 117
Co-branding 207
Commercialisation of culture 83

Commodification of culture 83
Comparative advantage 204
Competitive advantage 85, 91, 98, 101, 102, 109-111, 190, 199, 203, 206, 208, 211, 219, 223
Competitive performance 21
Competitive position 22
Consumer articulation 178, 180-182
Consumption experience 44, 45, 60
Content analysis 20, 22, 26, 66, 151
Cooperative branding 207
Costly signalling theory 115, 117, 118, 127
Country image 2-11, 14, 15
Creativity 241-243, 246, 247, 249, 252, 255, 257
Cuba 8
Cultural approach 2, 3
Cultural differences 4
Cultural events 247, 248, 250-252, 255, 256
Cultural heritage 100
Customer experience 58-61
Customer loyalty 5, 57, 72, 229, 267
Customer satisfaction 5, 42-46, 191, 194, 196, 199, 267, 270
Czech Republic 218, 230, 233

Denmark 230
Destination attributes 57, 63, 65, 71
Destination benchmarking 208, 211
Destination branding 21, 23, 24, 31, 206, 207
Destination competitiveness 203-205, 207, 208, 222
Destination development 139
Destination experience 24, 27, 57, 58, 61, 63, 64, 66, 71, 73

Destination image 2-11, 14, 15, 42,
    86, 87, 89-91
Destination information 139
Destination logos 22, 30-32
Destination loyalty 42, 64, 66, 68,
    71, 72, 206
Destination management 57, 71, 72,
    145, 211, 218, 222, 224, 241
    organisations 138, 139, 141,
        145, 147, 151, 152, 222-
        228, 237
    systems 138-142, 145-152
Destination marketing 21
    Association International 20, 25,
        27
    Organisations 25, 27, 207, 208
Destination slogans20, 22, 25-27,
    29-32
Disconfirmation theory 44, 45

e- word of mouth communication
    176
e-tourism 138, 147
Expectation-disconfirmation theory
    45
Experience economy 57, 58

Failure analysis 265, 273, 274
Failure detection 265, 273, 274
Finland 98, 102, 103, 106, 109-111,
    150
France 15, 21

Germany 179, 230, 233, 236
Green products 102, 110, 115, 116,
    118, 119, 130

High-season 43, 52
Hungary 218

Image 2, 3
    modification 6
Impression management theory 115,
    119, 127
Information asymmetry 156-158,
    160, 161, 163-167

Innovation 188-193, 195-199, 203-
    206, 208-212, 217-219, 241-
    247, 249, 250, 252, 254-257,
    261, 267, 270, 271
    orientation 191-193, 196
Inserve adverse selection 160
International peace 7
International security 7
Internet marketing 26
Ireland 230
Israel 2-15
Italy 15, 222, 223

Jordan 8

Knowledge theory 242, 244, 246-
    248, 250, 254-257

Latin America 15
Leisure experience 62
Low-season 42, 51, 52

Mallorca 42, 43
Malta 28
Market orientation 191
Market segmentation 21
Marketing activities 21
Mediterranean destinations 42
Modern innovation theory 205

Nepal 3
New Zealand 23
Norway 46

Online information search 179
Online social networks 115, 116,
    119, 121, 123, 127-130, 143,
    167, 183

Perceptual change 6
Pilgrimage tourism 7
Pioneering theory 44
Place attachment 92
Place branding 24
Poland 230, 233
Portugal 15

Positioning analysis 21
Positioning strategies 15, 21, 26
Product development 222, 225

Quality of life 81, 83, 84
Quasi-experimental research 2, 3, 8-10

Religious tourism 8
Reputation management 177
Russia 3

Satisfaction index 46
Service failures 262-267, 269, 271, 273, 274
Service recovery 261-267, 269, 271, 273, 274
Singapore 150
Slovakia 203, 209-212, 216, 218, 219
Slovenia 28
Snow tourism 224
Social dilemma theory 128
Social media 179, 182, 189
Social responsibility 98-111
Socio-cultural process 2, 4
South Africa 230
Spain 8-15, 196, 197, 261
Stereotyped prejudices 6
Sustainability 98-101, 103
Sustainable tourism 100, 117, 257

Sweden 46, 218
Switzerland 206, 207, 216, 217, 230
Syria 8

Technological turbulance 191-194, 196, 197, 199
Terrorist attacts 7
Total quality management 266
Tourism branding 23
Tourism competitiveness index 217
Tourism development 80-82, 84, 85, 87-92, 209-212, 216, 217
Tourism impacts 80-82, 84-92, 116, 117
Tourist experience 61-63, 81
Tourist loyalty 63, 66
Tourist motivations 43, 65, 72, 92
Tourist satisfaction 42, 43, 46, 48-52, 62, 63, 65
Turkey 3, 8-14, 21

UK 179, 230, 233
USA 31, 46, 216, 179
User rating 144, 146, 148, 151

Value creation 57, 58, 60, 61, 71, 72, 140, 265
Virtual opinion platforms 180, 181

Word of mouth communication 176, 177